EFFECTS OF CORPORATION INCOME TAX

EFFECTS OF CORPORATION INCOME TAX

PAPERS PRESENTED AT THE SYMPOSIUM
ON BUSINESS TAXATION
WAYNE STATE UNIVERSITY

arranged and edited by

Marian Krzyzaniak

papers by

Marian Krzyzaniak, Rice University

Arnold C. Harberger, University of Chicago

Richard A. Musgrave, Harvard University

Richard E. Slitor, Assistant Director at the
Office of Tax Analysis, U.S. Treasury

Richard Goode, the International Monetary Fund

WAYNE STATE UNIVERSITY PRESS   DETROIT 1966

Grateful acknowledgment is made to the Wayne State University Division of Graduate Studies for financial assistance in publishing this book.

CONTENTS

5

TABLES

V *Goode*

VI *Krzyzaniak and Musgrave*

GRAPHS

In the spring of 1963 I was named the recipient of the Wayne State University Alumni Fund Research Recognition Award. With the award went funds with which to organize a symposium on a subject of my choice and a reduced teaching load to enable me to prepare my own contribution.

The topic which I chose was business taxation. Several prominent economists were invited to come to Wayne State to discuss whatever aspect of this broader topic they wished. Both theoretical and empirical contributions were solicited; where the symposium participants felt some points needed further elaboration, discussion notes were exchanged.

This volume assembles the papers and discussion notes which resulted.

Marian Krzyzaniak
Rice University
Spring, 1965

INTRODUCTION

Professor Harberger's paper considers the waste that arises because the income generated from capital in the corporate sector of the economy is taxed at a considerably higher rate than the income from capital in the non-corporate sector. The theoretical analysis underlying Harberger's work is based on the assumption that variations in the rates of investment in these two sectors operate to bring about an allocation of capital such that net-of-tax average rates of return are (with possible adjustments for differential risk) equalized as between the two sectors. Put another way, Harberger assumes a degree of flexibility in the allocation of capital in the economy which is sufficient to ensure that differences in average rates of return between the two sectors (other than those associated with differential riskiness) will tend to be eliminated through time.

Working on the basis of this assumption, Harberger shows how the cost to the economy, induced by the differential taxation of the return to capital in the corporate and non-corporate sectors, depends upon the degree of substitutability between the products of the two sectors, and upon the degree of substitutability between labor and capital in each sector. Harberger then produces estimates of this cost for the U.S. economy, based on assumed degrees of substitutability, and on measures of the differential tax burden borne by the corporate sector during the period 1953–59. The estimated costs range from $1 billion to some $3 billion per year, with those reflecting the most plausible assumptions with regard to substitutability being concentrated between $1.5 billion and $2.5 billion per year.

The efficiency costs measured by Harberger are substantially independent of the incidence of taxes on income from capital.

Moreover, these costs are in a sense independent of the effects of taxation on capital accumulation itself. Basically, Harberger asks the question, how much less does the economy produce at any point in time because of tax-induced misallocations of the *existing* volume of resources? Even though the volume of (capital and labor) resources may be changing through time, there is always a cost of the type Harberger measures, representing the improvement which could be made by an appropriate reallocation of the then-existing stocks of resources.

When tax provisions lead to alterations in the rate of capital accumulation, special problems do, however, arise, among them that of assessing the effects of tax-induced changes in savings rates upon the relative shares of capital and labor in the national income. This problem provides the focus for my paper.

I theorize about the long-run developments in an economy in which a profits tax is imposed, defining long run as the period in which the supply of capital in the whole economy adjusts to the tax on profits. My model restricts itself to the perfectly competitive case, assumes the production function to be linear, homogeneous of degree one, and of either the Cobb-Douglas or the C.E.S. type, and considers, first, a general and, then, a non-general tax on profits. By this method I duplicate some of Professor Harberger's results.

The models start where the short-run "neoclassical" theory of shifting, either of the standard or of the Harberger version, leaves off. That is, it is assumed that in the short run there is no shifting if the tax is general, or that the Harberger adjustment through capital outflow is completed if the tax is not general.

If the tax is not shifted in the short run, it will impair new capital formation by various mechanisms. For example, the current and future rates of return on capital will decline, thereby reducing the incentive to invest. Without deviating from "neoclassical" thinking, I concern myself with the other side of the coin: the funds saved will be affected negatively since a tax on profits will substantially reduce the average propensity to save in such an economy. This follows from the fact that businesses and businessmen have a higher propensity to save than other groups in our society. Consequently, in the long run, capital will be less abundant and the equilibrium rate of return after tax, will tend to the pre-tax rate of return. Thus, when measured from changes in the rate of return, shifting is close to one hundred per cent. As for other measures of shifting—e.g., those based on changes in factor shares—shifting turns out to be mainly a function of the elasticity of substitution of factors. In the special Cobb-Douglas case, by the very nature of this production function, long-run shifting measured from gross factor shares remains zero.

While I doubt the "realism" of both the standard and Professor Harberger's "neoclassical" models, I find this study necessary for two reasons: 1) "neoclassical" models have normative uses—they often tell us the best attainable position for the economy; 2) the "neoclassicists" carefully worked out the short-run implications of their assumptions, but they were vague as to what would happen in the long run. And, since the long run is observable, the quantifiable implications of their model may be assessed both in theory and in empirical study.

Professor Musgrave asks what various taxes on business, including that on business profits, may do to international commodity flows. Much depends on whether the tax on an exporting business is shifted through an adjustment in prices or wages, or not shifted at all, and on what happens to the prices of competing goods in other countries. In addition, the international commodity flows will also be affected by changes in the exchange ratio between two countries.

Thus tax effects in an international setting are highly complex. Professor Musgrave considers the various alternatives and shows that in a closed economy the incidence of a tax is primarily a matter of relative prices; absolute price changes have little importance. However, in the case of an open economy the relative *international* prices are important, and these, in turn, depend largely on the movement of absolute domestic prices.

It is obvious that the subject is of great importance to countries which are merging into economic unions or communities such as the European Common Market, to all open economies, and to all export industries. Since little theorizing and even less research has been undertaken to explore this area, Professor Musgrave's paper is extremely welcome, but a vast area for further theorizing and research remains.

Doctors Goode and Slitor, in their respective papers, deal with another aspect of the same broad subject: they discuss critically Krzyzaniak and Musgrave's *The Shifting of the Corporation Income Tax*. Both discussants believe that our economy is sufficiently competitive that the "neoclassical" model, be it the standard or the Harberger version, is empirically relevant. And both claim that the Krzyzaniak–Musgrave econometric techniques fail to isolate the tax effects: in fact they claim that the results are highly biased upward. Their greatest concern, then, is with the Krzyzaniak–Musgrave measure of the profits tax as consistently shifted by more than one hundred per cent.

However, a joint presentation of the views of these two men does not do justice to their originality. For example, after reviewing critically the general standing of the theory of the shifting of the corporation income tax and the results of empirical research, Doctor Goode contends (see his Table 1) that the Krzyzaniak and Musgrave model assigns to changes in tax rates nearly the entire change in the before-tax rate of return on capital in all the U.S. manufacturing industries between the late thirties and the mid-fifties. He then points out that, in fact, the earlier period witnessed a relatively high level of unemployment which, when taken into account, should explain most of the increase in the before-tax rate of return between the periods. Doctor Goode also employs other data for the U.S. economy in continuing this particular line of reasoning.

One interesting point in Doctor Goode's discussion is that in his conclusions with respect to the long run he warns that "perhaps the narrow question of shifting is unanswerable because we cannot conceptually or statistically hold constant all the relevant variables except the corporation tax rates." This pessimistic note is correct to the extent that one cannot be certain of having found the truth. However, the scientific method does provide the means by which hypotheses are shown false.

Doctor Slitor uses computations to show that a rather different specification of the model will yield estimates of the degree of shifting somewhat lower than the Krzyzaniak and Musgrave result. For example, in his Table 1 he shows that by using a variable which measures the pressure in the economy (in fact, he uses the GNP gap) the measure of shifting is reduced from overshifting to shifting slightly less than 100 per cent. He concludes that the estimate of shifting might decline even further were mis–specification eliminated. Any shifting which than remains will be attributable to differential taxation along the Harberger line.

Doctor Slitor also looks for other and novel arguments to settle the dispute. For example, were the corporation income tax shifted in the short run as a result of increased prices, the less profitable companies would come under a "price umbrella" in that they would benefit more, relatively, than the more profitable ones. As evidence of the price umbrella, he considers various indicators showing that, as the tax rates increased after the thirties, the subgroup of submarginal loss companies in various industries declined in importance, a finding which has strong support in the regulated utilities, and clear, though somewhat less strong support, in the All Manufacturing group. In spite of such positive evidence for the Krzyzaniak and Musgrave results, Doctor Slitor withholds his judgment since the consequences of the full employment policies in the post-war period might also account for this phenomenon.

The Krzyzaniak–Musgrave discussion points out that the use of a pressure variable for the purpose of isolating tax effects is illegitimate because it assigns great importance to underemployment to explain changes in the before-tax rate of return on capital. This runs counter to the evidence of the late twenties, when both the average rate of return on capital for all manufacturing and the level of unemployment were low. In considering the price umbrella effect, Krzyzaniak and Musgrave show that the regulated utilities (for which Doctor Slitor found evidence of a strong price umbrella) are substantially overshifting.

In their rejoinder, Doctors Goode and Slitor show that the

divergent positions have not yet been bridged; the dispute cannot be settled until further evidence is offered. It is my contention, however, that the airing of all the evidence to date, and efforts to bring new evidence into consideration have brought us closer to a final answer on the question of who pays the corporation income tax. The price umbrella studies may turn out to be crucial.

We now leave it to the individual reader to judge for himself the significance of the steps which have been made in our understanding of the effects of taxes on business, and especially on business profits.

EFFECTS OF PROFITS TAXES: DEDUCED FROM NEOCLASSICAL GROWTH MODELS

Marian Krzyzaniak*

INTRODUCTION

The Main Objective

In 1963, Richard A. Musgrave and I published *The Shifting of the Corporation Income Tax*, a study of the short-run analysis of profits taxation. Our work, however, sought tax effects upon the rate of return on capital during a period too short to allow for changes in capital endowment.[1] Our findings clashed head-on with the well-established beliefs of many economists that profits taxes cannot be shifted in the short run. In a world of perfect markets, or pure monopolies and firms dedicated to short-run profit maximization, investors have no choice but to pay the tax out of the already maximized pretax profits. This is the essence of the "neoclassical" theory of shifting which we used, and it has been arrived at by a priori reasoning. It is chiefly

* In preparation of this paper many helpful comments were received from Dr. Richard Slitor and Dr. Kazuo Sato, and Professors Murray Brown, Thomas Finn, Arnold C. Harberger, Richard A. Musgrave, Karl Roskamp, and Lawrence Seltzer. Programming and simulating of Models B and D was done by the Wayne State University Computing and Data Processing Center operating with the support of National Science Foundation grant number 19981. In the remaining computations I was assisted skillfully by Mr. Willis Burris. Mr. Ben McCallum gave the paper a thorough reading.

[1] The study made little effort to measure short-run shifting on the gross or net share of capital. Shifting or no shifting on factor shares depends in a rather complicated way on the nature of the production function for the whole economy, on the nature of markets for factors and products, etc. Consequently, it is more difficult to isolate tax effects on factor shares than on the rate of return.

on this a priori foundation that Richard Goode and Richard Slitor (elsewhere in this volume) object to our finding that a high degree of short-run shifting characterizes our economy.

But what about the long run? "Long run" here means the end result of short-run changes after allowing adjustments in the total supply of capital by a change in the rate of new capital formation. The total supply of capital may be affected by a profits tax via changes in supply of investible funds and via lowered incentives to invest. Unfortunately very little is known about what determines the investment function in general, and neoclassical economists are less sure in their hypothesizing about the long-run shifting of a profits tax. As in the short-run analysis it is possible either (1) to try to find out empirically how our economy reacts to long-run imposition of a profits tax; or (2) to hypothesize about it by a priori reasoning.

Along the first line of reasoning M. Lerner and S. Hendriksen (13) assigned the changes they observed in the rate of return on capital in U.S. manufacturing between the twenties and early fifties wholly to tax rates on corporate profits. From the size of this tax effect, they concluded that the corporate profits tax was 100 per cent shifted. M. A. Adelman (1) reasoned similarly from changes in capital shares over the periods, and finding no change, claimed zero shifting. Since different economic variables underlie these diverging estimates, they need not be incompatible. One must, however, be aware of their nature. They assign as due to tax the whole change or lack of change in the respective economic variables; hence they do not isolate the tax effect from effects of changes in other exogenous variables that also changed between the two periods, nor do they remove growth effects on these variables. Further, the observed effects cannot be truly long run as (a) the periods compared are not far enough apart in time; and (b) the economy is subject to disturbances all the time; hence no observed period of comparison can present a truly long-run equilibrium. And finally, the theories these findings were supposed to reject or uphold were never clearly worked out, so that no one knows exactly which changes in variables should be measured and what size of change in them would matter.

This brings us to the second line of reasoning. Perhaps in the present unsatisfactory state of our understanding of the problem of long-run shifting, priority should be given to building various hypotheses about it. This paper presents my contribution toward this goal.

To arrive at a long-run theory of shifting one has to start from a known short-run position and then consider how it will affect new capital formation in a context of economic growth. One can first assume that the short-run neoclassical theory of shifting is valid [2] and then it becomes possible to look for long-run equilibrium values of relevant economic variables. It will be necessary to use growth models that adopt (a) a neoclassical investment function, claiming that available funds (i.e. saving) determine investment,[3] and (b) a neoclassical production function.[4] These various components set together present us with a model of a simplified economy that has a time path prescribed by its simultaneous equations. In order to write it up, let us note:

x = Tax rate on business profits.

$\mathcal{Q}_{x,t}$ = Product at time t when tax rate x was imposed in the period zero.

$I_{x,t}$ = Similarly defined new capital formation.

$S_{x,t}$ = Similarly defined total saving.

$s_{x,t}$ = Effective saving rate out of total income.

$K_{x,t}$ = Capital stock.

L_t = Labor force.

$F_{x,t}$ = Gross share of capital (profits before tax divided by value added).

[2] My findings (11) do not lend support to this view. I am trying here to build the first truly long-run "neoclassical" theory. More realistic ones may follow later, but they will be more complicated. This kind of theory needs to be built as it may have some normative uses in a welfare theory context as do most other neoclassical theories.

[3] Thus $I = S$ where I stands for investment and S for saving.

[4] Worked out first by R. Solow. In this paper I make use of production functions investigated by Swan (21), Arrow, Chenery, Minhas, and Solow (3), and Pitchford (18).

Then in the case of a general tax on profits (which is the case we start with) the model will consist of four basic equations:

1. $Q_{z,t} = f(K_{z,t}, L_t, t)$, production function,
2. $L_t = g(t)$, growth of labor force function,
3. $I_{z,t} = S_{z,t} = h(Q_{z,t}, s_{z,t})$, investment function,
4. $s_{z,t} = i(F_{z,t})$, saving rate,

where f, g, h and i are functionals.

Although there is only one exogenous variable, time t, the non-linear functions given initial inputs of capital and labor, and suitable parameters, allow us to determine any variable pertaining to this economy at any point of time. Note also that this model has already made use of any identities such as saving = investment. But it is overly general; the functionals and parameters involved need to be specified. It is here that I borrow heavily from modern neoclassicists without committing myself to the claim that neoclassical approaches describe the behavior of our economy adequately or better than alternative models.

To what use could such a model be put? Suppose one selects the functionals, parameters, and initial values of inputs, and then prescribes the path of the economy subject to this particular structure. If the model also possesses a long-run, stable equilibrium solution, certain key variables level off. If these levels are achieved, then this economy's path will turn into one of balanced growth. Further, for different values of the profits tax rate, these equilibrium values (if they exist) may differ, thereby allowing comparison of equilibrium values resulting from profits tax rate x with those resulting from zero tax. Especially, such comparisons for the rate of return on capital, and for gross and net share of capital, represent isolated long-run tax effects on these variables on which, in turn, degrees of shifting may be computed. And that was the main objective of this study.

As the study progressed its scope was somewhat enlarged. First, a profits tax may affect other long-run economic ratios of interest such as effective saving rate on total income and product-capital ratio. Second, ratios resulting from tax rate x

in period *t* may also be compared with equilibrium ratios when there is no profits tax. This allows us to find the dynamic path of adjustment to profits tax as well as the equilibrium position. Third, if in period zero such a tax was imposed and prior to this period our economy was moving along an equilibrium balanced growth path without tax, the tax effects in period zero collapse to those prescribed by the neoclassical theories of shifting.[5] Although these theories are well established on their own, they now become special cases of the dynamic neoclassical theory of shifting.

Basic Assumptions

The strictly mathematical aspects of the models here introduced can be and are relegated to Appendix I.[6] However, even the reader with adequate understanding of mathematics must be made fully aware of the hidden assumptions. This calls for spelling them out here in words.

As already stated the models considered consist of several simultaneous equations describing how the different important economic series change over time when a tax on business income is imposed. Such a tax may be general, falling on all business income, or non-general, falling for example on the capital earnings in the corporate sector only.[7] The basic neoclassical

[5] Be it of the standard short-run form for a general profits tax or of the "modern" Harberger version of the non-general profits tax (5).

[6] For the models themselves see Appendix I, Models A, B, C, and D.

[7] In the American economy income taxes are not integrated. In general one may consider:

    (1) income tax on profits of unincorporated business and on dividends;

    (2) corporate income tax;

    (3) capital gains tax.

Although in different sectors different taxes may apply, the combined tax rate applicable to investors in the corporate sector need not be very different from that to investors in unincorporated business. If these rates are equal, the income taxes are general despite the fact that in different legal units they are differently named. In such cases, the general tax models still apply.

Professor Musgrave and I ([11] Table 3-1, p. 28, column ix) found that an average investor in corporate business was somewhat discriminated against as compared with an investor in an unincorporated firm. The discrimination in the rate, which may be called a differential tax rate, was on the average close to twenty percentage points. One may, however, suspect that it was offset by the economic advantages of operating under the corporate form which lowers the investor's risk. If so, the differential rate

theory of shifting considered only the general tax on business profits. The case of a non-general tax was lately taken up and elaborated by A. C. Harberger ([5], [6]). His theory calls for adjusting flows of capital between the taxed and non-taxed sectors without affecting the total supply of capital in the economy. Such adjustment is no longer of a short-run nature, but in this paper it will be assumed to occur instantaneously. Starting with either of the above cases, this paper will allow adjustments in the total supply of capital as well, yielding a dynamic and long-run neoclassical theory of shifting of a general [8] *and* non-general [9] profits tax.

Thus we start with typically *neoclassical assumptions:*

(a) Factors are homogeneous.[10]

(b) Businessmen and workers maximize their returns.

(c) Markets for factors and products are purely competitive.[11]

(d) Marginal physical product of a factor is its real price.

(e) If a homogeneous factor is used in different sectors, its net reward (i.e. after tax) is the same in both sectors.

need not lead to any excess burden, and the individual marginal tax rate on business income paid by the average shareholder may still be considered general. Once more, the general tax model could be applied, and as will be shown, this would require a single producing sector only.

Nevertheless, one has to consider what a non-general tax, *if discriminatory*, does to the problem here studied. In such a case one needs at least two-sector models. In the models considered in this paper, sector one stands for corporations; sector two for unincorporated business; and their tax rate is the *corporate differential rate only*.

Harberger in the following chapter in this volume goes deeper into the matter of differential taxation of business noting that corporations are taxed rather unevenly, some, oils, etc., at a considerably lesser rate due to depletion allowance. If property taxes on business are added to profits taxes, the unevenness of tax rates is further increased. Hence, from an economic point of view the legal aspect of incorporation ceases to be a good line of division for business. He proposes simply to group business, irrespective of legal form, into heavily and lightly taxed. Under this new division of businesses, the differential tax rate is somewhat higher than our estimate. Harberger puts it at forty percentage points.

In this paper I use the terms corporated sector and non-corporate sector, but highly taxed and lightly taxed could be substituted.

[8] See Models A and B.

[9] See Models C and D.

[10] Only two factors are assumed to exist: labor and capital.

[11] Many neoclassical theorists require only maximization of returns, allowing monopoly or monopolistic competition. However, in a dynamic setting, for easier computation we need exhaustion of the product so that Euler's theorem may apply. For normative uses of the present theory this restriction would have to be imposed anyway.

(f) If sectoral prices of a factor differ, some units of this factor move to the sector where it is higher priced, until its price is equalized. This adjustment is assumed to be instantaneous.

In a dynamic setting, I impose other concepts modern neoclassicists use upon these assumptions underlying the neoclassical thinking. Thus I will require that:

(a) Production function be linear, homogeneous of degree one,[12] with elasticity of substitution constant.[13]

(b) Technological progress, if adopted in the model,[14] is neutral.[15]

[12] This assumes constant returns to scale, and in a pure competitive economy Euler's theorem will hold.

[13] Econometric estimation, if sought, would be facilitated by this constancy assumption.

For definition of elasticity of substitution of factors σ see R. G. D. Allen (2), pp. 341-43. I consider several special cases with constant elasticity of substitution parameter values; namely, 1 (Cobb-Douglas production function), 1.1,. 99, .8, 2/3, .6, and .5. The last six cases deal with Constant Elasticity of Substitution functions called CES by K. J. Arrow, A. B. Chenery, B. S. Minhas, and R. M. Solow (3) or SMAC by A. A. Walters (23), p. 25. The values 2/3, .6 and .5 are close to Arrow, Chenery, Minhas, and Solow's findings, and in agreement with an independent estimate by J. B. Kravis (8), p. 940. I did not try less plausible values of the elasticity of substitution parameter like 0 (a Leontieff-type model with constant capital-labor ratios would then result).

[14] Models with elasticity of factor substitution $\sigma = 1$ (Cobb-Douglas type productions functions) have stable equilibrium (21). The assumption of neutral technological progress changes equilibrium values but not stability.

Cases of $\sigma \neq 1$ (CES production functions) need not yield stable solutions. This has been shown by J. D. Pitchford [18]. Kazuo Sato [19] claims that unbalanced growth though possible in such cases is not very plausible. Fortunately all cases with zero technological progress rate considered in this study turned out to have stable solutions for the parameters adopted.

Where Hicks neutral technological progress rate was adopted models based on the CES production function (models B and D) yielded unbalanced growth. For $\sigma < 1$ the capital share and for $\sigma > 1$ the labor share persistently declined to zero. This is not a surprise as Hirofumi Uzawa has already shown [22] that neoclassical growth models based on the CES production functions remain balanced only if the technological progress is Harrod neutral. Unbalanced growth models for which the share of any factor declines to zero are contradicted by the apparent stability of factor shares in our economy.

In this study, consequently, in cases with $\sigma \neq 1$ (models B & D) the rate of technological progress is assumed to be zero. For $\sigma = 1$ (models A & C) a positive rate is also considered.

[15] An invention is Hicks neutral if for a constant capital-labor ratio the ratio of marginal physical product of capital to that of labor remains also unchanged. This may be expressed in mathematical terms as follows.
If a production function is subject to technological progress of any kind it shifts as time

(c) Capital goods last forever.[16]

(d) Labor force grows exponentially at a constant rate, independent of economic factors such as real wage rates, etc.

(e) Government taxes business only to buy the final product, it does not participate in any production, and its contribution to national product is nil.[17]

(f) Investment is determined by the availability of funds; namely, whatever is privately saved is privately invested.[18]

(g) Savings are determined by propensities to save, different for business and for individuals, the resulting effective saving rate on total income being a function of factor shares, of group propensities and of the tax rate. The group propensities are assumed constant over time, hence

goes by and may be written $Q_t = F(K_t, L_t, t)$. If this shifting process is Hicks neutral the effect of passage of time may be separated in the following way

$$Q_t = A_t f(K_t, L_t).$$

Harrod neutral technological progress would result in production function of the form

$$Q_t = F[K_t, (A_t L_t)].$$

One notes that in case of $\sigma = 1$ (Cobb Douglas type production function) the case of Harrod neutral technological progress rate cannot be distinguished from the Hicks neutral case.

The assumption of positive Hicks neutral technological progress in models A and C is controversial, subject to conceptual as well as measurement difficulties.

[16] There is no depreciation, and gross and net saving are equal as are gross and net investment. It is expected that finite life of capital goods would not change the results of this paper substantially.

[17] The problem of incidence of government expenditure is bothersome and, in this study, has to be abstracted out before "pure" effects of the tax are obtained. To assure that government purchases have no effect on a nation's welfare or social capital, it would be necessary that government buy only space rockets which when shot never return to earth and never yield any useful economic information, and that the government neither save nor invest.

[18] Thus Say's Law holds; there is never unemployment of labor, and capital is used to capacity.

This also excludes business cycle phenomena. Such an exclusion may be defended on the grounds that a full employment policy is a primary obligation of the federal government, and may be pursued *independently of taxation policies*. If these policies are independent of each other, any measure of tax effects which is affected by the stage of a current or past business cycle is not a measure of *ceteris paribus* tax effects.

marginal and average are equal. This is a proper assumption if we look at long-run propensities.[19]

(h) The product is either a homogeneous good, or if many goods are produced they are represented by an index number.[20]

Indicators and Measures

In this paper I try to find out how much different economic variables, in equilibrium and in the absence of a profits tax, will change if a profits tax of rate x is imposed. Such changes indicate the isolated tax effects on these variables, but only in a very raw way. For example, they will depend not only on the tax rate x but also on the level of the equilibrium value of the respective variable. For a more sophisticated analysis, these raw measures must be translated into relative ones: indicators and measures.

Specifically, a profits tax, if imposed on an economy moving along a balanced growth path (i.e., in equilibrium) in the absence of such a tax, may change:

[19] There is good ground to claim that business has a propensity to save far larger than that of individuals. (See Sergei P. Dobrovolsky [4]). The concepts here used are akin to N. Kaldors' (7), but owners of business, especially dividend receivers, have their own propensity to save independent of the amount of profits retained in business. To simplify matters, it is claimed here that individuals, whether wage earners or dividend receivers, have the same, rather small, propensity to save. In fact, cases are considered (a) in which individuals save barely anything (the "Marxist" variant) and (b) in which individuals save more. Businesses save somewhat less if about the same effective saving rate is to be observed, but still many times the individual's rate (the "capitalist" variant).

Luigi L. Pasinetti (17) is interested one step beyond the concern of this paper, namely, in what happens to the distribution of national income by income groups.

[20] For cases of a non-general tax the sectoral products are either two distinct homogeneous goods or two index numbers. Then another problem of indexing arises. These two goods or indexes have to be aggregated further into a real national product.

In case of a non-general tax it is also assumed that the two sectoral goods (or groups of goods) are distinct between the two sectors. This is in agreement with Harberger's (5) claim that the effect of imposition of a corporate income tax is not a wave of disincorporations in manufacturing industries, but a movement of capital from manufacturing to agriculture and real estate which are largely unincorporated. The problem of disincorporations is left out on purpose in this paper. Too little is known about it.

Richard Musgrave in this volume takes up the here omitted problem of different taxation rates on the profits of firms dealing in the same product. He sets this problem, however, in the context of international trade, as such taxation is there rather a rule, and he sees the great importance of it when the respective countries, members of an economic community, want to establish equitable taxation rules. His basic consideration is taxation rules for the European Common Market.

(a) the effective saving rate on total income,
(b) the product-capital ratio,
(c) the gross (before tax) rate of return on capital,
(d) the gross (before tax) share of profits in the total value added, and
(e) the net (after tax) share of profits in the total value added for private use (i.e., after subtracting tax liability from it).

The existence of a profits tax effect on the effective saving rate is crucial in this paper. Only if such an effect exists will investment be affected [21] and thus the total supply of capital change over time. It is this type of dynamic adjustment that we are interested in.

In turn, the product-capital ratio (other economists speak of the capital-output ratio, an inverse of the ratio here used) will be affected. This ratio was recently studied for the U.S. economy, and it showed significant variation over time. A great variety of forces in our economy were claimed to be determinants of this variation, but profits taxes were not considered significant, or worth closer analysis. The models here considered suggest, however, the opposite; hence, the omission of profits tax effects on the product-capital ratio may have been a serious error in empirical studies.

Profits tax effects on the gross rate of return, and on the gross and net share of capital were more widely studied ([1], [11], and [12]). Such effects need numerical expression, if possible, that is invariant for the initial level of these variables. This may be achieved by translating tax-induced changes in variables into various indicators and measures.

An indicator here is a numerical comparison of the variable in question in absence of, and with the tax, and it should be at least invariant as to the magnitude of the variable. Thus simple ratios could be indicators. For example, an indicator of the long-run tax effect upon the effective rate of saving on total income, if noted G_x, could be defined as a ratio of such an equilibrium saving rate with the tax, to that without the tax, or:

[21] The availability of funds theory of investment here assumed excludes tax effects on investment via incentive to invest (i.e., variable profitability rate).

$$G_x = \frac{S_{x,\infty}}{S_{0,\infty}}.$$

If there is no tax effect on saving, $G_x = 1$. If the tax lowers saving then $O < G_x < 1$. Thus, a decline in this indicator marks a positive tax effect. The reader will note that in general an indicator gives an impression of the existence of a tax effect but does not state clearly its direction or its relative magnitude.

Giving it some thought one can build indicators that do more than that. First, they can become zero whenever the variable shows no tax effect. Second, they may have an exactly defined position valued as one (100% of the tax effect). Third, they may take defined numerical positions in between the interval 0 to 1 and beyond it. Indicators of this type may be called measures.

The reader should be warned that indicators and measures may require arbitrary assumptions in their structure, hence, they are useful conventions only to present the data in a better perspective.

Let us now turn to product-capital ratios which will be noted $N_{x,t}$, thus:

$$N_{x,t} = \frac{Q_{x,t}}{K_{x,t}}.$$

One may propose here to note $E_{x,t}$ as the measure of tax effect upon the product-capital ratio and define it dynamically:

$$E_{x,t} = \frac{N_{x,t} - N_{0,\infty}}{N_{0,\infty}}.$$

In the long run this measure becomes:

$$E_x = \frac{N_{x,\infty} - N_{0,\infty}}{N_{0,\infty}}$$

where the sign ∞ denotes equilibrium level of the variable N.

This is a proper measure as it yields $E_x = 0$ for zero tax effect, and doubling of variable N corresponds to 100% of the tax effect.

Tax effects upon the gross rate of return and upon the gross and net share of capital will be measured by degrees of shifting on such variables. Krzyzaniak and Musgrave ([11], pp. 37–39) found that:

(a) It is not enough to determine zero and 100% shifting, one must determine also degrees of shifting within and outside this interval;

(b) Consequently a large, perhaps infinite number of ways to build measures of shifting are permissible;

(c) Two measures turned out to have an easy economic interpretation, the S and S^* measures of shifting.

Before considering these measures let us introduce additional notations and definitions.

Notations:

For Tax Rate $0 < x < 1$	Description of Variables
$y_{x,t}$	Gross (before tax) rate of return on capital
$\pi_{x,t}$	Gross (before tax) profits
$H_{x,t}$	Net share of profits in the total value added for private use.

To get such variables in absence of tax we substitute 0 for x in the subscript.

Definitions:

$$y_{x,t} = \frac{\pi_{x,t}}{K_{x,t}},$$

$$F_{x,t} = \frac{\pi_{x,t}}{\mathcal{Q}_{x,t}},$$

$$H_{x,t} = \frac{\pi_{x,t}(1 - x)}{\mathcal{Q}_{x,t} - x\,\pi_{x,t}}.$$

Following Krzyzaniak and Musgrave (11), the S measures of shifting are here adopted to measure shifting on the gross rate of return and on the gross share, the S^* measure of shifting on the net share, namely:

$$S_{y,t} = \frac{y_{x,t} - y_{0,\infty}}{x\,y_{x,t}}, \quad \text{and} \quad S_{y,\infty} = \frac{y_{x,\infty} - y_{0,\infty}}{x\,y_{x,\infty}},$$

$$S_{F,t} = \frac{F_{x,t} - F_{0,\infty}}{x F_{x,t}}, \qquad S_{F,\infty} = \frac{F_{x,\infty} - F_{0,\infty}}{x F_{x,\infty}},$$

$$S^{*}{}_{H,t} = \frac{H_{x,t} - (1 - x) H_{0,\infty}}{x H_{0,\infty}}, \qquad S^{*}{}_{H,\infty} = \frac{H_{x,\infty} - (1 - x) H_{0,\infty}}{x H_{0,\infty}}.$$

One may note that in case of a general profits tax for $t = 0$ the model should yield short-run neoclassical theory of shifting results, as it does.[22]

Another warning is due. In the short-run under standard neoclassical assumptions, shifting of a general profits tax remains zero. Some economists, anticipating empirical results disagreeing with this "theory," introduced additional concepts of forward and backward shifting. Any short-run shifting will be called forward if it results from increases in prices of products (price administration). Thus the burden of a profits tax falls partly or fully upon consumers. Any short-run shifting will be called backward if it results from lowering returns to other factors, in our case money wages. Thus money wages would have to decline, and the burden of the tax falls partly or fully on wage earners. Unfortunately these two distinctions have no meaning in this paper. First, in the short run we measure shifting from a model in *real* terms (money does not appear as a variable at all), and in real terms wages will decline and profits will rise in cases of both forward and backward shifting; hence, this distinction is lost for computing degrees of shifting. In the long run, which is more basic here, the vehicle of adjustment is neither price administration nor money wage rate depression but changes in capital formation, which is neither forward nor backward shifting as usually defined.

The indicators and measures so far introduced here apply especially to the cases of a general profits tax. Cases of a non-general tax will require several additional concepts of indicators and measures and further consideration of these is relegated to the chapter on non-general profits tax models.

[22] The short-run measure of shifting on the net share, however, is not zero as the neoclassical theory would require. This is entirely due to a peculiar definition for measures of shifting on shares (see [11], p. 11). Measures on shares agreeing completely with neoclassical theory, *e.g.*, tied to rate of return measures, are possible but become ambiguous if positive shifting either forward or backward or a combination of both is allowed in the construction of the measure.

GENERAL PROFITS TAX

The model introduced in my first section will now be considered in the context of a general tax on profits. The context of a non-general tax will be taken up later.

The linear, homogeneous of degree one, production function assumes constant elasticity of substitution of factors noted as σ.[23] For $\sigma = 1$ a Cobb-Douglas type production function applies and, with the help of a simple calculus, the model is easy to resolve for equilibrium values of variables. This case is noted here as Model A.

For $\sigma \neq 1$ the production function is of the CES type. Since equilibrium solutions are more difficult to get for this type, numerical solutions for the key variables were computed by IBM 7070 computer, for the different values of σ given and for the adopted values of the parameters. The following values of σ were considered:

$$\sigma = 1.1, .99, .8, .66667, .6, \text{ and } .5.$$

COBB-DOUGLAS PRODUCTION FUNCTION

Model A

Let us start with the case of the Cobb-Douglas production function and a general tax. This model is represented by the following set of equations:

A-1. $\mathcal{Q}_{x,t} = e^{gt} K_{x,t}^{a} L_t^{b}$, production function; [24]

A-2. $L_t = L_0 e^{ht}$, growth of labor force function;

A-3. $I_{x,t} = \dfrac{dK_{x,t}}{dt} = s_{x,t} \mathcal{Q}_{x,t}$, neoclassical investment function;

A-4. $s_{x,t} = bs_i + as_p (1 - x) + as_i (1 - s_p) (1 - x)$,

  (workers (retained (savings from distributed profits)
  savings) profits)

  effective saving rate out of total income

[23] For definition of σ see (2), pp. 341–43.

[24] As mentioned before, this model and Model C permit introduction of the rate of neutral technological progress. For comparison with Models B and D the cases of $g = 0$ will be also considered.

where $t =$ time (period),

$a =$ share of capital coefficient,

$b =$ share of labor coefficient,

$s_i =$ propensity to save by individuals,

$s_p =$ propensity to retain profits in business.

Note that the effective saving rate out of total income previously noted as $s_{x,t}$ here is not dependent on time; hence the time subscript is omitted further on. It may be rewritten as: $s_x = s_i + as_p (1 - s_i) - ax[s_p + s_i - s_p s_i]$, which, for zero tax, becomes:

A-4a. $s_o = s_i + as_p (1 - s_i)$; hence also,

$s_x = s_o - ax[s_p + s_i - s_p s_i]$.

As the last item to be subtracted is always positive:

$s_x < s_0$ for $0 < x < 1$.

If this model describes our economy adequately, imposition of a profits tax will affect private capital formation negatively.

Parameter Values

This model may be solved for equilibrium values of its variables.[25] These depend only on the values of parameters a, b, h, and g and the tax variable x, but not on time t.

To show what this means for our economy and to measure tax effects, more or less "realistic" values of such parameters were introduced in the model.

A parameter is here considered "realistic" if its value is plausible for the U. S. economy. Where the economic profession entertains divergent estimates, as for example with respect to elasticity of factor substitution σ, several values of parameters were selected over the range of this divergence.

In general the parameters here adopted have a common core but different group saving propensities result in two variants. In the "Marxist" variant, the propensity to save by individuals (mostly workers) is close to nil. In the "capitalist" variant, the propensity to save by individuals is more substantial though

[25] For the general way of solving for equilibrium values see Appendix I, Model A.

lower than the propensity to retain profits by business. It is of interest to find in what ways such differences in propensities to save influence the various tax effects. Specifically in this model the common core is:

$$g = .015,[26] \ h = .01, \ a = .3, \ b = .7, \text{ and } x = .5,$$

with two variants of propensities to save:[27]

(a) the Marxist variant assuming

$$s_p = .66667 \text{ and } s_i = .005, \text{ and}$$

(b) the capitalist variant assuming

$$s_p = .5 \text{ and } s_i = .05.$$

Equilibrium Solution

The equilibrium solution to this model,[28] and the variables of interest are shown as functions of parameters in Table 1. Measures and indicators of tax effects derived from this table are given in Table 2. One should note here that none of the measured tax effects depends on the rate of neutral technological progress, though the variables do.

In the short run, according to the measures of shifting on the rate of return and on the gross share, the tax falls on business due to the nature of the standard neoclassical model. Shifting measured on the net share of capital in the short run is a positive function, but this is a definitional matter (see n. 22).

However, there can be no long-run shifting on the gross share since, due to the particular production function (Cobb-Douglas type), the gross share is invariant to changes in the effective rate of saving. Thus business pays the tax (sharewise) in full, even in the long run.

[26] To allow comparison with the CES models (B and D), the case of zero neutral technological progress rate, i.e., $g = 0$ was also considered.

[27] To get more contrast, propensities to retain profits s_p are somewhat exaggerated. Those considered here are more realistic for the war periods than for the present, being now somewhat less for business.

In the CES models only the capitalist variant was studied. The Marxist variant was omitted to save computations as it was considered less applicable to the U.S. economic problems.

[28] See Appendix I, Model A.

Table 1
General Solution, Variables

Effective saving rate on total income		Product-capital ratio		Gross rate of return on capital		Gross share of capital		Net share of capital		
In Absence of Tax	With Tax	In Period Zero	Long Run with Tax	In Period Zero	Long Run with Tax	In Period Zero	Long Run with Tax	Long Run in Absence of Tax	In Period Zero	Long Run with Tax
s_0	s_x	$N_{0,\infty}=N_{x,0}$	$N_{x,\infty}$	$y_{0,\infty}=y_{x,0}$	$y_{x,\infty}$	$F_{0,\infty}=F_{x,0}$	$F_{x,\infty}$	$H_{0,\infty}$	$H_{x,0}$	$H_{x,\infty}$
$s_i+as_p(1-s_i)$	$s_0-ax[s_p+s_i-s_ps_i]$	$\dfrac{(g/b+h)}{s_0}$	$\dfrac{(g/b+h)}{s_x}$	$aN_{x,0}$	$aN_{x,\infty}$	a	a	a	$\dfrac{a(1-x)}{1-ax}$	$\dfrac{a(1-x)}{1-ax}$

Table 2
General Solution, Tax Effects

Shifting						Other tax effects on	
Short run			Long run			Saving	Product-Capital Ratio
On the Rate of Return	On the Gross Share	On the Net Share	On the Rate of Return	On the Net Share	On the Gross Share		
$S_{y,0}$	$S_{F,0}$	$S^*_{H,0}$	$S_{y,\infty}$	$S^*_{H,\infty}$	$S_{F,\infty}$	G_x	E_x
0	0	$\dfrac{a(1-x)}{1-ax}$	$\dfrac{1}{x}[1-G_x]$	$\dfrac{a(1-x)}{1-ax}$	0	s_x/s_0	$\dfrac{1}{G_x}-1$

s_0-ax

Table 3

Variables (tax rate $x = .5$)

Type of Propensity to Save	Effective saving rate on total income		Product-capital ratio		Gross rate of return on capital		Gross share of capital		Net share of capital		
	In Absence of Tax	With Tax	In Period Zero	Long Run with Tax	In Period Zero	Long Run with Tax	In Period Zero	Long Run with Tax	Long Run In Absence of Tax	In Period Zero	Long Run with Tax
	s_0	s_x	$N_{0,\infty} = N_{x,0}$	$N_{x,\infty}$	$y_{0,\infty} = y_{x,0}$	$y_{x,\infty}$	$F_{0,\infty} = F_{x,0}$	$F_{x,\infty}$	$H_{0,\infty}$	$H_{x,0}$	$H_{x,\infty}$
Neutral Technological Progress:[1]											
Marxist	.2040	.10375	.15406	.30293	.04622	.09088	.3	.3	.3	.17647	.17647
Capitalist	.1925	.11375	.16327	.27630	.04898	.08289	.3	.3	.3	.17647	.17647
No Neutral Technological Progress:[2]											
Marxist	.2040	.10375	.04902	.09639	.01471	.02892	.3	.3	.3	.17647	.17647
Capitalist	.1925	.11375	.05195	.08791	.01559	.02637	.3	.3	.3	.17647	.17647

[1] $g = .015$

[2] $g = 0$ (Note that variables N and y are small in this case.)

Table 4

Tax Effects[1]

(tax rate $x = .5$)

Type of Propensity to Save	Shifting						Other tax effects on	
	Short Run			Long Run			Saving	Product-Capital Ratio
	On The Rate of Return	On The Gross Share	On The Net Share	On The Rate of Return	On The Gross Share	On The Net Share		
	$S_{y,0}$	$S_{F,0}$	$S*_{H,0}$	$S_{y,\infty}$	$S_{F,\infty}$	$S*_{H,\infty}$	G_x	E_x
Marxist	0	0	.17647	.9295	0	.17647	.50858	.9627
Capitalist	0	0	.17647	.81818	0	.17647	.59091	.69231

[1] No distinction is made between cases with neutral technological progress rate $g = .015$ and for zero of such rate. Tax effects are independent of it.

Nevertheless, the long-run view, in general, is different from the short-run view. The numerical values of the variables involved are given in Table 3. These in turn are translated into measures and indicators of tax effects as given in Table 4.

We note that the long-run shifting, as measured on the rate of return, is substantial but somewhat less than 100 per cent. Apparently the tax on profits negatively affects new private capital formation. Thus, in the long run with the tax, capital becomes somewhat more scarce than in the absence of the tax, so the rate of return rises, allowing substantial but not full recoupment of the tax burden on the rate of return. As the negative tax effect on the effective saving rate on total income is more pronounced in the Marxist variant, businessmen fare better if the society's propensity to save is Marxist rather than capitalist.

There is one more lesson to be drawn. When capital formation is reduced, the tax on profits makes the product-capital ratio for the whole economy rise substantially, and this is a factor to be noted in exploring the historical trend of that ratio.

One finally may note that though some shifting on the rate of return occurs in the long run it cannot be classified either as forward or backward. As we noted it was all due to changes in capital formation. Only in the short run, shifting, if it occurs, may be forward (if the rate of return increases due to a tax-induced rise in product prices) or backward (if the rate of return increases due to a tax-induced lowering of other factor returns, especially money wage rates). In a neoclassical model in the short run there cannot be either forward or backward shifting as shifting is then nil anyway.

Time Path

Finally one may ask how long it takes to get to the long-run solution. By the nature of the model an infinite number of periods is needed. We may, however, change the question and ask how fast our variables converge to their long-run equilibrium levels.

As changes in the national product-capital ratio $N_{z,t}$ underlie changes in the other variables, we will pay attention to convergence in this particular variable only. Accordingly, speed of convergence will be defined by the number of periods after which the fraction k of the long-run equilibrium effect on the national product-capital ratio is reached.[29]

Table 5 gives us that insight for the cases with $g = .015$. We

Table 5

Speed of Adjustment[1]

(tax rate $x = .5$; neutral technological progress rate $g = .015$)

k	Marxist propensity to save		Capitalist propensity to save	
	t_k	S_{y,t_k}^2	t_k	S_{y,t_k}^2
.1	9.0	.176	6.8	.129
.2	15.0	.324	13.8	.243
.3	27.8	.449	21.4	.344
.4	38.1	.558	23.6	.434
.5	49.4	.652	38.8	.514
.6	62.5	.734	43.6	.587
.7	78.2	.807	62.7	.653
.8	99.2	.872	80.4	.713
.9	133.1	.930	109.3	.768
.95	165.8	.957	157.2	.794
.99	239.8	.978	237.3	.813
1.00	∞	.983	∞	.818

[1] Computed with respect to the fraction k of E_x. Then for the computed t_k the S_{y,t_k} is also shown. S_{y,t_k} stands here for shifting on the gross rate of return, measured from the period of tax imposition to period t_k.

[2] Estimated according to formula $S_{y,t_k} = \dfrac{E_{x,t_k}}{x E_{x,t_k} + 1}$.

note that a long time has to pass to get 90, 95 or 99 per cent of the tax effect. For 90 per cent between 100 to 140 periods,[30] and for 99 per cent close to 250 periods are needed. In cases with zero neutral technological progress rate,[31] the convergence would slow down by the factor $\dfrac{g + bh}{bh} \sim 3.1$; hence to get 90

[29] $k = \dfrac{E_{x,t_k}}{E_x}$. For derivation of the speed series see Appendix I, Model A.

[30] This is in agreement with Professor Ryuzo Sato's results (20).

[31] For derivation of this see Appendix I, Model A.

per cent of the tax effect we would have to wait 300 to 350 periods, to get 95 per cent we would have to wait 450 to 500 periods, and to get 99 per cent 700 to 750 periods would be needed. The zero neutral technological progress case is, however, less realistic than the $g = .015$ case. The resulting equilibrium values of gross rate of return on capital and of product-capital ratio are "realistic" for the $g = .015$ case and "unrealistically" small for the $g = 0$ case.

But what does the large number of periods required to get a fraction k of the total tax effect mean in terms of days, months, and years? One interpretation would be that periods represent four months.[32] This interpretation, however, violates the principles according to which we selected the values of parameters in this study. In particular, the rate of growth of the labor force is given values approximating the one observed for the economy as a whole on a per annum basis. Also, $g = .015$ refers to a rate in terms of years. Consequently the periods have to be assigned the length of one year. For the "realistic" $g = .015$ case several generations have to pass before approximately the full effect of the tax will be borne by this economy. In the case $g = 0$, the speed of adjustment is even slower and centuries have to pass, but we have noted this is a less "realistic" case.

What is then the importance of studying adjustments requiring such a long passage of time? A politician determining tax policies most likely will forget the long-run implications of his current actions if such implications are liable to appear only after his death. The statesman, however, should not. It is to him, then, that this study is addressed.

CES PRODUCTION FUNCTION

Model B

For elasticity of substitution $\sigma \neq 1$, the linear, homogeneous of degree one, production function takes the form:

$$\mathcal{Q}_{x,t} = [aK_{x,t}^{-r} + bL_t^{-r}]^{-1/r},$$

[32] An inverse of the velocity of income would yield periods of four months and over. See Fritz Machlup (14).

which may also be written:

$$\mathcal{Q}_{x,t} = \left[a + b\left(\frac{K_{x,t}}{L_t}\right)^r \right]^{-1/r} K_{x,t}\ ^{33}$$

where $r = \dfrac{1 - \sigma}{\sigma}$ or $\sigma = \dfrac{1}{1 + r}$.

Unfortunately, even if $(a + b) = 1$, the models based on the above production function are hard to resolve and their general solution eluded me. However, with some small changes in the structure of the model, I was able to simulate the model on a 7070 IBM computer by iterative computation of the model variables for consecutive periods. The computer, however, cannot run forever. Fortunately, if an equilibrium solution exists, the key variables asymptotically level off, and the model approaches a balanced growth path. Values of variables of the 750th period were adopted as it has been found that they approximated closely enough the long-run equilibrium values.

As in the previous model, the labor force is assumed to grow at a constant rate h, independent of taxes, thus:

$$L_t = L_0 e^{ht}.$$

The investment function had to be modified first. In Model A it was represented by a differential equation. Here, to facilitate computations, it was changed to a difference equation. The second change was in the definition of saving. The equality of saving with investment and the availability of funds, as in the neoclassical theory of investment, still holds, but saving now is defined in the Robertsonian [34] sense, i.e., saving in the current period is what was not consumed in the preceding period. Thus:

$$I_{x,t} = K_{x,t} - K_{x,t-1} = S_{x,t} = s_{x,t-1}\mathcal{Q}_{x,t-1}.$$

The need for such changes is obvious if one looks at the effective saving rate on total income. It is no longer a constant

---

[33] The CES models (B and D) yield persistently declining to zero share functions (capital or wage) if positive neutral technological progress is introduced. This seems to be unrealistic. Hence such a progress rate was here assumed to be zero.

[34] This change affects the dynamic path but not the long-run stable solution (if such exists). Fortunately, our main interest is in this solution and only secondarily in the path towards it.

because gross shares are now affected by the rate of tax on profits; even if the group propensities to save, s_i and s_p, remain unchanged, the effective rate of saving out of total income function takes a rather complicated form. By lagging saving, the production function turns with ease into a reduced form and the computer may take over the search for the numerical solution.

With tax rate x, we have by the Euler theorem:

$$s_{x,t} = \left[s_p \frac{K_{x,t}}{Q_{x,t}} \frac{\partial Q_{x,t}}{\partial K_{x,t}} + s_i (1 - s_p) \frac{K_{x,t}}{Q_{x,t}} \frac{\partial Q_{x,t}}{\partial K_{x,t}} \right] (1 - x)$$

(retained profits)   (withdrawals) $+ s_i \frac{L_t}{Q_{x,t}} \frac{\partial Q_{x,t}}{\partial L_t}.$

(wages)

This rather complicated formula may be somewhat simplified if we use the capital share concept $F_{x,t}$. Then for $0 \le x < 1$ we get:

$$s_{x,t} = s_i + F_{x,t} [s_p (1 - s_i) - x (s_p + s_i - s_i s_p)].$$

Note here that now the effective saving rate out of total income depends on time, hence the time subscript cannot be omitted.

Parameter Values

As in Model A, "realistic" values of parameters had to be adopted. Of course, these are an inference only. One would want those for which the resulting equilibrium variables are close to the ones observed for our economy.[35] Also, to save computer time, only the capitalist variant is taken up.[36]

[35] Note that for $\sigma \neq 1$ the equilibrium level of the capital or labor share in this economy differs from the share parameters a and b used in the model, i.e., $a \neq F_{x,\infty}$ and $b \neq 1 - F_{x,\infty}$. Only for $\sigma = 1$, with the Cobb-Douglas production function, do the parameters and the factor shares coincide.

To get realistic numerical levels of factor shares one should vary such parameters together with the elasticity of substitution of factors σ. To yield a long-run equilibrium realistic gross share of capital, i.e., between .2 and .3, the higher the σ, the lower should be the value of the parameter. Unfortunately, any hunt for the proper value of the a parameters would require many runs on the computer. Such runs are costly and restricted funds posed a prohibiting constraint.

The alternative to varying the values of parameters a and b is to use some of their constant values. For the Cobb-Douglas with $\sigma = 1$ case (Model A) and for the CES production function with $\sigma = 1.1$ (Model B), $a = .3$ was chosen. For $\sigma < 1$ (Model B), $a = .5$ was considered proper, though perhaps somewhat on the low side for elasticity σ low.

[36] The capitalist variant was considered more relevant for the U.S. economy.

Thus the following parameter values were adopted in Model B: for $\sigma = 1.1$,

$$g = 0, \ a = .3, \ b = .7, \ h = .01, \ s_p = .5, \ s_i = .05, \ x = .5;$$

and for $\sigma < 1$,

$$g = 0, \ a = .5, \ b = .5, \ h = .01, \ s_p = .5, \ s_i = .05, \ x = .5.$$

Equilibrium Solution

No general solution to the equilibrium values in terms of parameters for this model is offered. Instead numerical cases for several values of elasticity of substitution parameter σ are solved by simulation of the model on the 7070 IBM computer.[37] The 750th period variables are considered close enough to their equilibrium values. As noted before, only the capitalist variant and cases with zero neutral technological progress rate, i.e., $g = 0$ were considered. The speed in Model A in such a case assured us that about 99 per cent of the change in the product-capital ratio will be accounted by the 750th period.[38] As shown in Table 8, this appears to hold approximately in this case as well.

The numerical values of the variables sought are given in Table 6 and the resulting measures and indicators of tax effects in Table 7.

A simple way of reviewing the cases is to present the measures and indicators as functions of the elasticity of substitution of factors parameter σ. In the following graphs the solution for the capitalist variant with $g = 0$ is shown. The graphs themselves are disjointed between $\sigma = .99$ and $\sigma = 1$ because the embedded capital share parameter a differs; for $\sigma < 1$ it is $a = .5$, and for $\sigma \geq 1$, $a = .3$. Most of the measures and indicators are only slightly affected by this variation in parameter a as the break points on the curves are not far apart.

Graph 1 relates tax effects on the saving rate and on the

[37] For the simulation method see Appendix I, Model B.

[38] 700 to 750 periods were required to get 99 per cent accuracy in Model A with zero neutral technological progress.

Table 6
Variables[1]

(tax $x = .5$, $a = .5$, for $\sigma < 1$, $a = .3$ for $\sigma = 1.1$)

Elasticity of factor substitution	Effective saving rate			Product-capital ratio		Gross rate of return		Gross share of capital		Net share of capital		
	In Absence of Tax, Long Run	With Tax		In Absence of Tax, Long Run	With Tax, Long Run	In Absence of Tax, Long Run, and With Tax in Period Zero	With Tax, Long Run	In Absence of Tax, Long Run, and With Tax in Period Zero	With Tax, Long Run	In Absence of Tax, Long Run	With Tax	
		In Period Zero	Long Run								In Period Zero	Long Run
σ	$s_{0,750}$	$s_{z,0}^2$	$s_{z,750}$	$N_{0,750} = N_{z,0}$	$N_{z,750}$	$y_{0,750} = y_{z,0}$	$y_{z,750}$	$F_{0,750} = F_{z,0}$	$F_{z,750}$	$H_{0,750}$	$H_{z,0}^3$	$H_{z,750}$
1.1	.24012	.13505	.13053	.04195	.07649	.01679	.02899	.40025	.37898	.40025	.25019	.23379
.99	.27968	.15275	.15337	.03641	.06599	.01761	.03210	.48354	.48646	.48354	.31886	.32140
.8	.16753	.10258	.10858	.05998	.09240	.01484	.02547	.24744	.27567	.24744	.14119	.15987
.66667	.11902	.08088	.08624	.08445	.11634	.01227	.01984	.14530	.17054	.14530	.07834	.09322
.6	.10098	.07281	.07725	.09946	.12988	.01068	.01666	.10734	.12823	.10734	.05671	.06851
.5	.07987	.06336	.06612	.12575	.15171	.00791	.01151	.06287	.07585	.06287	.03245	.03942

[1] The "capitalist" variants assume that individuals (mostly workers) save more substantially, though their propensity to save is smaller than the propensity to retain profits by business. Here it means that business propensity to retain profits $s_p = .5$, and individuals propensity to save $s_i = .05$.

[2] Effective saving rate with rate x in period zero was computed according to formula $s_{z,0} = s_i + F_{z,0}[s_p(1-s_i) - x(s_p+s_i)] = .05 + .2125 F_{z,0}$.

[3] Computed according to formula $H_{z,0} = \dfrac{(1-x)F_{z,0}}{1-xF_{z,0}}$.

Table 7

Tax Effects

(tax $x = .5$, $a = .5$ for $\sigma < 1$, $a = .3$ for $\sigma = 1.1$)

Elasticity of factor substitution	Short-run shifting			Long-run shifting			Tax effects	
	On the Rate of Return	On the Gross Share	On the Net Share	On the Rate of Return	On the Gross Share	On the Net Share	On the Saving Rate	On the Product-Capital Ratio
σ	$S_{y,0}$	$S_{F,0}$	$S^*_{H,0}$	$S_{y,750}$	$S_{F,750}$	$S^*_{H,750}$	G_x	E_x
1.1	0	0	.25017	.84167	.11225	.16822	.54360	.82336
.99	0	0	.31886	.90280	.01201	.32936	.54838	.81241
.8	0	0	.14120	.83471	.20481	.29219	.64812	.54051
.66667	0	0	.07832	.76310	.29600	.28314	.72458	.37762
.6	0	0	.05664	.71789	.32582	.27650	.76500	.30585
.5	0	0	.03229	.62554	.34225	.25402	.82784	.20644

Table 8

Speed of Adjustment

Period[2]	Product-capital ratio in period t					Tax effect on the product-capital ratio in period t as a fraction of its long-run equilibrium effect[1]		
	0	500	600	700	750	500	600	700
σ	$N_{x,0}=N_{0,750}$	$N_{x,500}$	$N_{x,600}$	$N_{x,700}$	$N_{x,750}$	$\dfrac{E_{x,500}}{E_x}$	$\dfrac{E_{x,600}}{E_x}$	$\dfrac{E_{x,700}}{E_x}$
1.1	.04195	.07477	.07575	.07631	.07649	.95020	.97858	.99479
.8	.05998	.09147	.09207	.09233	.09240	.97131	.98982	.99784
.66667	.08445	.11452	.11578	.11624	.11634	.94293	.9244	.99686
.6	.09946	.12752	.12918	.12976	.12988	.92242	.97699	.99606
.5	.12575	.14789	.15063	.15153	.15171	.85285	.95840	.99307

[1] The formula for adjustment in period t is $\dfrac{N_{x,t}-N_{0,750}}{N_{x,750}-N_{0,750}}$.

[2] The earlier periods values, being too much contaminated by our arbitrary choice of initial inputs, are omitted.

Graph 1

Long-Run Tax Effect on the Effective
Saving Rate and on the Product-Capital Ratio
(capitalist variant, tax rate $x = .5$,
$a = .5$ for $\sigma < 1$, and $a = .3$ for $\sigma = 1.1$)

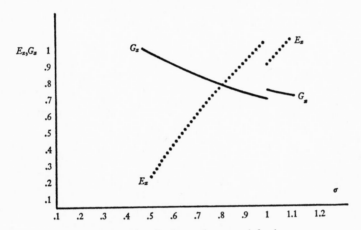

———————— G_x Tax effect on the effective saving rate, defined as

$$\frac{\text{long-run saving rate with tax } x}{\text{long-run saving rate in absence of tax}}.$$

· · · · · · · · · · · · E_x Tax effect on the product-capital ratio, defined as increase in the long-run product-capital ratio, due to imposition of tax x to the long-run capital-product ratio in absence of tax.

product-capital ratio to the parameter σ. The depressing tax effect on saving is related inversely to the elasticity of substitution of factors σ, and vice versa on the product-capital ratio. The reason is as follows. For smaller σ the gross share of capital for a constant implicit capital share coefficient a is also smaller. As the group propensity of firms to retain profits is higher than the propensity to save by individuals, it makes for a lesser decline in the over-all saving rate if the tax on profits is imposed.

We turn now to the short-run solution. The model starts from the standard neoclassical theory of shifting; hence there cannot be any short-run shifting either on the gross share or on the rate of return. The short-run shifting on the net share is not zero, but this is once more a definitional matter.

For the long run there is shifting on the rate of return as the profits tax negatively affects capital formation. Graph 2 relates

Graph 2

Long-Run Shifting on the Rate of Return
(capitalist variant, tax rate $x = .5$,
$a = .5$ for $\sigma < 1$, $a = .3$ for $\sigma \geq 1$)

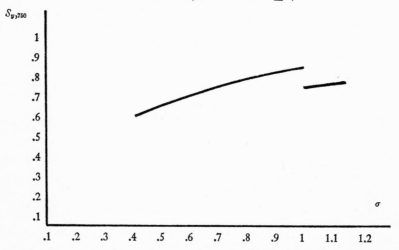

the long-run shifting on the gross rate of return to σ elasticity of substitution of factors. From Graph 2 we note that shifting is facilitated by the higher value of σ. We may note here that even for $\sigma = 1$ such shifting on the rate of return as occurs does not reach 100 per cent.[39] This would be of interest if one wanted to generalize a neoclassical investment function into a world in which investment depends not only on available funds but also on the expected level of the rate of return. Moreover, this model, if compared with Model A (case of $\sigma = 1$) is of great interest because it no longer preserves constancy of gross shares for variations in the tax rate. As shown on Graph 3, this results for small σ in a positive long-run shifting on gross shares; this shifting declines as σ increases, becomes zero for $\sigma = 1$, and turns negative for $0 > 1$. The relation appears to be monotonic giving

[39] For very small values of σ, the gross share of capital $F_{x,\infty}$ with tax, and $F_{0,\infty}$ in absence of tax, is small; hence a profits tax has little effect on the effective saving rate and new capital formation is affected very little. Consequently the gross rate of return will not rise much.

Graph 3

Long-Run Shifting on the Gross Share
(capitalist variant, tax rate $x = .5$,
$a = .5$ for $\sigma < 1$, $a = .3$ for $\sigma \geq 1$)

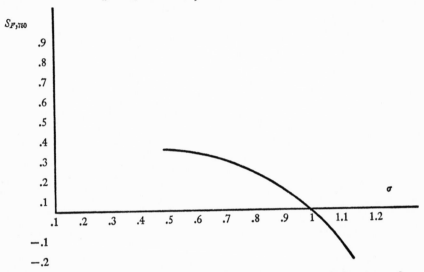

support to the methods of estimating σ from the behavior of the wage share.[40]

Graph 4 relates long-run shifting on the net share to the value of σ. It differs from the short-run picture which, as we have already noted, showed positive shifting for definitional reasons. The long-run shifting is substantial even for $\sigma = .5$, then it rises slowly, reaching its peak at $\sigma = 1$, then for $0 > 1$ it declines. One notes also that shifting on the net share is rather sensitive to the choice of the embedded capital share parameter a which for $\sigma < 1$ is set at $a = .5$ and for $\sigma \geq 1$ at $a = .3$. A more substantial gap between the two branches of the shifting function results.

The result that long-run shifting on both the gross and the net shares is variable over time for $\sigma \neq 1$ and for different rates of a profits tax, has important distributional implications around which a neoclassical theory of long-run tax effects may

[40] For example the Arrow, Chenery, Minhas and Solow paper (3) seems to be estimating σ that way, fitting wage shares by cross section analysis. According to E. Kuh (12), p. 208, such a cross-section is liable to yield longer-run parameters.

Graph 4
Short-Run and Long-Run Shifting on the Net Share
(capitalist variant, tax rate $x = .5$,
$a = .5$ for $\sigma < 1$, $a = .3$ for $\sigma \geq 1$)

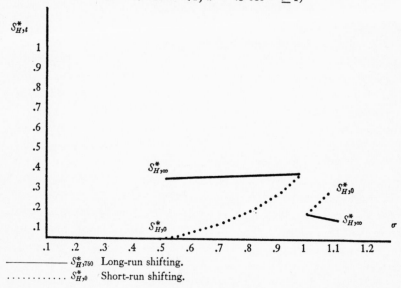

——————— $S^*_{H,750}$ Long-run shifting.
. . . . $S^*_{H,0}$ Short-run shifting.

be built. Because of limitation of funds, I confined myself to neoclassical theory of shifting.

NON-GENERAL PROFITS TAX

The Harberger Model

A. C. Harberger ([5], [6], and elsewhere in this book) notes that in the U.S. different businesses are taxed differently; thus the profits taxes are not completely general. Since the standard neoclassical theory does not consider this aspect, he worked out another theory of shifting for the case where the profits tax falls on profits in one business [41] but not in another.

[41] Note that, for two reasons, the differences in profit taxation under progressive personal income tax rates need not be considered:
    (a) Progressive rates of personal income taxes call for readjustments in investors' claims, each investor maximizing his own net income. These are more transfers of titles of property and ownership than transfers of physical capital assets between different uses. Only the last is the subject of both Harberger's theory of shifting and the one developed here.
    (b) The whole subject of personal income taxation will here be ruled out if the personal income tax is proportional. Such a rate would not have a "differential" part. Let this be assumed in this chapter.

This is a simplification of reality. In fact, different businesses even if subject to different tax rates are never completely tax exempt. There is always a "common" part of such taxation that falls on all businesses and a "differential" part that falls on some but not on others.

One way to study this problem would be to introduce different rates of taxation in two sectors, corporate and noncorporate, the corporate sector tax rate being the higher. This was thought to complicate the model too much and was not examined either by Harberger nor will it be in this study. Another way, adopted to some degree here, is to study the common and the differential profits tax effects separately, and then only for an economy subject to both, to arrive at a combined measurement of these tax effects. Such combined measures and indicators will be in the nature of weighted averages of common and differential tax effects. Such weights will most likely be of a very complex nature. In this paper only the simplest case is considered in footnote 54. There the common part of tax is subject to standard neoclassical shifting theory and the "differential" part is subject to Harberger's adjustment. Also the total supply of capital is considered given; hence no dynamic adjustment in the capital supply is superimposed.

In one respect Harberger's model is more general than its version here. He somewhat relaxes the perfect competition assumption for factors and for products, requiring only that investors, businesses, workers, etc., be maximizers of their returns and that markets be either perfect or monopolistic. I adopted the more restrictive assumption of perfectly competitive markets which not only simplifies the calculus involved in solving the model but also results in a "theory" of shifting for normative use.

Harberger further observes that the differently taxed sectors deal in different products.[42] The differential profits tax, if this tax is not shifted as neoclassicists claim, lowers the net (after

[42] The problem of differentially taxed firms in the same industry is bothersome and would require different analysis. Fortunately in the U.S. firms within one industry are usually taxed at the same rate, exemptions to this rule being rare or unimportant. This is not so for firms operating internationally or facing foreign competition in their domestic markets. R. A. Musgrave deals more closely with this aspect (elsewhere in this book).

tax) rate of return to capital in the taxed sector. Harberger adopts the neoclassical assumption that this would result in transfer of usage of capital goods [43] from the taxed to the non-taxed sector of our economy.[44] As time progresses, and more of capital goods are transferred from taxed to non-taxed sectors, they become more scarce in the first, more abundant in the second sector of industries. This, in turn, allows the before-tax rate of return in the taxed sector to rise and compels it to fall in the non-taxed sector. The movement of physical assets between the two sectors stops when the net rates of return on capital in both sectors are equalized.

If, after a lapse of time the gross rate of return in the taxed sector were to be observed, some shifting would be claimed as the gross rate of return in this sector rises; hence it might be concluded that the investor in this sector no longer bears the full burden of the differential tax. Such a claim, however, could be misleading. What happens to the gross rate of return on capital in the whole economy should be noticed. As the rate in the non-taxed sector falls, the over-all gross rate may remain unchanged showing that the capital-owning class still bears the burden of the tax in full and so there is zero shifting of the differential profits tax. In such a case any shifting observed in the taxed sector alone measures the transference of the tax burden within the capitalist class.

The Harberger adjustment to the differential profits tax obviously requires time; [45] hence it is not truly short run as the standard neoclassical tax effect is. Neither is it a long-run adjust-

---

[43] Disincorporations, and changes in portfolios including substitution of borrowed funds for equity, are not considered here.

[44] Harberger notes that agriculture and real estate are largely unincorporated. He is then willing to go further, leave the legal form of business entirely out of the picture, and lump together agriculture and real estate with industries exempted partially from taxation under depletion allowances, etc. Even differentials in property taxation are lumped together in what would then be the non-taxed (differentially) sector.

[45] One should note here that efforts to isolate the required capital flows have so far failed. Harberger (5) does not offer any data to prove they occur. The observed growth of corporate and non-corporate sectors seems unaffected by tax differentials. In a crude effort to isolate them, I regressed changes in equity capital in all manufacturing companies with and without profits given in *Statistics of Income* for the years 1936-42, 1949-59, on changes in the differential tax given in (11), Table 3-1, Col. ix, p. 28, lagged one period and unlagged. Least squares estimates of the regression function yielded:

ment similar to the one studied in this paper because he assumes the total supply of capital to be unaffected by the tax.[46] In

(1) $\Delta K_t = a_0 - .06236 \, \Delta Z_{t-1}{}^{**} + u_t,$
$\qquad [-.40346]$
$\quad R = 0;$

(2) $\Delta K_t = b_0 - .01536 \, \Delta Z_t{}^{**} + v_t,$
$\qquad [-.09129]$
$\quad R \quad = 0;$

where

ΔK_t = Change in total capital in all manufacturing in hundred billions of dollars.
$\Delta Z_t{}^{**}$ = Change in differential tax rate.
u_t and v_t = Stochastic variables $[N, O, \sigma^2]$.
= Square brackets contain the ratio of the regression coefficient to its standard error; i.e., the value of the t statistic.
R = Multiple correlation coefficient adjusted for degrees of freedom.

The apparent lack of a causal relation between the regressor and regressant variables as shown by R and t statistics is bothersome. One could claim the following alternatives:

(a) The capital flows do occur but over a period somewhat longer than two years. A distributed lag estimate of the above relation between ΔK_t and $\Delta Z_t{}^{**}$ could perhaps give the final answer as to whether such relation exists.

(b) Perhaps in a more general case in which elasticities of substitution of factors in both sectors and elasticity of product substitution differ, given realistic assumptions as to the values of these different σ's, we would get capital flows of a very small size. Unfortunately, Models A and B applicable to the case of general profits tax will then become good approximations, and Models C and D applicable to differential profits tax will become somewhat superfluous.

(c) One could dispense with Models C and D of this section if the tax differential is offset by advantages of operation under corporate form, with a result of no capital flows.

(d) Finally capital flows need not occur if the economy does not heed neoclassical assumptions. For example, if the tax is shifted 100 per cent in the short run, thus restoring the net rate of return on capital to its pretax level, this rationale for physical capital flows vanishes.

Be it as it may, we explore here in Models C and D the case in which neoclassical assumptions hold. The existence of adjusting capital flows of the Harberger type may be proven in the future by more refined methods (e.g., by distributed lag estimation).

[46] Perhaps one could call Harberger's flows medium-run as this adjustment may be speedier than the adjustment in the total supply of capital via new capital formation. If so, the measures of shifting observed would be of a mixed type partly due to Harberger's adjustment, partly due to adjustment in new capital formation.

In the dynamic theory here proposed the Harberger adjustment is assumed to be instantaneous; i.e., after imposition of a tax we start in period zero from an economy that already had adjusted itself along Harberger's lines. Thus, the variables for the whole economy and for its sectors are no longer those of the long-run equilibrium in the absence of the tax.

Denoting the corporate (more highly taxed) sector by subscript 1, we then have:

$y_{x,0} \neq y_{0,\infty}; \; y_{1, \, x,0} \neq y_{1,0,\infty},$
$F_{x,0} \neq F_{0,\infty}; \; F_{1,x,0} \neq F_{1,0,\infty},$ and
$N_{x,0} \neq N_{0,\infty}.$

Once more our variables collapse in period zero to a neoclassical model but this time the model is not the "standard" but the Harberger version of it, which is not short run.

cases of a general tax we have already found that this need not hold, and one may suspect that the differential profits taxation is subject to similar type of adjustment in the total supply of capital. This paper thus becomes a generalization of A. C. Harberger's theory by allowing adjustments in the total supply of capital as well. In some general sense this is very much similar to what was done in the general profits tax case. The difference is that, in the general profits tax case we start with the standard neoclassical theory and in the case of non-general profits tax with the Harberger version, then we apply the same type of dynamic adjustment to both: changes in new capital formation.

Our Model

In general our model for the differential tax case resembles the case with a general tax, but is more complex. Instead of one production function for the whole economy we need two: one for the corporate (taxed) and one for the non-corporate (non-taxed) business sector. The respective different sectoral products have to be aggregated into the real national product. This aggregation calls for *a priori* knowledge of the joint demand function for both the sectoral products (from which one could get a rate of substitution between the two). As this is not known, these sectoral products are aggregated by an index number formula subject to the condition of constant elasticity of substitution of products, defined in the same way as elasticity of substitution of factors.[47] Such an index number formula preserves a negative slope for the rate of substitution; thus it can be considered as resulting from demand functions, and that facilitates aggregation.

In addition, allocation of factors between the two sectors has to be resolved. One relation is simple, the sectoral capital must add to the total capital, and so must the sectoral labor add to total labor. A second set of equations results from the neoclassical assumption that net (after tax) returns to a factor must be equal in both sectors. Together the two sets of equations permit allocation of the factors between the two sectors.

[47] For the definition of elasticity of substitution used here see (2), pp. 341–43.

Additional Notation, Definitions, and Relations

Introduction of two sectors calls for additional notation of (a) the sectoral variables and (b) the aggregate variables for the whole economy. In this section this is resolved by adding subscript 1 to variables for the corporate (taxed) sector and subscript 2 to variables for the non-corporate (non-taxed) sector. For their national aggregate such subscripts are omitted. Thus we note:

Variable	For the Whole Economy	For the Corporate Sector	For the Non-Corporate Sector
Gross (before tax) Profits	$\pi_{x,t}$	$\pi_{1,x,t}$	$\pi_{2,x,t}$
Wages	$W_{x,t}$	$W_{1,x,t}$	$W_{2,x,t}$
Product	$Q_{x,t}$	$Q_{1,x,t}$	$Q_{2,x,t}$
Value Added	$Q_{x,t}$	$V_{1,x,t}$	$V_{2,x,t}$
Gross Rate of Return on Capital	$y_{x,t}$	$y_{1,x,t}$	$y_{2,x,t}$
Wage Rate	$w_{x,t}$	$w_{1,x,t}$	$w_{2,x,t}$
Gross Share of Capital	$F_{x,t}$	$F_{1,x,t}$	$F_{2,x,t}$
Net Share of Capital	$H_{x,t}$	$H_{1,x,t}$	$H_{2,x,t}$
Capital	$K_{x,t}$	$K_{1,x,t}$	$K_{2,x,t}$
Labor	L_t	$L_{1,t}$	$L_{2,t}$
Tax Liability in Units of National Product	$T_{x,t}$	$T_{1,x,t}$	——

and introduce the following definitions:

$$V_{1,x,t} = W_{1,x,t} + \pi_{1,x,t}$$

$$V_{2,x,t} = W_{2,x,t} + \pi_{2,x,t}$$

$$F_{x,t} = \frac{\pi_{x,t}}{Q_{x,t}}; \quad F_{1,x,t} = \frac{\pi_{1,x,t}}{V_{1,x,t}}; \quad F_{2,x,t} = \frac{\pi_{2,x,t}}{V_{2,x,t}}$$

$$H_{x,t} = \frac{\pi_{x,t} - T_{x,t}}{Q_{x,t} - T_{x,t}}$$

$$H_{1,x,t} = \frac{\pi_{1,x,t} - T_{1,x,t}}{V_{1,x,t} = T_{1,x,t}}$$

$$H_{2,x,t} = \frac{\pi_{2,x,t}}{V_{2,x,t}} = F_{2,x,t}$$

$$T_{1,x,t} = x\,\pi_{1,x,t}$$

Special Problems

A new problem in measurement of shifting arises when a non-general profits tax is introduced. As Krzyzaniak and Musgrave ([11], p. 9, Table 2-1) point out, in this case one could consider changes in earnings of capital either in the whole economy (p. 9, Table 2-1, indicators 8 and 14) or in the corporate sector only (p. 9, Table 2-1, indicators 5, 6, 9, and 10). Measures of shifting based on such indicators may differ and are meaningless unless they can be interpreted.

Obviously, changes in earnings of capital in the whole economy indicate which part of the tax burden was shifted onto consumers or factors other than capital. Consequently, such shifting will be referred to hereafter as *for the whole economy*. The notation for it remains the same as for the case of the general tax. Had the purpose of this paper been the tax incidence and not the tax effects on relative income variables the formulae for shifting in the whole economy would have to be more complex.

If the corporate sector alone is considered, changes in earning of its capital indicate to what extent the tax burden is shifted onto consumers, onto factors other than capital in both sectors, and onto capital earnings in the non-corporate sector. Apparently, the businessmen in the unincorporated sector need not escape the corporate income tax even if they are legally exempt from it. Consequently, such shifting will be called *corporate* as it includes the improvement in the position of corporate at the expense of non-corporate capital as well.

The variables for the corporate sector and the measures of corporate shifting will be denoted by introducing subscript 1 before other subscripts. Thus we define corporate shifting:

$$S_{1,y,t} = \frac{y_{1,x,t} - y_{1,0,\infty}}{x y_{1,x,t}} \qquad \text{on the gross rate of return,}$$

$$S_{1,F,t} = \frac{F_{1,x,t} - F_{1,0,\infty}}{x F_{1,x,t}} \qquad \text{on the gross share, and}$$

$$S^{*}_{1,H,t} = \frac{H_{1,x,t} - (1 - x) H_{1,0,\infty}}{x H_{1,0,\infty}} \qquad \text{on the net share.}$$

Let us introduce one more concept. The difference between corporate shifting and shifting for the whole economy may be called *differential* shifting as it measures the transference of the differential profits tax effects within the capitalist class. Differential shifting will be noted by adding the subscript d before other subscripts. Thus:

$$S_{d,y,t} = S_{1,y,t} - S_{y,t} \qquad \text{on the gross rate of return,}$$

$$S_{d,F,t} = S_{1,F,t} - S_{F,t} \qquad \text{on the gross share, and}$$

$$S^*_{d,H,t} = S^*_{1,H,t} - S^*_{H,t} \qquad \text{on the net share.}$$

In the real world both sectors are taxed; hence the corporate sector is subject to the common as well as to the differential tax rate. Consequently, tax effects in the corporate sector will be *combined* in a kind of weighted average of the common and the differential tax rate effects (see n. 54).

If business is taxed unevenly, as is assumed here, economists are able to show that in static conditions resources will be misallocated and the economy will become less efficient than the perfectly competitive norm for which a general profits tax calls. This is the co-called excess burden of a non-neutral tax, which Harberger calls waste. In the dynamic approach applied in this paper, an excess burden problem appears also. Moreover, given constant and equal elasticities of substitution of factors and of products, this excess burden takes a simple form: the production function for the whole economy is scaled down by a multiplicative constant u_x which is always a positive fraction, i.e., $0 < u_x < 1$. Thus, in the absence of a profits tax, this function may be written in the form:

$$\mathcal{Q}_{0,t} = M_0 f(K_{0,t}, L_t),$$

and, with tax x,

$$\mathcal{Q}_{x,t} = M_x f(K_{x,t}, L_t),$$

where

$$M_x = u_x M_0,$$

and M_x is a scaling factor with tax rate x and M_0 the same in absence of tax.

It is of interest to find that as neither M_0 nor M_x depends on time t, neither does u_x. Thus, if we accept u_x as an indicator of the excess burden of the differential profits tax, we find that this excess burden, as a per cent of national product, is a man-made constant over time. Excess burden here means that the same pair of capital and labor inputs will produce less in units of national product with the tax than in the absence of tax. In terms of an isoquant map, the isoquant curves remain unchanged but the number (value) assigned to each isoquant is lowered by a constant factor u_x.

Further, one should note that in this paper sectoral production functions and the aggregate production function differ in one important aspect. The corporate and non-corporate sector production functions are purely technological relations. As long as the tax does not affect the capital to labor ratio of inputs, the factor share remains unchanged. If such a ratio varies, the share is determined by the sectoral production function with its parameters unchanged. After all the parameters are determined by technology alone.

It is not so with the aggregate production functions and its parameters. This function incorporates technological relations and a demand function represented by an index. Various mixes of the sectoral products result in various welfare positions. Consequently, if an imposition of a tax changes the mix of the national product, the aggregate production function for the economy as a whole may show changed input ratios as well as changed values of parameters underlying the aggregate production function.

This paper is concerned only with the cases in which elasticity of substitution of factors in the corporate sector, and in the non-corporate sector, as well as elasticity of substitution of sectoral products, are constant and of the same value. This yields aggregate production functions which formally resemble the sectoral production functions, being either of the Cobb-Douglas type or the CES type. A change in the tax, however, affects (a) the scale of national product and (b), in the case of CES production functions, parameters determining factor shares. These changes in parameters are due to non-technological aspects of the aggregate production function.

Finally, the reader should distinguish between two terms used in this paper; *Harberger shifting* and *Harberger-type shifting*. Harberger shifting is what Harberger calls shifting. Harberger-type shifting is shifting as defined and measured by me in this paper. Both concepts are, however, reconcilable; the Harberger shifting being a partial, the Harberger-type shifting being a total isolated tax effect on a financial variable from which such shifting is computed.

In my interpretation, to get the Harberger shifting, assume an economy subject to Harberger's adjusting capital flows between corporate and unincorporated business; then correct my concept of shifting on the rate of return for the whole economy by assuming no waste due to misallocation of resources. I call my concepts Harberger-type shifting as they result from the Harberger adjustment. I distinguish between corporate and for-the-whole-economy Harberger-type shifting, each measured on the basis of financial data for either the corporate sector or the whole economy. Changes in variables, on which such measures are based, represent total effects of a differential tax. No correction is made for Harberger's waste or for the tax effects due to capital flows. The difference between the corporate and for-the-whole-economy Harberger-type shifting, I call differential shifting. It measures the improvement in corporate investor's position, at the expense of the unincorporated business, due to resulting capital flows.

I offer the following justification for the change away from the established Harberger definition. First, my measures, based on observable financial data, refer to total tax effects on certain economic variables which are easier to isolate than partial effects which require one to derive inferences from inferences. Second, since the corporate data are readily available and of superior quality to those for the whole economy, one is compelled to consider them first and trust them more. Third, where the question to be asked is how an investor facing differential profit taxation will behave, it is not the partial effect but the total effect on a key variable such as the rate of return on capital that matters to him. Finally, by expanding the concept of shifting, more information is acquired; for example, we may find how much of the tax burden on the corporate investor falls on the unincorporated business.

COBB-DOUGLAS PRODUCTION FUNCTIONS

Model C

As there are two sectors in the economy, producing two different goods, one may assume that in general their production functions may differ with respect to:

(a) rates of growth of technological progress,
(b) share parameters associated with different kinds of factors, and
(c) elasticities of substitution of factors in each sector.

One would prefer a most general treatment in which all these parameters, though constant for the sector,[48] differ between sectors. For the case here considered this may be easily assumed with respect to (a) and (b) type parameters, but we have difficulties if such a generalization is made about type (c), elasticities of substitution of factors; "unmanageable" mathematical formulae result. Special cases, however, with the same elasticity of substitution of factors in both sectors turn out to be "manageable." In Model C both sectoral production functions have $\sigma = 1$, i.e., are of the Cobb-Douglas type. Such an assumption is realistic for many products, but nevertheless is not a very general case. To generalize it further, Model D uses the same elasticity of substitution of factors in both sectors, but $\sigma \neq 1$. CES production functions result.

To keep in mind that the parameters now are describing economic relations within separate sectors we add subscript 1 when denoting parameters for the corporate (taxed) sector and subscript 2 for the non-corporate (not taxed) sector. Thus we note:

[48] Constancy of parameters over time makes their statistical estimation easier. Changes in them would be equivalent to a change in the structure of the model.

Parameters	In the Corporate Sector	In the Non-Corporate Sector
Rate of neutral technological progress	g_1	g_2
Capital share parameter	a_1	a_2
Labor share parameter	b_1	b_2

and to preserve linear homogeneity of degree one in these production functions we shall claim that

$$a_i + b_i = 1 \quad \text{for } i = 1,2.$$

As in both sectors the inputs are related to outputs by Cobb-Douglas type production functions, we write them

C-1a.
$$\mathcal{Q}_{1,x,t} = e^{g_1 t} K_{1,x,t}{}^{a_1} L_{1,t}{}^{b_1}$$
$$\mathcal{Q}_{2,x,t} = e^{g_2 t} K_{2,x,t}{}^{a_2} L_{2,t}{}^{b_2}$$

These products are measured in their respective sectoral units. To aggregate them we will use an index number formula. To compute it a knowledge of a joint demand function for the two products is required so that the rate of substitutability of one product for the other is known. Once more a constant rate of elasticity of substitution would facilitate statistical estimation. Also such a parameter of substitution of products need not be the same as that for substitution of factors within sectors. Unfortunately "unmanageable" mathematical formulae result in the general case. However, in a special case, with products substituting at the same elasticity of substitution as factors, the model may be resolved easily, and this is what we assume in this model.[49] Here we claim that elasticity of substitution of products must be also one, hence the index number formula takes the Cobb-Douglas function form.

There is a new parameter here to be introduced, namely the corporate product share parameter m in the total product. Such

[49] Despite the restrictive assumption that elasticities of substitution are equal, the models here are not overly specialized.

For example, Daniel McFadden (15), p. 75, introduces so-called block additive production functions which preserve constant input substitution. Such functions can be aggregated with ease but these aggregates are only special cases of the one here used. For example, the aggregate production function here becomes block additive for parameter value $m = .5$.

a parameter must be a positive fraction. Consequently the index number formula for aggregation of products becomes

C-1b. $$\mathcal{Q}_{x,t} = (\mathcal{Q}_{1,x,t})^m (\mathcal{Q}_{2,x,t})^{(1-m)}$$

or, after substitution of C-1a,

$$\mathcal{Q}_{x,t} = e^{[mg_1 + (1-m)g_2]t} K_{1,x,t}{}^{ma_1} K_{2,x,t}{}^{(1-m)a_2} L_{1,t}{}^{mb_1} L_{2,t}{}^{(1-m)b_2}$$

This aggregate production function for the whole economy is misleading in one respect; it shows more dimensions of freedom than it really has. Superficially one could think that it depends on a quadruple of independent inputs: $K_{1,x,t}$, $K_{2,x,t}$, $L_{1,t}$, and $L_{2,t}$. In fact, we have, in this aggregate production function, only pairs of inputs that are independent of each other; namely, the aggregated supplies of homogeneous factors $K_{x,t}$ and L_t.

First, the Harberger assumption calls for equating net returns (measured in units of a national product) to factors between sectors, or

C-1c. $$(1 - x)\frac{\partial \mathcal{Q}_{x,t}}{\partial K_{1,x,t}} = \frac{\partial \mathcal{Q}_{x,t}}{\partial K_{2,x,t}}$$

$$\frac{\partial \mathcal{Q}_{x,t}}{\partial L_{1,t}} = \frac{\partial \mathcal{Q}_{x,t}}{\partial L_{2,t}}, \text{ and second,}$$

these factors being homogeneous may be added between sectors. Thus we get:

$$K_{x,t} = K_{1,x,t} + K_{2,x,t} \quad \text{Aggregate capital,}$$
$$L_t = L_{1,t} + L_{2,t} \quad \text{Aggregate labor.}$$

Combining the two sets of information on factor allocation between sectors, we can find what proportion of a factor will be allocated in the corporate and what proportion in the non-corporate sector. It is of great interest to find that these proportions once achieved (here instantaneously, by assumption) will remain constant over time. To write them in an easy-to-remember way we may here introduce formulae for aggregation of sectoral parameters. That these are truly aggregation formulae will be seen when the aggregate production function is written in its final form.

Let the aggregate parameters be defined:

$g = mg_1 + (1 - m) g_2$ Aggregate rate of neutral technological progress

$a = ma_1 + (1 - m) a_2$ Aggregate share of capital parameter

$b = mb_1 + (1 - m) b_2$ Aggregate share of labor parameter.

One notes also that the aggregate share parameters add to 1 as they should, $a + b = 1$; thus the aggregated production function remains linear, homogeneous of degree one.

Finally let us introduce the aggregate production function scale factor M defined for the case with tax rate x:

$$M_x = \left\{ \left[\frac{a(1 - x)}{a - ma_1 x} \right]^{a_1} m \left[\frac{a_1}{a} \right]^{a_1} \left[\frac{b_1}{b} \right]^{b_1} \right\}^m$$

$$\cdot \left\{ \left[\frac{a}{a - ma_1 x} \right]^{a_2} (1 - m) \left[\frac{a_2}{a} \right]^{a_2} \left[\frac{b_2}{b} \right]^{b_2} \right\}^{(1 - m)}.$$

For the case with zero tax this collapses to:

$$M_0 = \left\{ m \left[\frac{a_1}{a} \right]^{a_1} \left[\frac{b_1}{b} \right]^{b_1} \right\}^m \cdot \left\{ (1 - m) \left[\frac{a_2}{a} \right]^{a_2} \left[\frac{b_2}{b} \right]^{b_2} \right\}^{(1 - m)};$$

hence the rescaling factor u_x will become:

$$u_x = \frac{M_x}{M_0} = \frac{[a(1 - x)]^{ma_1} [a]^{(1-m)a_2}}{[a - ma_1 x]^a}$$

and will always be a positive fraction.

With this new notation the four equations C-1c lead to the following allocation of factors:

C-1e.
$$K_{1,x,t} = \frac{ma_1(1 - x)}{a - ma_1 x} K_{x,t},$$

$$K_{2,x,t} = \frac{(1 - m)a_2}{a - ma_1 x} K_{x,t},$$

$$L_{1,t} = \frac{mb_1}{b} L_t,$$

$$L_{2,t} = \frac{(1 - m)b_2}{b} L_t.$$

If C-1e equations are substituted in C-1b, the aggregate production function takes the following form:

C-1f. In absence of tax $\mathcal{Q}_{0,t} = M_0\, e^{gt}\, K_{0,t}{}^a\, L_t{}^b$.

With tax $\mathcal{Q}_{x,t} = M_x\, e^{gt}\, K_{x,t}{}^a\, L_t{}^b$.

This extremely useful result is the payoff of choosing equal constant elasticities of substitution. We may compare the aggregate production function with formula A-1. The only difference is that now we have the same form of production function scaled by factor M_0 or M_x, which, for given tax rate x, is a constant. Consequently, the solution to this model may follow the method used to solve the Model A. The reader already has been warned that this aggregate production function is not a purely technological relation. It embodies demand for a mix of products as well.

The aggregate labor supply function is of the same form as in Model A, namely:

C-2. $$L_t = L_0\, e^{ht}.$$

This shows that, by assumption, labor grows independently of the real wage rate levels and also, in consequence, of the profits tax rate x. In addition, a look at equations C-1e shows that the allocation of labor between the corporate and non-corporate sector does not depend on the level of the profits tax rate.

The neoclassical investment function, under which available funds determine investment irrespective of the level of the rate of return on it, is here assumed in the same form as in Model A, namely:

C-3. $$I_{x,t} = \frac{dK_{x,t}}{dt} = S_{x,t} = s_{x,t}\, \mathcal{Q}_{x,t}.$$

To find the effective saving rate $s_{x,t}$, we need to know the gross (before) tax earnings of capital and labor in both sectors. As Euler's theorem holds (the aggregate as well as the sectoral production functions are linear and homogeneous of degree one), for $0 \le x < 1$ the effective saving rate is:

C-4a. With tax x

$$s_x = s_i b + s_p m a_1 (1 - x) + (1 - s_p) s_i m a_1 (1 - x) + s_p (1 - m) a_2 +$$
$$\text{(wages)} \quad \text{(corporate} \qquad \text{(dividends)} \qquad \text{(non-corpor-}$$
$$\text{profits)} \qquad\qquad\qquad\qquad \text{ate profits)}$$

$$+ (1 - s_p) s_i (1 - m) a_2, \text{ or}$$
$$\text{(withdrawals)}$$

C-4b. $\qquad s_x = s_i + a s_p (1 - s_i) - m a_1 x [s_p + s_i - s_p s_i].$

For zero tax this becomes:

C-4c. $\qquad s_0 = s_i + a s_p (1 - s_i);$ [50] hence also

C-4d. $\qquad s_x = s_0 - m a_1 x [s_p + s_i - s_p s_i].$

Once more the effective saving rate is independent of time, and so the time subscript may be omitted. Introduction of the tax will lower this rate since the right-hand term to be subtracted in formula C-4d is always positive.

Parameter Values

Model C is more complex than Model A, requiring, among other things, the assignment of values to more parameters than was the case for Model A. Since these have to be realistic, they can be chosen in a way that will yield aggregated parameters equal to those accepted as realistic in Model A.

In Model C we adopt the following parameter values:

Common Core

$$h = .01, x = \quad .2,\,[51] \quad m = .6\,[52],$$
$$a_1 = .2, \quad b_1 = \quad .8, \qquad g_1 = .015\,[53],$$
$$a_2 = .45, \quad b_2 = 55, \qquad g_2 = .015.$$

[50] Note that in the absence of a differential tax the effective saving rate is formulated the same way as in the preceding Model A (see formula A-4a) but now the notation stands for the aggregate of single sector parameters.

[51] The differential rate as measured by K & M (11), Table 3-1, Column ix, p. 28, varied from -.006 to .36 the last 25 years. An average would be close to the value of .2 here adopted. Harberger elsewhere in this volume estimates this differential tax rate at .40, but he excludes the depletion industries from his highly taxed industry group and considers differentials in property taxation as well.

[52] The observed corporate sector capital share is lower than the share of capital in the unincorporated business. Consequently, the aggregation parameters m, a_1, and a_2 are chosen so that the aggregate capital share for the whole economy is the same as in Model A; namely: $a = m a_1 + (1-m) a_2 = .3$.

[53] The corporate and non-corporate sector technological progress rates do not differ much in the U.S. economy.

For comparison with Model D $g_1 = g_2 = 0$ is also tried. Propensities to consume are:

In the capitalist variant $s_p = .5$, $s_i = .05$;
In the Marxist variant $s_p = .6667$, $s_i = .005$.

The Magnitude of the Capital Outflow

Now let us consider the problem of size of capital flows required by the Harberger model. Using relation C-1 we note that Harberger's adjustment, here assumed to be instantaneous, calls for the following outflow of capital from the corporate to the non-corporate sector:

$$K_{1,0,\infty} - K_{1,x,0} = \frac{ma_1}{a} K_{0,\infty} - \frac{ma_1}{a} \frac{(1-x)}{\left(1 - \frac{ma_1}{a}x\right)} K_{x,0}.$$

In the medium run the supply of capital is fixed; hence

$$K_{0,\infty} = K_{x,0}.$$

Consequently, percentagewise, the formula for the outflow of capital is:

$$100 \frac{K_{1,0,\infty} - K_{1,x,0}}{K_{1,0,\infty}} = \frac{100 \left(1 - \frac{ma_1}{a}\right)}{\left(1 - \frac{ma_1}{a}x\right)}.$$

Substituting adopted parameter values and different values of differential tax, we get:

For x	Percentage Outflow
.1	6.1%
.2	13.0%
.3	20.5%
.4	28.6%

These are amazingly high figures, and one should be able to observe them from the data on our economy, even if such movements were also subject to disturbances due to non-tax causes. Such disturbances most likely will be of a lesser size and probably of a random, at least not of an exactly offsetting

Table 9

General Solution, Variables

Effective saving rate		Scale factor		Product-capital ratio		
In Absence of Tax	With Tax	In Absence of Tax	With Tax	In Absence of Tax, Long Run	With Tax, in Period Zero	With Tax, Long Run
s_0	s_x	M_0	M_x	$N_{0,\infty}$	$N_{x,0}$	$N_{x,\infty}$
$s_0 = s_i + a s_p(1-s_i)$	$s_0 - ma_1x[s_p + s_i - s_p s_i]$	$\left\{m\left[\frac{a_1}{a}\right]^{a_1}\left[\frac{b_1}{b}\right]^{b_1}\right\}^m \cdot$ $\left\{(1-m)\left[\frac{a_2}{a}\right]^{a_2}\left[\frac{b_2}{b_2}\right]^{b_2}\right\}^{(1-m)}$	$\left\{\left[\frac{a(1-x)}{a-ma_1x}\right]^{a_1} m\left[\frac{a_1}{a}\right]^{a_1}\left[\frac{b_1}{b}\right]^{b_1}\right\}^m \cdot$ $\left\{\left[\frac{a}{a-ma_1x}\right]^{a_2}(1-m)\left[\frac{a_2}{a}\right]^{a_2}\left[\frac{b_2}{b}\right]^{b_2}\right\}^{(1-m)}$	$M_0\frac{g/b+h}{s_0}$	$M_x\frac{g/b+h}{s_0}$	$M_x\frac{g/b+h}{s_x}$

For the whole economy

Gross rate of return			Gross share of capital			Net share of capital		
In Absence of Tax, Long Run	With Tax, in Period Zero	With Tax, Long Run	In Absence of Tax, Long Run	With Tax, in Period Zero	With Tax, Long Run	In Absence of Tax, Long Run	With Tax, in Period Zero	With Tax, Long Run
$y_{0,\infty}$	$y_{x,0}$	$y_{x,\infty}$	$F_{0,\infty}$	$F_{x,0}$	$F_{x,\infty}$	$H_{0,\infty}$	$H_{x,0}$	$H_{x,\infty}$
$aM_0\frac{g/b+h}{s_0}$	$aM_x\frac{g/b+h}{s_0}$	$aM_x\frac{g/b+h}{s_x}$	a	a	a	a	$\frac{a-ma_1x}{1-ma_1x}$	$\frac{a-ma_1x}{1-ma_1x}$

For the corporate sector

Gross rate of return			Gross share of capital			Net share of capital		
In Absence of Tax, Long Run	With Tax, in Period Zero	With Tax, Long Run	In Absence of Tax, Long Run	With Tax, in Period Zero	With Tax, Long Run	In Absence of Tax, Long Run	With Tax, in Period Zero	With Tax, Long Run
$y_{1,0\infty}$	$y_{1,x,0}$	$y_{1,x,\infty}$	$F_{1,0\infty}$	$F_{1,x,0}$	$F_{1,x,\infty}$	$H_{1,0\infty}$	$H_{1,x,0}$	$H_{1,x,\infty}$
$y_{0\infty}$	$\frac{a-ma_1x}{a(1-x)}\cdot y_{x,0}$	$\frac{a-ma_1x}{a(1-x)}\cdot y_{x,\infty}$	a_1	a_1	a_1	a_1	$\frac{a_1(1-x)}{1-a_1x}$	$\frac{a_1(1-x)}{1-a_1x}$

Table 10

General Solution, Tax Effects

	For the whole economy			Differential			Corporate		
Shifting	On the Gross Rate of Return	On the Gross Share	On the Net Share	On the Gross Rate of Return	On the Gross Share	On the Net Share	On the Gross Rate of Return	On the Gross Share	On the Net Share
	$S_{y,0}$	$S_{F,0}$	$S^*_{H,0}$	$S_{d,y,0}$	$S_{d,F,0}$	$S^*_{d,H,0}$	$S_{1,y,0}$	$S_{1,F,0}$	$S^*_{1,H,0}$
a. Harberger Type	$\dfrac{M_z - M_0}{xM_z} = \dfrac{1}{x}\left(1 - \dfrac{1}{u_z}\right)$	0	$1 - \dfrac{bma_1}{a(1-ma_1x)}$	$\dfrac{1}{u_z}\cdot\dfrac{(a-ma_1)}{(a-ma_1x)}$	0	$\dfrac{bma_1}{a(1-ma_1x)} - \dfrac{b}{1-a_1x}$	$\dfrac{1}{x}\left[1 - \dfrac{a(1-x)}{(a-ma_1x)u_z}\right]$	0	$\dfrac{a_1(1-x)}{1-a_1x}$
b. Long Run	$S_{y,\infty}$ [1] $\quad\dfrac{1}{x}\left[1 - \dfrac{G_z}{u_z}\right]$	$S_{F,\infty}$ $\quad 0$	$S^*_{H,\infty}$	$S_{d,y,\infty}$ [2] $\quad G_z S_{d,y,0}$	$S_{d,F,\infty}$ $\quad 0$	$S^*_{d,H,\infty}$	$S_{1,y,\infty}$ [3] $\quad\dfrac{1}{x}\left[1 - \dfrac{a(1-x)}{a-ma_1x}\cdot\dfrac{G_z}{u_z}\right]$	$S_{1,F,\infty}$ $\quad 0$	$S^*_{1,H,\infty}$
Other Effects	Rescaling factor (indicator of excess burden) $\quad u_z \quad \dfrac{M_z}{M_0}$			Effect on saving $\quad G_z \quad \dfrac{s_z}{s_0}$			Effect on product-capital ratio $\quad E_z$ [4] $\quad \left[\dfrac{u_z}{G_x} - 1\right]$		

[1] Shifting is now less than in preceding model as u_z is a fraction. Thus the non-general tax not only affects production function but also disallows some shifting that, under a general tax, would have been possible.

[2] In words, the long-run differential shifting declines to a fraction of its short-run value (G_z is a fraction). Thus at least in the long run, fellow businessmen in the non-corporate sector suffer less from non-general tax.

[3] As G_z is a fraction, shifting is now slightly higher than under the Harberger adjustment alone.

[4] The effect is now smaller than in previous model. There we had $E_z = \dfrac{1}{G_z} - 1$ and u_z is a positive fraction.

type. However (see n. 45), no clear proof exists of capital movements of that size in the U.S. economy and this is disturbing because the importance of Harberger's version of neoclassical theory of shifting and of its extension in the form of Models C and D is here based upon the existence of these flows. But, although the question of the existence of such flows is not finally resolved, the Harberger neoclassical theory of shifting may have normative uses even if it turns out to be an empty box, so let us proceed with our analysis.

Equilibrium Solution

As noted before, Model C in its aggregated form resembles Model A. Consequently as in Model A, we may seek an equilibrium solution in its general form by finding equilibrium values of interesting key variables as functions of parameters. These values are shown in Table 9, and are translated into measures and indicators of tax effects in Table 10.

Already from this general formulation one could draw important conclusions about the Harberger adjustment. First, it results in an excess burden of a very simple form. The production function retains its general form after the differential tax has been imposed but the same pair of capital and labor inputs will produce less in units of the index for the national product, the reduction as a percentage of the national product being equal to $100 \, (1 - u_x)$ which is a positive fraction. As a result of this excess burden, the Harberger type of shifting on the gross rate of return for the whole economy becomes negative. That is, because of intersectoral movement of capital adjusting to the differential profits tax and the resulting inefficiency, the gross rate of return on capital for the whole economy declines from the pretax level. Further, the Harberger type corporate shifting on the gross rate of return shows that capital in the unincorporated sector bears part of the burden of the differential profits tax on the corporate sector because the corporate returns rise and the non-corporate returns decline. If the legislative intent was to put the burden of tax on capital in the corporate sector only, this is somewhat thwarted.

Turning now to the long-run adjustment we find that adjustment to the differential profits tax due to changes in new capital formation leaves the multiplicative indicator of excess burden u_x unchanged. Thus, percentagewise the inefficiency of the economy resulting from a differential profits tax remains the same over time. The long-run shifting of this tax as measured on the gross rate of return for the whole economy is substantial, though not so large as if this tax were general. Further, the long-run differential shifting measured on the gross rate of return is lower than in the short run but only slightly so, thus the unincorporated business still suffers from lower rates of return to support higher gross rates in the corporate sector. Also the corporate long-run shifting on the gross rate of return compared with its initial position after Harberger's adjustment increases. All shifting measures on the gross share, however, remain zero for all periods, reflecting the basic property of the Cobb-Douglas production function—the gross share remains constant. The net shares, because of the definition of the S^* measures, are affected by the tax, Harberger-type and long-run measures remaining unchanged. Finally, the tax effect on the product-capital ratio is also slightly lower than it is for the case of a general tax of the same rate.

Numerical solutions to our model both for values of our variables and for measures or indicators of tax effects, give an idea not only of direction but also of the magnitudes here involved. They are shown in Tables 11 and 12 and have to be in line with what was, above, deduced in a general way.

First we note that excess burden as a percentage of national product is very small. For .2 differential tax rate the product declines by less than .2 per cent. In absolute terms, in a 500 billion dollar GNP economy this is not so small, a decline of approximately one billion dollars. A. C. Harberger having differently defined the taxed and non-taxed sectors arrives at a higher differential tax rate and, thus, a higher measure of this waste.

As the indicator of excess burden shows small percentagewise decline in efficiency of the economy as a whole, the Harberger-

Table 11

Variables (differential tax rate x = .2)

For the Whole Economy — Effective saving rate, Scale factor, Product-capital ratio

	Effective saving rate — In Absence of Tax s_0	Effective saving rate — With Tax s_x	Scale factor — In Absence of Tax M_0	Scale factor — With Tax M_x	Product-capital ratio — In Absence of Tax, Long Run $N_{0,\infty}$	Product-capital ratio — With Tax, in Period Zero $N_{x,0}$	Product-capital ratio — With Tax, Long Run $N_{x,\infty}$
Neutral Technological Progress Rate g		0 .015		0 .015	0 .015	0 .015	0 .015
Propensity to Save: Marxist	.2040	.18796	.52854	.52761	.02591 / .08143	.02586 / .08128	.02807 / .08822
Propensity to Save: Capitalist	.1925	.17990	.52854	.52761	.02746 / .08629	.02741 / .08614	.02933 / .09217

(For each Product-capital ratio cell the two figures correspond to $g = 0$ / $g = .015$.)

For the Whole Economy — Gross rate of return, Gross share of capital, Net share of capital

	Gross rate of return — In Absence of Tax, Long Run $y_{0,\infty}$	Gross rate of return — With Tax, in Period Zero $y_{x,0}$	Gross rate of return — With Tax, Long Run $y_{x,\infty}$	Gross share of capital — In Absence of Tax, Long Run $F_{0,\infty}$	Gross share of capital — With Tax, in Period Zero $F_{x,0}$	Gross share of capital — With Tax, Long Run $F_{x,\infty}$	Net share of capital — In Absence of Tax, Long Run $H_{0,\infty}$	Net share of capital — With Tax, in Period Zero $H_{x,0}$	Net share of capital — With Tax, Long Run $H_{x,\infty}$
Neutral Technological Progress Rate g	0 .015	0 .015	0 .015						
Propensity to Save: Marxist	.00777 / .02443	.00776 / .02439	.00842 / .02647	.3 / .3	.3 / .3	.3 / .3	.3 / .3	.28279 / .28279	.28279 / .28279
Propensity to Save: Capitalist	.00824 / .02589	.00822 / .02584	.00880 / .02609	.3 / .3	.3 / .3	.3 / .3	.3 / .3	.28279 / .28279	.28279 / .28279

For the Corporate Sector

	Gross rate of return — In Absence of Tax, Long Run $y_{1,0,\infty}$	Gross rate of return — With Tax, in Period Zero $y_{1,x,0}$	Gross rate of return — With Tax, Long Run $y_{1,x,\infty}$	Gross share of capital — In Absence of Tax, Long Run $F_{1,0,\infty}$	Gross share of capital — With Tax, in Period Zero $F_{1,x,0}$	Gross share of capital — With Tax, Long Run $F_{1,x,\infty}$	Net share of capital — In Absence of Tax, Long Run $H_{1,0,\infty}$	Net share of capital — With Tax, in Period Zero $H_{1,x,0}$	Net share of capital — With Tax, Long Run $H_{1,x,\infty}$
Neutral Technological Progress Rate g	0 .015	0 .015	0 .015						
Propensity to Save: Marxist	.00777 / .02443	.00892 / .02805	.00968 / .03044	.2 / .2	.2 / .2	.2 / .2	.2 / .2	.16667 / .16667	.16667 / .16667
Propensity to Save: Capitalist	.00824 / .02589	.00945 / .02972	.01012 / .03000	.2 / .2	.2 / .2	.2 / .2	.2 / .2	.16667 / .16667	.16667 / .16667

(For each cell the two figures correspond to $g = 0$ / $g = .015$.)

Table 12
Tax Effects
(differential tax rate $x = .2$)

Shifting

Variants of the Propensity to Save	For the whole economy			Differential			Corporate		
	On the Gross Rate of Return	On the Gross Share	On the Net Share	On the Gross Rate of Return	On the Gross Share	On the Net Share	On the Gross Rate of Return	On the Gross Share	On the Net Share
Harberger Type:	$S_{y,0}$	$S_{F,0}$	$S^*_{H,0}$	$S_{d,y,0}$	$S_{d,F,0}$	$S^*_{d,H,0}$	$S_{1,y,0}$	$S_{1,F,0}$	$S^*_{1,H,0}$
Marxist	−.00882	0	.71317	.65217	0	−.54640	.64335	0	.16667
Capitalist	−.00882	0	.71317	.65217	0	−.54640	.64335	0	.16667
Long Run:	$S_{y,\infty}$	$S_{F,\infty}$	$S^*_{H,\infty}$	$S_{d,y,\infty}$	$S_{d,y,\infty}$	$S^*_{d,H,\infty}$	$S_{1,y,\infty}$	$S_{1,F,\infty}$	$S^*_{1,H,\infty}$
Marxist	.38501	0	.71317	.60090	0	−.54640	.98591	0	.16667
Capitalist	.31901	0	.71317	.61056	0	−.54640	.92957	0	.16667

Other Effects

	Rescaling factor (indicator of excess burden)	Tax effects on saving	Tax effect on the product-capital ratio
	$u_x = \dfrac{M_x}{M_0}$	$G_x = \dfrac{s_x}{s_0}$	E_x
Marxist	.99824	.92137	.08343
Capitalist	.99824	.93455	.06816

type shifting for the whole economy, though negative, is also very small, less than 1 per cent. Further, the Harberger-type differential shifting on the gross rate of return is about 65 per cent, resulting in a substantial increase in the corporate rate of return yielding 64 per cent corporate shifting.[54] Obviously, the Harberger shifting on the gross rate of return comes to a large degree at the expense of investors in unincorporated business.

Let us turn now to numerical results for tax effects in the long run. The long-run shifting on the gross rate of return for the whole economy is between 30 to 40 per cent only. As the differential shifting on the rate of return declined slightly to 60–61 per cent, the corporate shifting on the gross rate of return for the corporate investors was once higher, more than 90 per cent. These figures show, however, that because of restriction of new capital formation, two-thirds of this shifting occurred at the expense of the fellow businessmen in the unincorporated sector whom the tax supposedly was not intended to burden, and only one-third at the expense of consumers.

Due to the adoption of Cobb-Douglas production functions there is no long-run shifting of any kind on the gross share. As for the long-run shifting on the net share, it is all due to definitions of S^* measures of shifting. It is interesting to note that long-run shifting on the net share for the whole economy is

[54] One should not interpret the 64 per cent Harberger-type corporate shifting on the gross rate of return as the degree of shifting one would "observe" in the corporate sector. In our economy the corporate sector is also subject to a tax rate common to both sectors. Hence what one would observe in the corporate sector is the combined degree of corporate shifting.

Suppose the common tax rate is .3 and the differential tax rate is .2. Under the standard and Harberger neoclassical theory of shifting, the corporate rate rises only due to the differential tax rate and, for the capitalist variant,

becomes..	.2972.
In absence of taxes, it would have been..........................	.2589.
The increase is..	.0383.
The combined tax liability, however, is (.5) (.2972)................	.1486.

Hence the combined rate of corporate
shifting on the rate of return is the ratio of the above.............. .25773.

This is a comparatively small degree of shifting and, given the size of errors statistical estimation is usually subject to, its existence would be hard to prove. K & M (11) found a substantially higher degree of shifting for all manufacturing corporations; hence their finding cannot be explained by non-generality of profits taxes alone.

higher than corporate shifting which yields negative differential shifting on the share.[55] We also noted previously (see Graph 4) that shifting on the net share is somewhat more sensitive to changes in the value of the embedded share parameter a. This goes for all kinds of shifting on the net share in this model, the relevant parameters being a_1, a_2, and their aggregate a. Further, the non-general tax has only a small effect on the effective saving rate as indicated by G_x. This is partly due to the smallness of the differential tax.[56] Similar argument explains why the product-capital ratio is now only slightly affected.

The convergence of this model is very much like that of Model A.[57] For the capitalist variant with neutral technological progress rate $g = .015$ and differential tax rate $x = .2$, it takes 108.6 periods to get 90 per cent of the tax effect on national product-capital ratio. For 95 per cent, one has to wait 140.3 periods and for 99 per cent 213.5 periods. In the case of zero neutral technological progress, as in Model A, the number of periods has to be multiplied by a factor 3.1.

CES PRODUCTION FUNCTIONS

Special Problem

When elasticity parameters for substitution of factors and of products are no longer equal to one, the constant elasticity of substitution production functions cease to be the Cobb-Douglas type and become the CES type. For the same reasons as in the case of Model B the rate of neutral technological progress must be assumed zero (see n. 33). An interesting property that is new in this case is that the differential profits tax also affects the aggregate share parameters of the aggregate production function. This, we noted, is due to the hybrid nature of the aggregate production function. The nature of the underlying sectoral parameters is technological hence they

[55] Note that Harberger's short-run and long-run shifting on the net share are the same.

[56] In our world where the corporate and unincorporated sectors are subject also to a common rate, the combined tax effect on the saving rate will be somewhere between that for Model A and for this model, thus the saving rate will decline more substantially.

[57] For proof see convergence formula, Appendix I, Model C.

remain unchanged. The mix of national products is, however, changed, which in turn affects the formula under which these parameters are aggregated into the aggregate production function parameters. In all preceding Models, A, B, and C, for any level of profits tax, the share parameters in the production function for the whole economy were independent of the tax; hence there was no need for showing the tax rate x in the notation of the share parameters. Now this no longer holds and we will have to distinguish these parameters for cases of a positive differential tax rate x, or for a zero rate, by introducing subscripts x or 0. Thus we will have:

	With Tax	*In Absence of Tax*
Aggregate capital share parameter	a_x	a_0
Aggregate labor share parameter	b_x	b_0

As linear homogeneity of degree one holds we will have the relation:

$$a_x + b_x = 1 \text{ for } 0 \leq x < 1$$

What is the interpretation and importance of this dependence of share parameters on the differential tax rate? It is obvious that it represents a change in the slopes of isoquants. One could perhaps call this a tilt in the aggregate production function. Thus the rate of substitution of factors is affected even if the elasticity is not (we assume no change in σ). This in turn means that capital and labor shares will move in opposite directions, as will the gross rate of return and the real wage rate.

It is obvious that measures of shifting computed for any case here reflect now a very complex set of relations. For example, the long-run corporate shifting on the gross rate of return may be positively affected by a decline in new capital formation, by the transference of the tax burden in part to the non-corporate investor, and by the increased profitability of capital due positively to a change in isoquant slopes and negatively to an excess burden resulting from imposition of a differential profits tax.

Perhaps these various partial effects should be separated to find out how much of the corporate shifting came via new capital formation, via decline in the non-corporate rate, via the tilt in the aggregate production function, and via the excess burden effect. The little that was done to explore these aspects quantitatively is discussed later.

Model D

The production functions [58] in the sectors take the form

D-1a.
$$Q_{1,x,t} = [a_1 K_{1,x,t}^{-r} + b_1 L_{1,t}^{-r}]^{-1/r},$$
$$Q_{2,x,t} = [a_2 K_{2,x,t}^{-r} + b_2 L_{2,t}^{-r}]^{-1/r},$$

and are to be aggregated under the following index number formula:

D-1b.
$$Q_{x,t} = [m Q_{1,x,t}^{-r} + (1-m) Q_{2,x,t}^{-r}]^{-1/r}.$$

The following aggregate production function results:

$$Q_{x,t} = [ma_1 K_{1,x,t}^{-r} + (1-m)a_2 K_{2,x,t}^{-r} + mb_1 L_{1,t}^{-r} + (1-m)b_2 L_{2,t}^{-r}]^{-1/r}.$$

The parameter r is related to the elasticity of substitution parameter σ as follows:

$$\sigma = \frac{1}{1+r}, r = \frac{1-\sigma}{\sigma}.$$

The aggregate production function may be further compressed by a change from sectoral inputs of capital and labor to their aggregates for the whole economy. To accomplish this we use first the information that these factors are homogeneous and so also additive. Another set of relations between them results from the neoclassical assumption that the net sectoral rate of return to a factor must be equal for the same factor in both sectors. Combining this information we will arrive, as in Model C, at a unique allocation of these factors between sectors. The formulae are, however, very complex, and we need to use not only the notation for aggregate parameters but even some intermediate notation as well. For derivation of this notation the reader is referred to Appendix I, Model D.

Let us introduce first the intermediate notation

[58] See n. 33. The neutral technological progress rate $g_1 = g_2 = g = 0$ must be assumed.

D-1c. $A_x = [(1 - x)ma_1]^{1/(r+1)} + [(1 - m)a_2]^{1/(r+1)},$

$B_x = B_0 = B = [mb_1]^{1/(r+1)} + [(1 - m)b_2]^{1/(r+1)},$

$\mathcal{J}_x = \left[\dfrac{ma_1}{(1 - x)^r}\right]^{1/(r+1)} + [(1 - m)a_2]^{1/(r+1)}.$

Then the aggregate parameters and scale coefficients with the differential profits tax x take the form:

$a_x = \dfrac{A_x^r \mathcal{J}_x}{A_x^r \mathcal{J}_x + B^{r+1}}$ aggregate capital share parameter,

$b_x = \dfrac{B^{r+1}}{A_x^r \mathcal{J}_x + B^{r+1}}$ aggregate labor share parameter,

$M_x = [A_x^r \mathcal{J}_x + B^{r+1}]^{-1/r}$ scale coefficient,

and for $x = 0$ we get the same in the absence of the tax: a_0, b_0 and M_0.

As in Model B the rescaling factor is defined:

$$u_x = \frac{M_x}{M_0}.$$

In this new notation, factors are allocated between sectors according to formulae:

D-1d. $K_{1,x,t} = \dfrac{[(1 - x)\, ma_1]^{1/(r+1)}}{A_x} K_{x,t}$,

$K_{2,x,t} = \dfrac{[(1 - m)\, a_2]^{1/(r+1)}}{A_x} K_{x,t}$,

$L_{1,t} = \dfrac{[mb_1]^{1/(r+1)}}{B} L_t$,

$L_{2,t} = \dfrac{[(1 - m)\, b_2]^{1/(r+1)}}{B} L_t$.

Substituting D-1d in D-1b and using the notation introduced in D-1c we finally get the aggregate production function *in absence of tax:*

D-1e. $$\mathcal{Q}_{0,t} = M_0 [a_0 K_{0,t}{}^{-r} + b_0 L_t{}^{-r}]^{-1/r},$$

and *with tax:*

$$\mathcal{Q}_{x,t} = M_x [a_x K_{x,t}{}^{-r} + b_x L_t{}^{-r}]^{-1/r}.$$

Once more the nature of this aggregate production function for the whole economy resembles that in Model B for the general profits tax case, but now introduction of the tax changes the scale of output toward less output for the same input, as well as changing shares of factors expressed in units of the index for the national product in favor either of capital (if $a_x > a_0$) or of labor (if $a_x < a_0$).

The aggregate labor supply function is once more of the form:

D-2. $$L_t = L_0 e^{ht}.$$

The neoclassical investment function is of the form modified for Model B, namely:

D-3. $$I_{x,t} = K_{x,t} - K_{x,t-1} = S_{x,t} = s_{x,t-1} \mathcal{Q}_{x,t-1}.$$

The effective saving rate may be derived from the following formula:

D-4a. $$s_{x,t} = \left[s_p \frac{K_{1,x,t}}{\mathcal{Q}_{x,t}} \frac{\partial \mathcal{Q}_{x,t}}{\partial K_{1,x,t}} + s_i(1 - s_p) \frac{K_{1,x,t}}{\mathcal{Q}_{x,t}} \frac{\partial \mathcal{Q}_{x,t}}{\partial K_{1,x,t}} \right](1 - x)$$

(corporate profits)   (dividends)

$$+ \left[s_p \frac{K_{2,x,t}}{\mathcal{Q}_{x,t}} \frac{\partial \mathcal{Q}_{x,t}}{\partial K_{2,x,t}} + s_i(1 - s_p) \frac{K_{2,x,t}}{\mathcal{Q}_{x,t}} \frac{\partial \mathcal{Q}_{x,t}}{\partial K_{2,x,t}} \right] +$$

(non-corporate profits)   (withdrawals)

$$+ s_i \frac{L_t}{\mathcal{Q}_{x,t}} \frac{\partial \mathcal{Q}_{x,t}}{\partial L_t},$$

(wages)

which in terms of parameters and total capital share [59] may be written *in absence of tax:*

D-4b. $$s_{0,t} = s_i + F_{0,t} [s_p (1 - s_i)],$$

and *with tax:*

$$s_{x,t} = s_i + F_{x,t} \left\{ s_p (1 - s_i) - x \frac{s_p + s_i - s_p s_i}{\mathcal{F}_x} \left[\frac{m a_1}{(1 - x)^r} \right]^{1/(1+r)} \right\}.$$

[59] For derivation see Appendix I, Model D.

Parameter Values

As in Model C the number of parameters is here larger than in the case of a general profits tax. Sectoral parameters have to be given realistic values here, and this is not the only complication. Equilibrium values of sectoral and aggregate variables, and thus measures and indicators of tax effects, depend on the share parameters a_1, a_2, b_1, and b_2, and on the value of the elasticity of substitution parameter σ as well. In fact, the higher the σ parameter is, the smaller should be the values of a_1 and a_2 which yield the long-run gross capital share at realistic levels. This complex relationship between sectoral share parameters, elasticity of substitution, and gross share of capital cannot be stated easily in a simple mathematical formula. A large computer could, of course, search for realistic parameters that would yield the required gross share of capital, but this was considered too costly a procedure for the purpose at hand.

The alternative to this approach is to use more than one set of parameters, a_1, a_2, b_1, and b_2, for different values of the parameter σ without paying regard to the same gross shares requirement as done for Model B. We still hope to approximate it adopting the following parameter values for Model D:

for $\sigma = 1.1$,

$$g = g_1 = g_2 = 0, \ a_1 = .2, \ a_2 = .45, \ h = .01, \ m = .6, \ x = .2,$$
$$s_p = .5, \ s_i = .05;$$

for $\sigma < 1$,

$$g = g_1 = g_2 = 0, \ a_1 = .33333, \ a_2 = .75, \ h = .01, \ m = .6, \ x = .2,$$
$$s_p = .5, \ s_i = .05.$$

The Magnitude of Capital Outflow

Let us now consider the magnitude of capital flows implied by the Harberger model. The total outflow is determined by formula:

$$K_{1,0,\infty} - K_{1,x,0} = \frac{[ma_1]^{1/(r+1)}}{A_0} K_{0,\infty} - \frac{[(1-x)ma_1]^{1/(r+1)}}{A_x} K_{x,0},$$

and $K_{x,0} = K_{0,\infty}$ as initially the total supply of capital is fixed. Consequently, the percentage outflow is:

$$100 \frac{K_{1,0,\infty} - K_{1,x,0}}{K_{1,0,\infty}} = 100 \left[1 - \frac{A_0}{A_x} (1 - x)^{1/(r+1)} \right].$$

For various differential tax rates and various elasticities of substitution, *the following percentage outflows of capital from the taxed sector* are implied by the Harberger adjustment:

σ Elasticity of Substitution	Differential Tax Rate x	.1	.2	.3	.4
1.1		7.0	14.5	22.7	31.5
.99		6.2	12.9	20.2	28.3
.8		4.9	10.2	16.1	22.7
.66667		4.0	8.3	13.2	18.7
.6		3.5	7.4	11.8	16.7
.5		2.9	6.1	9.7	13.8

In Model C the differential tax rate $x = .2$ called for a 13 per cent outflow of capital from the corporate sector. The above figures show that this outflow is more moderate for lower values of σ; but even for $\sigma = .5$ it is substantial, and one would think it should be observable by modern econometric techniques.[60]

Equilibrium Solution

Equilibrium values of variables in Model D cannot be found easily with the help of a simple calculus. Instead, the model was simulated on IBM computer 7070. A large computer, however, cannot run forever (or one cannot wait or pay for it), and it is necessary to settle for a point in time in which the model is not yet in the long-run equilibrium but close to it. As noted before, by long-run equilibrium we mean those values of the variables in the model for which the economy will grow along a balanced growth path.

In the case of a general profits tax with a Cobb-Douglas production function (Model A) and a zero neutral technological progress rate, about 700 periods were required to yield a 99 per cent approximation. In Model B, where the CES production

[60] The qualifying remarks in n. 45 hold here as well.

function was adopted instead of the Cobb-Douglas, we adopted 750 periods as a good approximation. In Model C we changed to a differential profits tax and found for the case of the Cobb-Douglas production function that the speed of the adjustment process is not substantially changed. Combining all this information with a desire to be on the safe side led to the adoption of 1,000 periods as a number which should provide values close enough to the long-run levels of the variables of interest. Table 13 supports this procedure well.

The approximate values of the variables of the model are given in Table 14 and these in turn are translated into indicators and measures of tax effects in Table 15. As before, we will start from an initial position which now represents the end of the Harberger adjustment. Because of the assumption of instantaneous adjustment, we get this by setting the time variable $t = 0$.

We note that the Harberger adjustment in this model is more complicated than in Model C. Shifting for the whole economy is negative for larger σ because of excess burden (waste), which pulls down the over-all rate of return to all factors. For smaller σ values such shifting becomes positive. Apparently a tilt in the aggregate production function resulting from an increase in the aggregate capital share parameter with tax over that in the absence of tax (i.e., $a_x > a_0$) increases returns to capital at the expense of returns to labor sufficiently to offset a decline due to excess burden. Numerical strength of this change in the capital share parameter is given by the tax effect denoted as v_x, for which the formula is:

$$v_x = \frac{a_x}{a_0}, \text{ and}$$

$$a_x > a_0 \text{ when } v_x > 1,$$

$$a_x < a_0 \text{ when } v_x < 1.$$

Although percentagewise excess burden and embedded capital share parameter effects are small, their absolute effects are quite powerful. The excess burden for a .2 differential tax may result

Table 13

Speed of Adjustment
(differential tax rate $x = .2$, neutral technological progress rate $g = 0$)

Period[2]		Product-capital ratio in period t						Tax effect on product-capital ratio in period t, as a fraction of its long-run equilibrium effect[1]				
	0	500	600	700	800	900	1000	500	600	700	800	900
σ	$N_{0,1000}$	$N_{x,500}$	$N_{x,600}$	$N_{x,700}$	$N_{x,800}$	$N_{x,900}$	$N_{x,1000}$	$\dfrac{E_{x,500}}{E_{x,1000}}$	$\dfrac{E_{x,600}}{E_{x,1000}}$	$\dfrac{E_{x,700}}{E_{x,1000}}$	$\dfrac{E_{x,800}}{E_{x,1000}}$	$\dfrac{E_{x,900}}{E_{x,1000}}$
1.1	.05458	.06040	.06094	.06118	.06129	.06134	.06136	.85895	.93900	.97450	.99013	.99700
.8	.04445	.04877	.04987	.05050	.05087	.05107	.05118	.64201	.80504	.89923	.95281	.98305
.66667	.07257	.07844	.07940	.07974	.07986	.07990	.07992	.79832	.92884	.97582	.99211	.99796
.6	.08356	.08926	.09047	.09087	.09099	.09103	.09104	.76151	.92403	.96417	.99307	.99835
.5	.10309	.10790	.10975	.11027	.11041	.11045	.11046	.65275	.90183	.97442	.99334	.99858

[1] The formula for adjustment in period t is $\dfrac{N_{x,t} - N_{0,1000}}{N_{x,1000} - N_{0,1000}}$

[2] As the initial inputs are not long-run equilibrium inputs in the absence of tax, early periods are contaminated too much by the arbitrariness of our choice.

Table 14
Variables

(differential tax rate $x = .2$; $a_1 = .3333$; $a_2 = .75$; for $\sigma < 1$, $a_1 = .2$; $a_2 = .45$; for $\sigma = 1.1$)

Elasticity of Substitution	Effective saving rate			Embedded capital share parameter		Scale factor		Product-capital ratio		
	In Absence of Tax, Long Run	With Tax, in Period Zero	With Tax, Long Run	In Absence of Tax	With Tax	In Absence of Tax	With Tax	In Absence of Tax, Long Run	With Tax, in Period Zero	With Tax, Long Run
σ	$s_{0,1000}$	$s_{z,0}$	$s_{z,1000}$	a_0	a_z	M_0	M_z	$N_{0,1000}$	$N_{z,0}$	$N_{z,1000}$
1.1	.22793	.21273	.19781	.29895	.29883	.53128	.53026	.04445	.04434	.05118
.99	.28123	.26047	.24341	.50043	.50044	.55565	.55403	.03617	.03607	.04176
.8	.18596	.17312	.16540	.50900	.50931	.54576	.54443	.05458	.05450	.06136
.66667	.13987	.13104	.12700	.51540	.51591	.53851	.53738	.07257	.07251	.07992
.6	.12148	.11432	.11149	.51871	.51932	.53479	.53377	.08356	.08352	.09104
.5	.09847	.09348	.09189	.52578	.52655	.52913	.52828	.10308	.10305	.11046

For the Whole Economy

Elasticity of Substitution	Gross rate of return			Gross share of capital			Net share of capital		
	In Absence of Tax, Long Run	With Tax, in Period Zero	With Tax, Long Run	In Absence of Tax, Long Run	With Tax, in Period Zero	With Tax, Long Run	In Absence of Tax, Long Run	With Tax, in Period Zero	With Tax, Long Run
σ	$y_{0,1000}$	$y_{z,0}$	$y_{z,1000}$	$F_{0,1000}$	$F_{z,0}$	$F_{z,1000}$	$H_{0,1000}$	$H_{z,0}$	$H_{z,1000}$
1.1	.01665	.01660	.01892	.37459	.37445	.36960	.37459	.32381	.31928
.99	.01761	.01756	.02036	.48681	.48682	.48755	.48681	.43159	.43218
.8	.01562	.01561	.01810	.28623	.28645	.29509	.28623	.24311	.25088
.66667	.01373	.01374	.01590	.18920	.18951	.19896	.18920	.15758	.16576
.6	.01257	.01259	.01454	.15047	.15079	.15972	.15048	.12439	.13199
.5	.01052	.01054	.01212	.10204	.10232	.10968	.10204	.08357	.08971

For the Corporate Sector

Elasticity of Substitution	Gross rate of return			Gross share of capital			Net share of capital		
	In Absence of Tax, Long Run	With Tax, in Period Zero	With Tax, Long Run	In Absence of Tax, Long Run	With Tax, in Period Zero	With Tax, Long Run	In Absence of Tax, Long Run	With Tax, in Period Zero	With Tax, Long Run
σ	$y_{1,0,1000}$	$y_{1,z,0}$	$y_{1,z,1000}$	$F_{1,0,1000}$	$F_{1,z,0}$	$F_{1,z,1000}$	$H_{1,0,1000}$	$H_{1,z,0}$	$H_{1,z,1000}$
1.1	.02182	.02182	.02341	.24974	.24709	.24324	.24974	.20794	.20454
.99	.02053	.02053	.02068	.32285	.32558	.32379	.32285	.26752	.27696
.8	.01784	.01784	.01808	.18286	.18676	.19334	.18286	.15520	.16089
.66667	.01563	.01563	.01650	.13264	.12834	.13534	.13264	.10535	.11129
.6	.01429	.01429	.01370	.10050	.10518	.11184	.10050	.08596	.09152
.5	.01192	.01192	.01192	.07117	.07544	.08104	.07117	.06128	.06590

Table 15
Tax Effects

(differential tax rate $x = .2$, and $a_1 = .33333$, $a_2 = .75$ for $\sigma < 1$, $a_1 = .2$, $a_2 = .45$ for $\sigma = 1.1$)

Harberger Type:

Elasticity of Substitution σ	Shifting for the whole economy			Differential shifting			Corporate shifting		
	On the Gross Rate of Return $S_{y,0}$	On the Gross Share $S_{F,0}$	On the Net Share $S^{*}_{H,0}$	On the Gross Rate of Return $S_{d,y,0}$	On the Gross Share $S_{d,F,0}$	On the Net Share $S^{*}_{d,H,0}$	On the Gross Rate of Return $S_{1,y,0}$	On the Gross Share $S_{1,F,0}$	On the Net Share $S^{*}_{1,H,0}$
1.1	−.01383	−.00181	.32225	.66810	.05196	−.15915	.65427	.05377	.16310
.99	−.01293	.00139	.43282	.72520	.03864	−.28975	.71227	.04003	.14307
.8	−.00262	.00428	.24675	.62348	.10002	−.00298	.62086	.10430	.24377
.66667	.00423	.00817	.16439	.60276	.17498	.09710	.60699	.18315	.26149
.6	.00802	.11054	.13306	.59224	.21220	.14341	.60026	.22274	.27648
.5	.01224	.01380	.09488	.57652	.26958	.21041	.58876	.28338	.30529

Long Run:

Elasticity of Substitution σ	On the Gross Rate of Return $S_{y,1000}$	On the Gross Share $S_{F,1000}$	On the Net Share $S^{*}_{H,1000}$	On the Gross Rate of Return $S_{d,y,1000}$	On the Gross Share $S_{d,F,1000}$	On the Net Share $S^{*}_{d,H,1000}$	On the Gross Rate of Return $S_{1,y,1000}$	On the Gross Share $S_{1,F,1000}$	On the Net Share $S_{1,H,1000}$
1.1	.59944	−.06749	.26175	.58641	.06620	−.16670	1.18585	−.13369	.09505
.99	.67633	.00755	.43888	.56273	.00692	−.14950	1.23906	.01447	.28938
.8	.68601	.15009	.38243	.53764	.12088	.01688	1.22365	.27097	.39931
.66667	.68250	.24515	.38054	.52091	.18720	.11990	1.20341	.43235	.50044
.6	.67644	.28935	.38580	.51294	.21762	.16739	1.18938	.50697	.55318
.5	.65894	.34827	.39591	.50177	.26095	.23414	1.16071	.60922	.63005

Other Effects:

Elasticity of Substitution σ	Tax effect on the embedded share parameter $v_x = \dfrac{a_x}{a_0}$	Rescaling factor (indicator of excess burden) $u_x = \dfrac{M_x}{M_0}$	Tax effect on saving rate G_x	Tax effect on product-capital ratio E_x
1.1	.99960	.99810	.86786	.15156
.99	1.00002	.99709	.86551	.15468
.8	1.00061	.99755	.88941	.12423
.66667	1.00099	.99791	.90796	.10130
.6	1.00118	.99810	.91780	.08953
.5	1.00147	.99839	.93320	.07156

for the U.S. economy in about one billion dollars annual waste. The embedded capital share parameter effect would, for small σ, increase the capital share parameter by .1 per cent, but in absolute terms for an economy of the size of ours this would mean a rise in earnings of capital by approximately 200–300 million dollars at the expense of labor earnings.[61] Harberger type differential shifting on the gross rate of return is substantial. It declines somewhat for lower values of σ but still accounts for about two-thirds of the loss; hence corporations are able to shift that same amount of the tax burden, mostly to non-corporate business. Once more, a lower σ makes it more difficult to shift.

Harberger-type shifting on the gross share for the whole economy only slightly deviates from zero (for $\sigma = 1$ it is zero, for $\sigma > 1$ it is negative, and for $\sigma < 1$ it is positive). This deviation is entirely due to changes in the aggregate embedded capital share parameter a_x, and it reflects the tax burden that falls on labor.[62] Harberger-type differential shifting is positive and rises with the decline in σ. Apparently, sharewise, corporate business benefits more the lower the elasticity of substitution parameter σ is. The corporate shifting on the gross share, being the sum of differential shifting plus shifting for the whole economy (the last being rather small), varies quite similarly to Harberger-type differential shifting on the gross share.

Harberger-type shifting on the net share for the whole economy is positive but declines steeply as σ declines. Such differential shifting is negative for $\sigma \geq .8$ and positive for $\sigma < .8$. The Harberger-type corporate shifting on the net share is

[61] This figure is estimated as follows. The excess burden for a .2 differential tax is for a 600 billion dollar economy estimated at about 1 billion dollars (Harberger uses a higher differential tax and arrives at a figure of 3 billion). The capital share of this burden is about 20–30 per cent, hence its loss will be from 200 to 300 million dollars. We note, however, that a rise in the embedded capital share parameter more than offsets this loss for all business investors.

The reader should be aware that this loss and its offset at the expense of labor results only if Harberger's adjustment in fact operates in our society and elasticities of substitution are in fact low. Then not only unincorporated business, but labor as well are suffering from a tax that was intended to burden only investors in corporate business.

[62] As noted before, this should not be interpreted as backward shifting, which may occur in a non-neoclassical world where money wages can be administered.

positive and rises as σ declines because differential shifting more than offsets Harberger-type shifting for the whole economy.

Let us now turn to the long-run solution. Imposition of the tax resulted in an excess burden for any level of σ already under the Harberger adjustment. The resulting waste varied from .16 to .3 per cent of the national product. We may note that this waste as a percentage of national product persists even in the long run.

The differential profits tax has a negative effect on savings, but it is smaller for several reasons. First, the tax falls on some profits but not on others, and second, the differential here applied is $x = .2$ against the general tax $x = .5$. For the same differential tax rate the tax effect on savings is larger if σ is larger and vice versa.

As the tax affects the effective saving rate negatively, the product-capital rate rises. Here too, a larger σ, facilitating a higher cut in investment, tends to produce a larger increase in the product-capital ratio.

The long-run shifting on the gross rate of return for the whole economy varies little around the two-thirds value. Higher aggregate share parameters help and so does higher elasticity of substitution. In addition, the long-run differential shifting on the gross rate of return exceeds 50 per cent, and so the corporate shifting exceeds 100 per cent.

The long-run shifting on the gross share for the whole economy follows the pattern for the general profits tax in Model B as shown in Graph 3. Shifting is higher for low σ, becomes zero for $\sigma = 1$, and then turns negative; the only difference is that the slope of the decline is less. Differential shifting is positive and rises as we move away from $\sigma = 1$ value. The resulting long-run corporate shifting on the gross share is high for low σ, declines to zero as σ approaches one, and becomes negative for $\sigma > 1$.

The long-run shifting on the net share for the whole economy is positive. Low σ makes it more difficult to shift the tax burden sharewise. The differential long-run shifting on the net share is about one-fourth for $\sigma = .5$, and it turns negative even before reaching $\sigma = 1$. The resulting long-run corporate shifting on the net share is positive and exceeds .6 for $\sigma = .5$, declines to less than .3 for values of σ approaching one, and declines further for $\sigma > 1$. Note that all shifting measures on the net share are sensitive to changes in adopted values of the embedded capital share parameters.

CONCLUSION

The four models here considered allow a comprehensive review of the effects of a general and of a non-general tax on profits, providing the behavior of our economy is well-described by the neoclassical model. Even if this proviso is doubted, the neo-classical model is still of interest in a "normative" way within the context of a general welfare theory.

There are two clear definitions of the neoclassical theory of tax incidence and shifting. In the case of a general profits tax, the standard neoclassical model claims that in the short run this tax cannot be shifted because its burden falls on the owner of capital assets used in business. Neoclassicists recognized that this must have negative effects on capital formation, but they did not work out their knowledge with any precision. Neo-classicists were, in fact, rather vague when questioned about what happens to incidence and shifting in the long run.

In the case of a non-general profits tax the Harberger version of a neoclassical theory of shifting saw the non-neutrality effects of the kind of tax which brings forth flows of capital from the taxed to non-taxed sectors and results in inefficiency. In this case, the taxed sector may show shifting under my definitions, but the burden of the tax is passed not to the owners or factors other than capital or consumer but to investors in the non-taxed sector, i.e., the burden is passed within the capitalist class. The Harberger adjustment requires time but cannot be considered long-run in the sense of this paper because Harberger assumes that such a tax will have no effect on new capital formation. This assumption is here removed.

The crucial idea for both versions is that investible funds (saving) determine investment. This paper explores what will happen to an economy in a neoclassical world if the tax affects new capital formation in a context of economic growth. The standard and the Harberger versions are here only starting points in an adjustment process that is basically the same for all of the four models considered.

In this long-run growth process a crucial role is played by several determinants. First, a profits tax always reduces savings, and thus investment too. Second, profits tax effects depend to a degree on elasticity of substitution of factors and of products. Third, the values of share parameters embedded in the production functions are important (at least when studying distribution effects of this tax on the net shares). Let us bring these aspects out clearly.

Reduction in savings and in investment raises the product-capital ratio—an extremely interesting point that has always been missed by students reviewing the many possible determinants of this ratio.

The resulting increase in productivity of capital (made comparatively more scarce by the tax on profits) allows the gross rate of return to rise, thus at least partially restoring incentives to invest. This result has no meaning for a neoclassicist whose investment function does not depend on incentives to invest, but in a more general investment function where incentives and available funds determine investment it would be of great importance. Our study of shifting measured on the gross rate of return gives a partial answer to this particular question.

If the profits tax is non-general, incentives to invest in the taxed sector may be restored by capital outflow from the taxed to the non-taxed sectors. This Harberger type of adjustment to a differential profits tax, assumed in this paper to come about instantaneously, persists under the dynamic adjustment in which the new capital formation is affected.

The gross shares of factors are affected by general or non-general profits taxes in the long run and seem to be monotonically related to the elasticity of substitution parameter σ. Such shares rise after imposition of tax for $\sigma < 1$, remain unchanged for $\sigma = 1$, and decline for $\sigma > 1$. Varying of share parameters embedded in the production function affects the slope of gross shares as a function of elasticity of substitution σ.

The net shares of factors turn out to be very complex functions of tax rates, elasticity of substitution, and embedded factor share parameters.

Besides these major points several other points of interest were noted. The speed of adjustment through changes in new capital formation turned out to be rather slow. For the case of zero neutral technological progress rate, 700 to 1000 periods are required to be assured of 99 per cent of the long-run tax effect on the product-capital ratio. Various, reasonable interpretations of the length of such periods suggest that the adjustment takes 100–150 years, hence the long-run implications of such taxes may be often forgotten by politicians with a much shorter time horizon.

The non-general tax cases provided four more special points. First, the size of Harberger capital outflows becomes measurable as a function of a differential tax rate, elasticity of substitution, and embedded capital share parameters. Second, these outflows are of considerable size and if they in fact do occur in our economy, should be observable. Third, the resulting inefficiency of the economy can be measured from shifts towards the origin in the isoquants of the production function. And finally, for $\sigma \neq 1$ the isoquants of the aggregate production function may change their slope as well, leading to further deterioration or improvement in the gross and net capital share and in the gross rate of return. Improvement in the gross share of capital and the gross rate of return due to this phenomenon is at the expense of labor.

APPENDIX I

Model A

Model A may be written:

(1) $\mathcal{Q}_{x,t} = e^{\varrho t} K_{x,t}^{a} L_{t}^{b}$, production function,

(2) $L_t = L_0 e^{ht}$, growth of labor force function,

(3) $I_{x,t} = \dfrac{dK_{x,t}}{dt} = S_{x,t} = s_{x,t}\, \mathcal{Q}_{x,t}$, neoclassical theory of investment,

(4) $s_{x,t} = \quad bs_i \quad + as_p\,(1-x) + as_i\,(1-s_p)\,(1-x)$, effective saving rate.
      (wages)   (retained   (withdrawals)
              profits)

The effective saving rate may be rewritten:

$$s_x = s_i + as_p\,(1-s_i) - ax\,[s_p + s_i - s_p s_i].$$

In absence of tax, it becomes:

$$s_0 = s_i + as_p\,(1-s_i),$$

and with tax:

$$s_x = s_0 - ax\,[s_p + s_i - s_p s_i].$$

As the last term to be subtracted is always positive, $s_x < s_0$ for $0 < x < 1$.

To find the pattern of growth for this economy, we may consider what happens to the product-capital ratio.

(5) $$N_{x,t} = \frac{\mathcal{Q}_{x,t}}{K_{x,t}} = e^{gt}\left(\frac{K_{x,t}}{L_t}\right)^{-b}.$$

Taking logarithms, differentiating with respect to time, substituting L_t and $I_{x,t}$, and rearranging the terms we get:

$$\frac{dN_{x,t}}{N_{x,t}} - \frac{d[g + bh - bs_x\,N_{x,t}]}{[g + bh - bs_x\,N_{x,t}]} = (g + bh)\,dt.$$

Integration after a further rearrangement yields:

(6) $$N_{x,t} = \frac{[g + bh]}{[bs_x + C^{-1}\,e^{-(g+bh)t}]};$$

hence also

$$N_{0,t} = \frac{[g + bh]}{[bs_0 + C^{-1}\,e^{-(g+bh)t}]},$$

where $C^{-1} = \dfrac{1}{C}$ is a constant to be determined from initial conditions and e

is the base of natural logarithms.

$$As \qquad (g + bh) > 0,\; \lim_{t \to \infty} e^{-(g+bh)t} \to 0.$$

Hence, in equilibrium the product-capital ratio is finite and constant, namely:

(7a) $$N_{x,\infty} = \frac{(g/b + h)}{s_x},$$

$$N_{0,\infty} = \frac{(g/b + h)}{s_0}.$$

Also:

(7b)
$$E_x = \frac{N_{x,\infty} - N_{0,\infty}}{N_{0,\infty}} = \frac{s_0}{s_x} - 1 = \frac{1}{G_x} - 1 = \frac{s_0 - s_x}{s_x}.$$

On the assumption that factors are paid their marginal product, we have for $0 < x < 1$:

(8)
$$y_{x,t} = \frac{\partial \mathcal{Q}_{x,t}}{\partial K_{x,t}} = a \, N_{x,t},$$

$$\pi_{x,t} = y_{x,t} \, K_{x,t} = a \, \mathcal{Q}_{x,t},$$

$$F_{x,t} = \frac{\pi_{x,t}}{\mathcal{Q}_{x,t}} = a,$$

$$H_{x,t} = \frac{\pi_{x,t} - x\pi_{x,t}}{\mathcal{Q}_{x,t} - ax \, \mathcal{Q}_{x,t}} = \frac{a\,(1 - x)}{1 - ax}.$$

One gets the tax effects by substituting these variables in formulae for measures and indicators.

Finally, we would like to know something about the speed of adjustment. If we start in period zero from an equilibrium with respect to zero tax then $N_{x,0} = N_{0,\infty}$, and the constant of integration is determined from the formula:

(9a)
$$C = \frac{1}{b\,(s_0 - s_x)} \quad \text{or} \quad C^{-1} = b\,(s_0 - s_x) = abx \,[s_p + s_i - s_p s_i].$$

This allows us to explore the speed of adjustment of any variable of interest to us. The long-run tax effect on the change in the product-capital ratio was selected for this analysis because that ratio is most fundamental.

To get k fraction of E_x, we have the following relation:

(9b)
$$E_{x,t_k} = kE_x = \frac{N_{x,t_k} - N_{0,\infty}}{N_{0,\infty}}.$$

Applying relations (6), (7), and (9a) we get:

$$e^{(g + bh_{tk})} = \frac{k(s_0 - s_x) + s_x}{(1 - k)\,s_x} = \frac{E_{x,t_k} + 1}{(1 - k)}.$$

Hence the time required to get k fraction of E_x is:

(9c)
$$t_k = \frac{\ln\,[E_{x,t_k} + 1] - \ln\,(1 - k)}{g + bh}.$$

This ends the computation of a general solution to our problem.

Model B

In Model B we deal with the equations:

(1) $\quad \mathcal{Q}_{x,t} = [aK_{x,t}^{-r} + bL_t^{-r}]^{-1/r}$, $\qquad\qquad$ production function,

(2) $\quad L_t = L_0 e^{ht}$, $\qquad\qquad\qquad\qquad\qquad$ growth of labor function,

(3) $\quad I_{x,t} = K_{x,t} - K_{x,t-1} = S_{x,t} = s_{x,t-1}\mathcal{Q}_{x,t-1}$, $\qquad$ neoclassical theory of investment.

The effective saving rate now depends on factor shares which themselves are not constant, hence the rate depends on time t, and carries subscript t:

(4) $\quad s_{x,t} = s_i(1 - F_{x,t}) + s_p(1 - x)\,F_{x,t} + s_i(1 - s_p)(1 - x)\,F_{x,t}$

$\qquad\quad$ (wages) $\qquad\quad$ (retained $\qquad\qquad$ (dividends)
$\qquad\qquad\qquad\qquad\quad$ profits)

or:

$$s_{x,t} = s + F_{x,t}\,[s_p\,(1 - s_i) - x(s_p + s_i - s_p s_i)].$$

For zero tax this becomes:

$$s_{0,t} = s_i + F_{0,t}\,[s_p\,(1 - s_i)].$$

This completes our model.

Unfortunately the general solution to this model is difficult to find, and so changes in variables from period to period were simulated on the 7070 I.B.M. computer and their value for the 750th period was assumed to be close to the equilibrium value.

To standardize the variables, the initial inputs were selected to satisfy the relation $K_{x,0} + L_0 = 1$. In fact we chose for $0 \leq x < 1$:

(5) $\quad I_{x,0} =$ any constant. The actual value of $I_{x,0}$ has no effect on the outcome because $I_{x,1} = s_{x,0}\,\mathcal{Q}_{x,0}$.

$$K_{x,0} = .99,$$
$$L_0 = .01.$$

These inputs are arbitrary and obviously are not those for which the economy described by the model would show balanced growth in absence of tax. A more proper procedure would have been for $0 < x < 1$ to find the long-run equilibrium ratio of capital to labor in absence of tax and set the initial rates of capital and labor equal to it, or

$$\frac{K_{x,0}}{L_0} = \frac{K_{0,750}}{L_{750}},$$

which with relation $K_{x,0} + L_0 = 1$ would determine initial values of $K_{x,0}$ and L_0. However, to speed estimation of long-run relations, inputs (5) were used as initial inputs in all cases. Consequently, we cannot get the standard neoclassical results by setting $t = 0$ in the model. Also the dynamic path is affected; fortunately the long-run equilibrium values are not. As initial values of variables with the tax were also needed, they were computed by hand.

Having adopted initial inputs, the machine computed other variables of interest for period zero according to the following formulae:

(6)
$$N_{z,0} = \left[a + b \left(\frac{K_{z,0}}{L_0} \right)^r \right] - 1/r,$$

$$\mathcal{Q}_{z,0} = N_{z,0} K_{z,0},$$

$$F_{z,0} = \frac{K_{z,0}}{\mathcal{Q}_{z,0}} \frac{\partial \mathcal{Q}_{z,0}}{\partial K_{z,0}} = a \left[a + b \left(\frac{K_{z,0}}{L_0} \right) r \right]^{-1},$$

$$y_{z,0} = N_{z,0} F_{z,0},$$

$$H_{z,0} = \frac{\pi_{z,0} - x\pi_{z,0}}{\mathcal{Q}_{z,0} - x\pi_{z,0}} = \frac{(1-x) F_{z,0}}{1 - x F_{z,0}},$$

$$s_{z,0} = s_i + F_{z,0} [s_p (1 - s_i) - x(s_p + s_i - s_p s_i)].$$

In the next step the machine computed inputs for period 1 from formulae:

(7)
$$I_{z,1} = s_{z,0} \mathcal{Q}_{z,0},$$

$$K_{z,1} = K_{z,0} + I_{z,1},$$

$$L_1 = L_0 e^h,$$

and then found values for other variables for this period which then allowed it to compute inputs in period 2, and so on. By iteration consecutive periods' inputs and variables were computed. As the values of variables after a larger number of periods began levelling off, the variables for the 750th period were adopted as close enough approximations to the long-run balanced growth values.

Model C

We start with:

(1-a) $\mathcal{Q}_{1,z,t} = e^{g_1 t} K_{1,z,t}{}^{a_1} L_{1,t}{}^{b_1},$ corporate sector production function,

$\mathcal{Q}_{2,z,t} = e^{g_2 t} K_{2,z,t}{}^{a_2} L_{2,t}{}^{b_2},$ non-corporate sector production function.

These products are aggregated according to formula:

(1-b) $\mathcal{Q}_{z,t} = (\mathcal{Q}_{1,z,t})^m (\mathcal{Q}_{2,z,t})^{(1-m)},$ quantity index number.

Substituting values of $\mathcal{Q}_{1,z,t}$ and $\mathcal{Q}_{2,z,t}$ into formula (1-b) and denoting $g = mg_1 + (1-m)g_2$ we get:

$$\mathcal{Q}_{z,t} = e^{gt} K_{1,z,t}{}^{ma_1} K_{2,z,t}{}^{(1-m)a_2} L_{1,t}{}^{mb_1} L_{2,t}{}^{(1-m)b_2}.$$

The inputs in sectors, if homogeneous, are additive; hence also:

(1-c) $K_{1,z,t} + K_{2,z,t} = K_{z,t},$

$L_{1,t} + L_{2,t} = L_t.$

Further on the basis of neoclassical assumptions and instantaneous adjustment between sectors, we claim for $0 \leq x < 1$

$$(1 - x) \frac{\partial \mathcal{Q}_{x,t}}{\partial K_{1,x,t}} = \frac{\partial \mathcal{Q}_{x,t}}{\partial K_{2,x,t}},$$

$$\frac{\partial \mathcal{Q}_{x,t}}{\partial L_{1,t}} = \frac{\partial \mathcal{Q}_{x,t}}{\partial L_{2,t}} = \frac{\partial \mathcal{Q}_{x,t}}{\partial L_t}.$$

which instantaneously allocates the sectoral inputs as follows:

(1–d)
$$K_{1,x,t} = \frac{m a_1 (1 - x)}{a - m a_1 x} K_{x,t},$$

$$K_{2,x,t} = \frac{(1 - m) a_2}{a - m a_1 x} K_{x,t},$$

$$L_{1,t} = \frac{m b_1}{b} L_t,$$

$$L_{2,t} = \frac{(1 - m) b_2}{b} L_t,$$

where $a = m a_1 + (1 - m) a_2$,
$b = m b_1 + (1 - m) b_2$.

Note that $a + b = 1$.

If we denote further,

$$M_0 = \left\{ m \left[\frac{a_1}{a} \right]^{a_1} \left[\frac{b_1}{b} \right]^{b_1} \right\}^m \left\{ (1 - m) \left[\frac{a_2}{a} \right]^{a_2} \left[\frac{b_2}{b} \right]^{b_2} \right\}^{(1-m)},$$

$$M_x = \left\{ \left[\frac{a(1 - x)}{a - m a_1 x} \right]^{a_1} m \left[\frac{a_1}{a} \right]^{a_2} \left[\frac{b_1}{b} \right]^{b_1} \right\}^m \cdot$$

$$\cdot \left\{ \left[\frac{a}{a - m a_1 x} \right]^{a_2} (1 - m) \left[\frac{a_2}{a} \right]^{a_2} \left[\frac{b_2}{b} \right]^{b_2} \right\}^{(1-m)},$$

and substitute the sectoral inputs by their fractions of aggregated inputs, **we** get for the aggregate production function: *in absence of tax,*

(1–e)
$$\mathcal{Q}_{0,t} = M_0 e^{gt} K_{0,t}^a L_t^b;$$

with tax,

$$\mathcal{Q}_{x,t} = M_x e^{gt} K_{x,t}^a L_t^b.$$

This result is extremely useful, and is the payoff for choosing equal constant elasticities of substitution. We may compare the aggregate production function with formula (1), Appendix, Model A. As we see, the only difference is that now we have the same form of production function scaled by factor M_0 or

M_x, which for given tax rate x, is a constant. Consequently, the solution to this model can follow the method used to solve the Model A.

Let us pay some attention to the fact that $M_0 \neq M_x$. Apparently, the tax affects the scale of productivity. To get this into the open, let us form the rescaling factor u_x. We now have:

$$u_x = \frac{M_x}{M_0} = \frac{[a(1-x)]^{ma_1} [a]^{(1-m)a_2}}{[a - ma_1 x]^a},$$

which in this model is always a fraction [63] and may be thought of as an indicator of excess burden, i.e., of the decline in efficiency of production of the economy as a whole, due to non-neutrality (non-generality) of the tax.

Further

(2) $\qquad L_t = L_0 e^{ht},$ $\qquad\qquad$ growth of labor function,

and

(3) $\qquad I_{x,t} = \dfrac{dK_{x,t}}{dt} = S_{x,t} = s_{x,t} \mathcal{Q}_{x,t},$ $\qquad$ neoclassical theory of investment.

To find the effective saving rate $s_{x,t}$, we need to know the gross (before tax) earnings of capital in the sectors and in the whole economy. As Euler's theorem holds (the aggregate as well as sectoral production functions are linear and homogeneous of degree one), we have for $0 \leq x < 1$:

(4-a) $\qquad\qquad y_{1,x,t} = \dfrac{\partial \mathcal{Q}_{x,t}}{\partial K_{1,x,t}} = \dfrac{a - ma_1 x}{1-x} N_{x,t},$

$\qquad\qquad \pi_{1,x,t} = y_{1,x,t} K_{1,x,t} = ma_1 \mathcal{Q}_{x,t},$

$\qquad\qquad y_{2,x,t} = \dfrac{\partial \mathcal{Q}_{x,t}}{\partial K_{2,x,t}} = (a - ma_1 x) N_{x,t},$

$\qquad\qquad \pi_{2,x,t} = y_{2,x,t} K_{2,x,t} = (1-m) a_2 \mathcal{Q}_{x,t},$

$\qquad\qquad y_{x,t} = \dfrac{\partial \mathcal{Q}_{x,t}}{\partial K_{x,t}} = a N_{x,t},$

$\qquad\qquad \pi_{x,t} = a \mathcal{Q}_{x,t},$ and

the effective saving rate is determined as follows:

(4b) $s_x = s_i b + s_p ma_1 (1-x) + s_i (1-s_p) ma_1 (1-x) + s_p (1-m) a_2 +$
$\quad$ (wages) $\qquad$ (retained $\qquad$ (dividends) $\qquad\qquad$ (non-corporate
$\qquad\qquad\qquad$ profits) $\qquad\qquad\qquad\qquad\qquad$ profits)
$\quad + s_i (1-s_p)(1-m) a_2,$ $\qquad\qquad\qquad\qquad$ effective saving rate,
$\quad$ (withdrawals)

[63] In this model $0 < \dfrac{ma_1}{a} < 1$ and if $0 < x < 1$, then by the mean value theorem:

$[1-x]^{ma_1/a} < 1 - \dfrac{ma_1}{a} x$, or $0 < u_x < 1$.

or, *with tax:*

(4c) $s_x = s_i + as_p(1 - s_i) - ma_1 x[s_p + s_i - s_p s_i],$

and *in absence of tax:*

$$s_0 = s_i + as_p(1 - s_i);$$

thus s_x may also be written:

$$s_x = s_0 - ma_1 x[s_p + s_i - s_p s_i].$$

Once more the average structural savings rate is independent of time as in Model A; hence the time subscript may be omitted. Introduction of a differential profits tax will reduce this rate as the right-hand term to be deducted in the last formula above is always positive.

This completes our model.

The general solution to this model may be obtained as in Model A by differentiating the product-capital ratio, integrating, and solving for $t = 0$ and $t = \infty$.

In general for $0 \leq x < 1$ we find:

(5a) $$N_{x,t} = M_x \frac{g + bh}{bs_x + C^{-1} e^{-(g+bh)t}}.$$

Further, the product-capital ratio with tax under the Harberger-type of adjustment is not equal to that ratio in the long run in the absence of tax, as:

(5b) $$N_{0,\infty} = M_0 \frac{g + bh}{bs_0},$$

(5c) $$N_{x,0} = M_x \frac{g + bh}{bs_0},$$

and finally

(5d) $$N_{x,\infty} = M_x \frac{g + bh}{bs_x}.$$

Consequently,

(5e) $$E_x = \frac{M_x}{M_0} \cdot \frac{s_0}{s_x} - 1 = \frac{u_x}{G_x} - 1,$$

(6) $$F_{x,t} = \frac{T_{x,t}}{\mathcal{Q}_{x,t}} = a.$$

To get sectoral variables not computed so far additional sectoral values are required. For these it is possible to start from the information that, in the neoclassical model, wage rates are the same in all sectors, or

(7a) $$w_{x,t} = w_{1,x,t} = w_{2,x,t} = \frac{\partial \mathcal{Q}_{x,t}}{\partial L_t} = \frac{b\mathcal{Q}_{x,t}}{L_t}.$$

Hence the sectoral wage bills are:

(7b)
$$W_{1,x,t} = w_{1,x,t} L_{1,t} = mb_1 \mathcal{Q}_{x,t},$$
$$W_{2,x,t} = w_{2,x,t} L_{2,t} = (1-m) b_2 \mathcal{Q}_{x,t},$$
$$W_{x,t} = W_{1,x,t} + W_{2,x,t} = b\mathcal{Q}_{x,t},$$

and sectoral values added are:

$$V_{1,x,t} = \pi_{1,x,t} + W_{1,x,t} = m\mathcal{Q}_{x,t},$$
$$V_{2,x,t} = \pi_{2,x,t} + W_{2,x,t} = (1-m) \mathcal{Q}_{x,t}.$$

It follows also that:

$$F_{1,x,t} = \frac{\pi_{1,x,t}}{V_{1,x,t}} = a_1,$$

$$F_{2,x,t} = \frac{\pi_{2,x,t}}{V_{2,x,t}} = a_2,$$

and

(7e)
$$H_{x,t} = \frac{\pi_{x,t} - x\pi_{1,x,t}}{\mathcal{Q}_{x,t} - x\pi_{1,x,t}} = \frac{a - ma_1 x}{1 - ma_1 x},$$

$$H_{1,x,t} = \frac{\pi_{1,x,t}(1-x)}{V_{1,x,t} - x\pi_{1,x,t}} = \frac{a_1(1-x)}{1 - a_1 x}.$$

The speed of convergence in this model may be ascertained by a procedure similar to that for Model A. First we determine the constant in equation (5a) by assuming that our economy was already in equilibrium in the absence of tax. Then intersectoral flows of capital instantaneously result in the short-run equilibrium value of variable $N_{x,0}$ as given by equation (5a). Thus the constant C^{-1} in equation (5a) may be determined by equating it for $t = 0$ with (5c) relation, or

$$M_x \frac{g + bh}{bs_0} = M_x \frac{g + bh}{bs_x + C^{-1}},$$

which yields

(8a)
$$C^{-1} = b(s_0 - s_x).$$

To get the fraction k of E_x we start from the following relation:

(8b)
$$E_{x,t_k} = kE_x = \frac{N_{x,t_k} - N_{0,\infty}}{N_{0,\infty}}.$$

Substituting (5a), (5d), (5e), and (8a), and rearranging we get

$$e^{(g+bh)t_k} = \frac{(E_{x,t_k} + 1)\left(\dfrac{s_0}{s_x} - 1\right)}{E_x(1 - k)}$$

or

(8c)
$$t_k = \frac{ln(E_{x,t_k} + 1) + 1n\left(\dfrac{1}{G_x} - 1\right) - ln\left(\dfrac{u_x}{G_x} - 1\right) - ln(1 - k)}{g + bh}$$

as the time required to get the fraction k of the total tax effect on the product-capital ratio.

Relation (8c) differs from (9c), Appendix, Model A, by the two terms in the middle of the numerator which, however, offset each other to a degree. As u_x is a fraction, the model converges somewhat more slowly than Model A for the same effective tax rate and parameters. Note also that taking logarithms is allowed only if all the terms are positive, especially one must require relation

$\dfrac{u_x}{G_x} - 1 > 0$ to hold, which as $G_x > 0$ is equivalent to $u_x - G_x > 0$ or

(8d)
$$\frac{M_x}{M_0} > \frac{s_x}{s_0}.$$

This is a new restriction and is satisfied for a small differential tax rate but not for a large one. [64] Thus there exists an upper limit to the differential tax rate.

Model D

Model D is represented by the following equations:

(1a)　$\mathcal{Q}_{1,x,t} = [a_1 K_{1,x,t}^{-r} + b_1 L_{1,t}^{-r}]^{-1/r}$,　　　corporate sector
production function,

　　　$\mathcal{Q}_{2,x,t} = [a_2 K_{2,x,t}^{-r} + b_2 L_{2,t}^{-r}]^{-1/r}$,　　　non-corporate sector
production function,

aggregated according to:

(1b)　$\mathcal{Q}_{x,t} = [m\mathcal{Q}_{1,x,t}^{-r} + (1-m)\mathcal{Q}_{2,x,t}^{-r}]^{-1/r}$,　　　quantity index
number,

which after substitution results in:

$$\mathcal{Q}_{x,t} = [ma_1 K_{1,x,t}^{-r} + (1-m)a_2 K_{2,x,t}^{-r} + mb_1 L_{1,t}^{-r} + (1-m)b_2 L_{2,t}^{-r}]^{-1/r}.$$

[64] Relation (8d) may be written as:

$$\frac{[a(1-x)]^{ma_1}[a]^{(1-m)a_2}}{[a-ma_1 x]^a} > 1 - \frac{ma_1 x (s_p + s_i - s_p s_i)}{s_i + as_p (1-s_i)}$$

and for $x = 1$ is not satisfied, as it collapses to $0 > C$ and C is a positive number. No effort was made here to find the maximum x admissible under this condition.

Another restriction which is perhaps related to the above is the impossibility of negative capital inputs. For high values of the differential tax rate x (i.e., close to $x = 1$), the outflow of capital from the corporate sector required for equalization of net rates of return between both sectors may be larger than the initial endowment in capital in the corporate sector. If so, the obvious condition that

$$K_{i,x,0} \geq 0 \text{ for } i = 1.2$$

will not be satisfied. This condition was never stated openly in this paper as for small tax x and the adopted parameter values, it was satisfied. Nevertheless for high values of x it need not be. This case also was left out without further consideration.

The inputs are assumed homogeneous; hence additive, i.e.,

(1c)
$$K_{1,x,t} + K_{2,x,t} = K_{x,t}$$
$$L_{1,t} = +L_{2,t} = L_t.$$

Further, on the basis of neoclassical assumptions and instantaneous adjustment we claim $0 \leq x < 1$:

$$(1 - x)\frac{\partial \mathcal{Q}_{x,t}}{\partial K_{1,x,t}} = \frac{\partial \mathcal{Q}_{x,t}}{\partial K_{2,x,t}},$$

$$\frac{\partial \mathcal{Q}_{x,t}}{\partial L_{1,t}} = \frac{\partial \mathcal{Q}_{x,t}}{\partial L_{2,t}}.$$

We denote:

$$A_x = [(1 - x)ma_1]^{1/(r+1)} + [(1 - m)a_2]^{1/(r+1)}$$
$$B = [mb_1]^{1/(r+1)} + [(1 - m)b_2]^{1/(r+1)}$$

(in the B notation no subscript x is needed as B is not a function of the differential tax rate x).

Combining the above relations with the addition of homogeneous inputs we get the following formulae for allocation of resources between sectors:

(1d)
$$K_{1,x,t} = \frac{[(1 - x)ma_1]^{1/(r+1)}}{A_x} K_{x,t},$$

$$K_{2,x,t} = \frac{[(1 - m)a_2]^{1/(r+1)}}{A_x} K_{x,t},$$

$$L_{1,t} = \frac{[mb_1]^{1/(r+1)}}{B} L_t,$$

$$L_{2,t} = \frac{[(1 - m)b_2]^{1/(r+1)}L_t}{B} L_t.$$

If we denote further:

$$\mathcal{J}_x = \left[\frac{ma_1}{(1 - x)^r}\right]^{1/(r+1)} + [(1 - m)a_2]^{1/(r+1)},$$

$$a_x = \frac{A_x^r}{A_x^r \mathcal{J}_x + B^{r+1}},$$

$$b_x = \frac{B^{r+1}}{A_x^r \mathcal{J}_x + B^{r+1}},$$

$$M_x = [A_x^r \mathcal{J}_x + B^{r+1}]^{-1/r},$$

then [65] the aggregate product becomes *with tax:*

[65] Note the interesting relations:
$$A_0 = \mathcal{J}_0,$$
$$A^r_0 \mathcal{J}_0 = \{[ma_1]^{1/(r+1)} + [(1-m)a_2]^{1/(r+1)}\}$$

(1e)
$$\mathcal{Q}_{x,t} = M_x \left[a_x K_{x,t}^{-r} + b_x L_t^{-r} \right]^{-1/r},$$

and *in absence of tax:*

$$\mathcal{Q}_{0,t} = M_0 \left[a_0 K_{0,t}^{-r} + b_0 L_t^{-r} \right]^{-1/r}.$$

Once more the result is extremely useful. In aggregated terms this model has the same form as Model B. Also there is an inefficiency effect as in Model C because $M_x < M_0$ and finally the slopes of isoquants change, as $a_x \neq a_0$, and conversely $b_x \neq b_0$.

Further:

(2) $L_t = L_0 e^{ht}$,   growth of labor function,

(3) $I_{x,t} = K_{x,t} - K_{x,t-1} = S_{x,t} = s_{x,t-1}\mathcal{Q}_{x,t-1}$,   neoclassical theory of investment.

The effective saving rate is once more dependent on time as it is a function of shares and these are not constant except at a long-run equilibrium. The formula for $0 \leq x < 1$ is arrived at as follows:

(4a) $s_{x,t} = \left[s_p \quad\quad + s_i(1 - s_p) \right] \dfrac{K_{1,x,t}}{\mathcal{Q}_{x,t}} \dfrac{\partial \mathcal{Q}_{x,t}}{\partial K_{1,x,t}} (1 - x) +$
            (corporate   (dividends)
             profits)

$+ \left[s_p \quad\quad + s_1(1 - s_p) \right] \dfrac{K_{2,k,t}}{\mathcal{Q}_{x,t}} \dfrac{\partial \mathcal{Q}_{x,t}}{\partial K_{2,x,t}} + s_i \dfrac{L_t}{\mathcal{Q}_{x,t}} \dfrac{\partial \mathcal{Q}_{x,t}}{\partial L_t}.$
    (non-corpor-   (withdrawals)   (wages)
     ate profits)

This relation in terms of gross shares becomes *with tax:*

(4c) $s_{x,t} = s_i + s_p(1 - s_i) F_{x,t} - x \dfrac{\pi_{1,x,t}}{\mathcal{Q}_{x,t}} \left[s_p + s_i - s_p s_i \right]$

or

$$s_{x,t} = s_i + F_{x,t} \left\{ s_p(1 - s_i) - x \frac{s_p + s_i - s_p s_i}{\mathcal{J}_x} \left[\frac{ma_1}{(1-x)^r} \right]^{1/(r+1)} \right\}, \quad [66]$$

and *in absence of tax:*

$$s_{0,t} = s_i + F_{0,t} \left[s_p (1 - s_i) \right].$$

This completes our model.

[66] Computation of $\pi_{1,x,t}$ calls for the following steps:

$$y_{1,x,t} = \frac{\partial \mathcal{Q}_{x,t}}{\partial K_{1,x,t}} = \frac{A_x}{(1-x)\,\mathcal{J}_x}\ y_{x,t},$$

$$y_{x,t} = \frac{\partial \mathcal{Q}_{x,t}}{\partial K_{x,t}} = N_{x,t}\,F_{x,t},$$

$$\pi_{1,x,t} = y_{1,x,t}\,K_{1,x,t}.$$

Thus the sectoral variables are related to the variables for the whole economy.

The solution to this model was found by simulation of changes in variables on the 7070 IBM computer. As in the Model B the initial aggregate inputs in time zero were set for $0 \leq x < 1$

(5) $$I_{x,0} = \text{constant,}$$

$$K_{x,0} = .99,$$

$$L_0 = .01.$$

As in Model B for $x \neq 0$, more appropriate inputs should have been sought, so that the period zero capital-labor ratio might have equalled the long-run ratio in absence of tax, subject to conditions $K_{x,0} + L_0 = 1$.

To speed computations, relation (5) was fed into the computer, and for period zero with tax rate x the variables were computed by hand. [67] (The arbitrary initial inputs affect the dynamic path but not the long-run equilibrium.) Then the machine computed remaining variables for period zero, according to formulae:

(6) $$F_{x;0} = a_x \left[a_x + b_x \left(\frac{K_{x,0}}{L_0} \right)^r \right]^{-1},$$

$$s_{x,0} = s_i + F_{x,0} \left\{ s_p(1 - s_i) - x \frac{s_p + s_i - s_p s_i}{\mathcal{J}_x} \left[\frac{ma_1}{(1-x)^r} \right]^{1/(r+1)} \right\},$$

$$N_{x,0} = M_x \left[a_x + b_x \frac{(K_{x,0})^r}{L_0} \right]^{-1/r},$$

$$\mathcal{Q}_{x,0} = N_{x,0} \, K_{x,0},$$

$$y_{x,0} = N_{x,0} \, F_{x,0},$$

$$H_{x,0} = \frac{(1-x) \, F_{x,0}}{1 - x \, F_{x,0}},$$

$$L_{1,0} = \frac{[mb_1]^{1/(r+1)}}{B} L_0,$$

$$K_{1,x,0} = \frac{[(1-x)ma_1]^{1/(r+1)}}{A_x} K_{x,0},$$

$$y_{1,x,0} = \frac{\partial \mathcal{Q}_{x,0}}{\partial K_{1,x,0}} = \frac{A_x}{(1-x) \, \mathcal{J}_x} y_{x,0},$$

[67] Note: $F_{0,1000} = \dfrac{a_0}{a_0 + b_0 \left[\dfrac{K_{0,1000}}{L_{1000}} \right]^r}$, and assume $\left[\dfrac{K_{x,0}}{L_0} \right]^r = \left[\dfrac{K_{0,1000}}{L_{1000}} \right]^r =$

$\dfrac{a_0}{b_0} \dfrac{1 - F_{0,1000}}{F_{0,1000}}$, then $F_{x,0} = \dfrac{a_x}{a_x + b_x \left[\dfrac{K_{x,0}}{L_0} \right]^r}$ which allows us to compute other variables

for the zero period as well.

$$F_{1,x,0} = \frac{\left[\dfrac{ma_1}{(1-x)^r}\right]^{1/(r+1)} \cdot \dfrac{F_{x,0}}{\mathcal{J}_x}^{\,68}}{\left[\dfrac{ma_1}{(1-x)^r}\right]^{1/(r+1)} \dfrac{F_{x,0}}{\mathcal{J}_x} + \dfrac{(1 - F_{x,0})\,[mb_1]^{1/(r+1)}}{B}},$$

$$H_{1,x,0} = \frac{[(1-x)ma_1]^{1/(r+1)} \cdot \dfrac{F_{x,0}}{\mathcal{J}_x}}{[(1-x)ma_1]^{1/(r+1)} \dfrac{F_{x,0}}{\mathcal{J}_x} + \dfrac{(1 - F_{x,0})\,[mb_1]^{1/(r+1)}}{B}}.$$

In the next step the machine computed inputs in period 1 according to formulae:

$$I_{x,1} = s_{x,0}\,\mathcal{Q}_{x,0},$$

$$K_{x,1} = K_{x,0} + I_{x,1},$$

$$L_1 = L_0\,e^h,$$

and the computation of other variables for this period followed. This in turn allowed computation of inputs and other variables in period 2 and so on. By iteration any distant period inputs and variables can be computed. Since the values of variables of interest started levelling off, settling towards their long-run equilibrium values, the computer stopped after computing variables for the period 1000. These values were adopted as approximating closely enough the long-run equilibrium values.

Notation, Measures, Indicators, and Definitions

Parameters:

s_p = marginal and average propensity to retain profits in business.

s_i = marginal and average propensity to save by individuals (from wages, dividends, and withdrawals of profits).

a = share of profits in national product as embedded in the production function.

a_i = such shares of sectoral profits (i describes the sector).

b = share of wages in national product as embedded in the production function. (Note $a + b = 1$.)

b_i = such share of sectoral wages. (Note $a_i + b_i = 1$.)

$m, (1-m)$

= coefficients of allocation of goods between the two sectors.

[68] $F_{1,x,t}$ variable requires finding corporate value added $V_{1,x,t}$ first. See also Appendix, Model C.

x = effective rate of tax on business profits. (If x is in subscript, it denotes that such tax has been imposed in period zero and applied ever since. In two sector models, this is the differential profits tax falling on investment in corporations.)

g = rate of growth due to neutral technological progress.

g_i = sectoral rate of growth due to neutral technological progress.

h = rate of growth of the labor force.

σ = elasticity of substitution of factors.

r = coefficient of substitution related to above concept: $r = \dfrac{1 - \sigma}{\sigma}$ or $\sigma = \dfrac{1}{1 + r}$.

t = time (usually as a subscript), takes only integer values: ($t = 0$, $1, 2, \ldots, 750, \ldots, 1000, \ldots, \infty$).

i = in a subscript denotes sector: $i = 1$ stands for the corporate sector; $i = 2$ stands for the unincorporated business sector.

Variables for the whole economy:

$S_{x,t}$ = effective saving rate for the economy as a whole, if tax x has been imposed in period zero.

$\mathcal{Q}_{x,t}$ = national product in real terms (quantity) in period t if tax x has been imposed in period zero.

$K_{x,t}$ = total stock of capital in the economy.

L_t = labor force. (Note that this is independent of tax; hence no tax notation in subscript.)

$N_{x,t}$ = product-capital ratio.

$I_{x,t}$ = investment.

$w_{x,t}$ = wage rate. (Note that wage rate depends on the rate of tax, though the supply of labor does not.)

$W_{x,t}$ = wage bill.

$y_{x,t}$ = gross (before tax) rate of return on capital in the whole economy.

$\pi_{x,t}$ = gross (before tax) profits.

$T_{x,t}$ = tax liability.

$F_{x,t}$ = actual share of gross profits in the national product.

$H_{x,t}$ = actual share of net (after tax) profits in the national product for private use (i.e., after tax liability).

Variables for the i*th sector:*

$Q_{i,x,t}$ = product of the ith sector (quantity).

$K_{i,x1,t}$ = stock of capital in the ith sector.

$L_{i,t}$ = labor force employed in the ith sector.

$V_{i,x,t}$ = value added in the ith sector.

$\pi_{i,x,t}$ = gross (before tax) profits in the ith sector, in units of the national product.

$y_{i,x,t}$ = gross (before tax) rate of return in the ith sector.

$w_{i,x,t}$ = wage rate in the ith sector.

$W_{i,x,t}$ = wage bill in the ith sector.

$T_{i,x,t}$ = tax liability in the ith sector in units of national product.

$F_{i,x,t}$ = share of gross profits in the ith sector in its value added.

$H_{i,x,t}$ = share of net (after tax) profits in the ith sector in the ith sector value added for private use (i.e. after tax liability).

Measures and Indicators:

E_x = long-run tax effect upon product-capital ratio.

E_{x,t_k} = a fraction k of E_x to achieve which t_k time has to pass.

t_k = time required to realize E_{x,t_k}.

G_x = tax effect upon effective saving rate in the long run.

M_x = scale of aggregate production function in two sector models for tax rate x, $0 \leq x < 1$.

u_x = rescaling factor, indicating inefficiency introduced by a differential profits tax.

v_x = comparative change in slopes of aggregate production function isoquants in two sector models, indicating transference of the tax burden between various factors in the economy.

$S_{y,t}$ = shifting on the gross rate of return for the whole economy in period t.

$S_{F,t}$ = same on gross share.

$S_{H,t}$ = same on net share.

$S_{1,y,t}$ = corporate shifting on the gross rate of return.

$S_{1,F,t}$ = same on gross share.

$S^*_{1,H,t}$ = same on net share.

$S_{d,y,t}$ = differential shifting on the gross rate of return.

$S_{d,F,t}$ = same on gross share.

$S^*_{,H,t}$ = same on net share.

$S_{1,C,t}$ = combined corporate shifting on the gross rate of return, i.e. due to common and differential tax.

For time zero these measures in the models here adopted collapse to results for the standard (general tax on profits) or the Harberger (non-general tax on profits) version of neoclassical theory of shifting. For $t = \infty$ we get the long-run measures which are the main interest of this study.

Definitions:

1. $N_{x,t} = \dfrac{\mathcal{Q}_{x,t}}{K_{x,t}}$.

2. $y_{x,t} = \dfrac{\pi_{x,t}}{K_{x,t}}$.

   $y_{1,x,t} = \dfrac{\pi_{1,x,t}}{K_{1,x,t}}$.

3. $T_{x,t} = x\pi_{x,t}$ if tax is general.

   $T_{1,x,t} = x\pi_{1,x,t}$ if tax is non-general.

4. $V_{1,x,t} = y_{1,x,t} K_{1,x,t} + w_{1,x,t} L_{1,t}$.

5. $F_{x,t} = \dfrac{\pi_{x,t}}{\mathcal{Q}_{x,t}}$.

   $F_{1,x,t} = \dfrac{\pi_{1,x,t}}{V_{1,x,t}}$.

6. $H_{x,t} = \dfrac{\pi_{x,t} - T_{x,t}}{\mathcal{Q}_{x,t} - T_{x,t}}$, if tax is general.

   $H_{x,t} = \dfrac{\pi_{x,t} - T_{1,x,t}}{V_{x,t} - T_{1,x,t}}$, if tax is non-general.

   $H_{1,x,t} = \dfrac{\pi_{1,x,t} - T_{1,x,t}}{V_{1,x,t} - T_{1,x,t}}$.

7. $E_x = \dfrac{N_{x,\infty}}{N_{0,\infty}} - 1$.

8. $E_{x,t_k} = kE_x = \dfrac{N_{x,t}}{N_{0,\infty}} - 1$. (From this one may compute the time t_k required to get E_{x,t_k} effect.)

9. $G_x = \dfrac{S_{x,\infty}}{S_{0,\infty}}$.

10. $u_x = \dfrac{M_x}{M_0}$.

11. $v_x = \dfrac{a_x}{a_0}$.

12. Short-run standard neoclassical and Harberger-type shifting *for the whole economy:*

   a) $S_{y,0} = \dfrac{y_{x,0} - y_{0,\infty}}{xy_{x,0}}$.

   b) $S_{F,0} = \dfrac{F_{x,0} - F_{0,\infty}}{xF_{x,0}}$.

   c) $S^*_{H,0} = \dfrac{H_{x,0} - (1-x)H_{0,\infty}}{xH_{0,\infty}}$. [69]

13. Harberger-type corporate shifting:

   a) $S_{1,y,0} = \dfrac{y_{1,x,0} - y_{1,0,\infty}}{xy_{1,x,0}}$.

   b) $S_{1,F,0} = \dfrac{F_{1,x,0} - F_{1,0,\infty}}{xF_{1,x,0}}$.

   c) $S^*_{1,H,0} = \dfrac{H_{1,x,0} - (1-x)H_{1,0,\infty}}{xH_{1,0,\infty}}$.

14. Harberger-type differential shifting:

   a) $S_{d,y,0} = S_{1,y,0} - S_{y,0}$.

   b) $S_{d,F,0} = S_{1,F,0} - S_{F,0}$.

   c) $S^*_{d,H,0} = S^*_{1,H,0} - S^*_{H,0}$. [69]

15. Long-run shifting for the whole economy:

   a) $S_{y,\infty} = \dfrac{y_{x,\infty} - y_{0,\infty}}{xy_{x,\infty}}$.

[69] Following K & M (13), pp. 37–39 and 83–91, the S measure of shifting was adopted for the rate of return and gross share concepts and S^* for the net share concept. Formula for the Harberger-type shifting for the whole economy would be more complex if the purpose of this study was the incidence and not the tax effects.

b) $S_{F,\infty} = \dfrac{F_{x,\infty} - F_{0,\infty}}{xF_{x,\infty}}$.

c) $S_{H,\infty}^{*} = \dfrac{H_{x,\infty} - (1 - x)\, H_{0,\infty}}{xH_{0,\infty}}$.

16. Long-run corporate shifting:

a) $S_{1,y,\infty} = \dfrac{y_{1,x,\infty} - y_{1,0,\infty}}{xy_{1,x,\infty}}$.

b) $S_{1,F,\infty} = \dfrac{F_{1,x,\infty} - F_{1,0,\infty}}{xF_{1,x,\infty}}$.

c) $S_{1,H,\infty}^{*} = \dfrac{H_{1,x,\infty} - (1 - x)\, H_{1,0,\infty}}{xH_{1,0,\infty}}$.

17. Long-run differential shifting:

a) $S_{d,y,\infty} = S_{1,y,\infty} - S_{y,\infty}$.

b) $S_{d,F,\infty} = S_{1,F,\infty} - S_{F,\infty}$.

c) $S_{d,H,\infty}^{*} = S_{1,H,\infty}^{*} - S_{H,\infty}^{*}$.

18. Combined corporate shifting is a weighted average of shifting of the common and of the differential tax rate measured from the corporate sector data only.

BIBLIOGRAPHY

1. Adelman, M. A. "The Corporate Income Tax in the Long-Run," *The Journal of Political Economy*, LXV (April 1957), 151–157.
2. Allen, R. G. D. *Mathematical Analysis for Economists*. London: MacMillan and Company, Ltd., 1947.
3. Arrow, K. J., A. B. Chenery, B. S. Minhas, and R. M. Solow. "Capital-Labor Substitution and Economic Efficiency," *The Review of Economics and Statistics*, XLII (August 1961), 225–248.
4. Dobrovolsky, Sergei P. *Corporation Income Retention, 1915–43*. New York: National Bureau of Economic Research, 1951.
5. Harberger, Arnold C. "The Incidence of the Corporation Income Tax," *The Journal of Political Economy*, LXX (June 1962), 215–240.
6. ——. "The Measurement of Waste," *American Economic Review, Papers and Proceedings*, No. 3 (May 1964), pp. 58–76.
7. Kaldor, Nicholas. "Alternative Theories of Distribution," *Review of Economic Studies*, XXIII (February 1956), 83–100.

*The works listed here are cited in the text by having their numbers placed in parentheses.

8. Kravis, J. B. "Relative Shares in Fact and Theory," *The American Economic Review*, XLIX (December 1959), 917–949.

9. Kuznets, Simon. *National Product Since 1869*. New York: National Bureau of Economic Research, 1946.

10. ———. *National Income: A Summary of Findings*. New York: National Bureau of Economic Research, 1946.

11. Krzyzaniak, Marian, and Richard A. Musgrave. *The Shifting of the Corporation Income Tax*. Baltimore: The Johns Hopkins University Press, 1963.

12. Kuh, Edwin. "The Validity of Cross-Sectionally Estimated Behavior Equations in Time Series Applications," *Econometrica*, XXVII (April 1959), 197–214.

13. Lerner, Eugene M., and Eldor S. Hendricksen. "Federal Taxes on Corporate Income and the Rate of Return on Investment in Manufacturing, 1927 to 1952," *National Tax Journal*, IX (September 1956), 193–202.

14. Machlup, Fritz. "Period Analysis and Multiplier Theory," *Quarterly Journal of Economics*, LIV (November 1939), 1–27, also reprinted in *Readings in Business Cycle Theory*. Philadelphia: The Blakiston Company, 1944.

15. McFadden, Daniel. "Further Results on CES Production Functions," *The Review of Economic Studies*, XXX (2) (June 1963), 73–83.

16. Meade, J. E. *A Neo-Classical Theory of Growth*. New York: Oxford University Press, 1961.

17. Pasinetti, Luigi L. "Rate of Profit and Income Distribution in Relation to the Rate of Economic Growth," *Review of Economic Studies*, XXIX, 4 (October 1962), 267–279.

18. Pitchford, J. D. "Growth and the Elasticity of Factor Substitution," *Economic Record*, XXXVI (November 1960), 491–504.

19. Sato, Kazuo. "Growth and the Elasticity of Factor Substitution: A Comment—How Plausible is Imbalanced Growth?" *Economic Record*, XXXIX (September 1963), 355–361.

20. Sato, Ryuzo. "Fiscal Policy in a Neo-Classical Growth Model: An Analysis of Time Required for Equilibrating Adjustment," *The Review of Economic Studies*, XXX, 1 (February 1963), 16–23.

21. Swan, T. W. "Economic Growth and Capital Accumulation," *Economic Record*, XXXII (November 1956), 334–343.

22. Uzawa, Hirofumi. "Neutral Inventions and the Stability of Growth Equilibrium," *The Review of Economic Studies*, XXVIII, 1 (February 1961), 117–124.

23. Walters, A. A. "Production and Cost Functions: An Econometric Survey," *Econometrica*, XXXII (January-April 1963), 1–66.

**EFFICIENCY EFFECTS OF TAXES ON
INCOME FROM CAPITAL**

Arnold C. Harberger

NATURE OF THE EFFICIENCY COST OF TAXES ON INCOME FROM CAPITAL

The effects of the taxation of income from capital can be conveniently classified into (a) those affecting the distribution of income, and (b) those affecting economic efficiency. The first class of effects concerns the question of incidence, about which no general consensus of professional opinion has yet emerged. Although this paper is concerned with the second class of effects, I should like to emphasize at the outset the distinction between the issues that arise in the two classes of problems. This can perhaps best be seen within the confines of the simple model developed in my paper, "The Incidence of the Corporation Income Tax," (1), where it was shown that, so long as the elasticity of substitution between labor and capital is the same in both the taxed sector X and the untaxed sector Y and so long as the elasticity of substitution between the final products of X and Y is the same as the elasticities of substitution between factors of production within the two sectors, then the burden of a tax on income from capital in sector X (the corporate sector) falls exclusively on capital as a factor of production ([1], p. 230). Thus, regardless of whether the three elasticities of substitution in question are all equal to -1, or all equal to -4, or all equal to $-\frac{1}{4}$, the answer to the incidence problem

107

will be the same. However, the efficiency costs of the tax in question will vary greatly, according as the elasticities of substitution are large or small.

To demonstrate the measurement of efficiency costs graphically, Figure 1a represents the schedule of the rate of marginal productivity of capital (net of depreciation but gross of tax) in the corporate sector, while Figure 1b represents the corresponding schedule for the non-corporate sector.

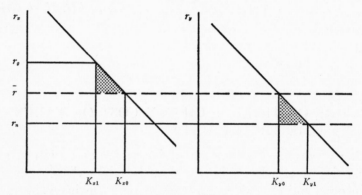

In the absence of any tax, the equilibrium rate of return would be $\bar{r}$, equal in both sectors. However, when a tax is imposed on the income from capital in sector X, the rate of return gross of tax rises there to r_g, while the rate of return net of tax falls in both industries to r_n. The quantity of capital employed in sector X falls from K_{x0} to K_{x1}, while the quantity of capital employed in sector Y rises by an equal amount, from K_{y0} to K_{y1}. The economy thus transfers capital from high productivity applications in the taxed sector to low productivity applications in the untaxed sector, with a consequent loss in over-all economic efficiency equal to the sum of the two shaded triangles in Figures 1a and 1b. That this loss equals $\frac{1}{2}(r_g - r_n)(K_{x0} - K_{x1})$ can easily be seen once it is recognized that $(K_{y1} - K_{y0}) = (K_{x0} - K_{x1})$. In shorthand form the loss can be written as $-\frac{1}{2}T_x \Delta K_x$, where $T_x(=[r_g - r_n])$ is the amount of tax per unit of capital employed in sector X, and ΔK_x is simply $(K_{x1} - K_{x0})$, the tax-induced change in employment of capital in industry X.

This measure of the loss in efficiency stemming from a tax

on capital in industry X is an application of a more general formulation of the efficiency losses arising from a general set of differential taxes on income from capital in various industries in the economy. This more general formulation is $-\frac{1}{2} \sum_i T_i \Delta K_i$, where T_i is the tax per unit of capital in the ith industry and ΔK_i is the change in the amount of capital in the ith industry arising as a result of the whole set of taxes $(T_1, T_2, \ldots, T_n)$. The derivation of this formula can be found in my paper, "The Measurement of Waste" (2), especially section IIIA.

Now the size of the loss depicted in Figures 1a and 1b obviously depends on the slopes of the marginal productivity schedules. For a given tax T_x, the size of the loss will be proportional to ΔK_x, and it can be shown, for the case in question, that ΔK_x will be proportional to the elasticity of substitution. When the three critical elasticities of substitution are all the same, the expression for ΔK_x is $\Delta K_x = S_x(K_x K_y/[K_x + K_y])T_x$. Thus, for given initial conditions $(K_x K_y/[K_x + K_y])$, and for a given amount of tax per unit of capital in the corporate sector, the size of ΔK_x, and therefore the size of the efficiency cost of the tax, will be proportional to S_x. The general expression for efficiency cost in this class of cases is $-\frac{1}{2} S_x(K_x K_y/[K_x + K_y])T_x^2$. It will clearly be 4 times as great for an elasticity of substitution of -1 as for one of $-\frac{1}{4}$, and 16 times as great for an elasticity of -4 as for one of $-\frac{1}{4}$. Since the incidence of the corporation income tax is identical for the whole class of cases here treated, there can obviously be no close linkage between the effects of the tax in terms of incidence and its effects in terms of economic efficiency. The formulas for efficiency cost, $-\frac{1}{2} T_x \Delta K_x$ for a tax in capital in a single sector and $-\frac{1}{2} \sum T_i \Delta K_i$ for a set of differential taxes on capital in a variety of sectors, are valid regardless of the incidence of taxes in question. They depend only on three assumptions: (a) a fixed supply of capital to the economy as a whole; (b) equilibrium in the capital market, in the sense that net rates of return are equalized in all uses of capital; and (c) absence of distortions of types other than taxes on capital (or on the income from capital) in different uses. Even these assumptions can be relaxed, but only at a cost of complicating the formulas in question. (See [2].)

DISTRIBUTION OF THE TAX BURDEN ON INCOME FROM CAPITAL BY MAJOR SECTORS

This section of my paper develops a rough measure for the efficiency costs of an assumed pattern of taxation on income from capital. The basic data are drawn from the U.S. economy in the period 1953–59, but the results should be taken as merely suggesting the possible orders of magnitude for the efficiency costs involved, because the values of the relevant elasticities represent plausible assumptions rather than exact estimates. Table 16 presents the basic data.

Table 16

Taxes on Income From Capital, By Major Sectors
(annual averages, 1953–1959, in millions of dollars)

	Total Income from Capital	Property and Corp. Income Taxes	Other Tax Adjustments	Total Tax on Income from Capital	Net Income from Capital
"Non-Corporate" Sector	26,873	6,639	1,724	8,363	18,510
Agriculture	7,481	1,302	927[a]	2,229	5,252
Housing	18,429	5,140	797[b]	5,937	12,492
Crude Oil and Gas	963	197	—[c]	197	766
"Corporate" Sector	52,399	22,907	9,945[d]	32,852	19,547
Total	79,272	29,546	11,669	41,215	38,057

[a] Fifteen per cent of (1) minus (2). Assumes a typical effective tax rate of 15 per cent on farm income.

[b] Assumes 70 per cent of (1) generated by owner-occupied housing, on which income no personal tax liability is incurred. Assumes 30 per cent of (1) and (2) generated by rental housing, with personal tax of 20 per cent paid on the excess of income over property taxes. Thus (3) = 6 per cent of the difference between (1) and (2).

[c] Assumes personal tax offsets on account of depletion; expensing and similar privileges counterbalance personal taxes on dividends and capital gains arising out of crude petroleum and natural gas operations.

[d] Twenty per cent of (1)–(2). Assumes a 50 per cent dividend distribution rate, and a "typical" effective tax rate of 40 per cent on dividend income.

Source: For cols. 1 and 2, Leonard G. Rosenberg, "Taxation of Income from Capital by Non-Financial Industry Groups" (unpublished Ph.D. Dissertation, University of Chicago, 1963), Table 14.

The terms "Corporate" sector and "Non-Corporate" sector are really misnomers: it might perhaps be better to call them the "Heavy-Tax" sector and the "Light-Tax" sector. Agriculture and Housing (i.e., the industry that provides residential housing services) are relatively lightly taxed and also predominantly unincorporated, but the Crude Oil and Gas Industry, although it is largely incorporated, is nonetheless favored by special tax treatment. Likewise, one finds within what I have called the "Corporate" sector a few industries (e.g., personal and business services and wholesale and retail trade) that are not over-whelmingly corporate in structure. These are, however, heavily enough taxed that, even without allowing for taxes on their dividends, approximately 30 per cent of the income from capital generated by them is taken in the form of taxes. For the great bulk of the industries in the "Corporate" sector, corporation and property taxes together take 45 or more per cent of the total income from capital. Thus no great damage is done by lumping together all non-financial industries other than Agriculture, Housing, and Crude Oil and Gas into a single "Corporate" sector for the purposes of this analysis.

The second aspect of Table 16 that requires emphasis is that, to my knowledge, it is the first attempt to approximate the total weight of taxation on the income from capital in various sectors. Leonard Rosenberg, from whose work the basic data in columns 1 and 2 are taken, has made a painstaking effort to allocate property tax receipts among industries. His complete results, which cover some fifty separate industries, will be made available in a forthcoming Brookings Institution volume. Here I have aggregated his data into the two broad sectors previously defined. In addition to Rosenberg's allocations, I have attempted to take into account the personal income tax burdens (or offsets) attaching to the income from capital generated in the sectors considered. In making the adjustments in column 3, I have tried consciously to err on the side of being conservative. Thus I have tried not to overstate the personal tax burden arising out of the corporate sector, both by assuming a compara-tively low (for dividend recipients) effective tax rate on dividends and by neglecting capital gains taxes altogether. Capital gains themselves are indirectly taken into account by the fact that retained earnings are counted as part of the income from capital generated in the corporate sector, but no tax liability whatsoever is imputed to them. Similarly, I have attempted not to understate the personal tax liabilities nor to overstate the personal tax offsets arising in the non-corporate sector. For example, the effective tax rate on farm income is probably not as high as the 15 per cent figure assumed in Table 16. Similarly, it is conservative, in the case of Oil and Gas, to assume that the personal tax payments due on the dividends, etc., arising out of Crude Oil and Gas operations are just barely counterbalanced by the personal tax offsets (depletion, expensing, etc.) generated by this set of activities—in fact the personal tax offsets probably far outweigh the personal tax liabilities arising from Oil and Gas.

From columns 4 and 5 of Table 16, it can be seen that total taxes on income from capital in the "Non-Corporate" sector amounted to $8.36 billion, on the average, in 1953–59, or approximately 45 per cent of the annual average net income from capital generated in this sector during the period. On the other hand, in the "Corporate" sector, total taxes on income from capital averaged some $32.8 billion per year during the same period, which amounted to some 168 per cent of the annual average net income from capital here. (The figures are not so shocking when taxes are expressed as percentages of gross income—31.0 per cent for the non-corporate and 62.7 per cent for the corporate sector—but convenience in applying the formula for efficiency cost dictates the use of taxes expressed as a percentage of net income.) The taxation of income from capital in the United States can therefore be very roughly approximated by a general tax of 45 per cent on all net income from capital plus a surtax equal to some 85 per cent of the net income from capital generated in the corporate sector ($1.45 \times 1.85 = 2.68$).

If we treat a general tax on all income from capital as neutral, as the analysis underlying the first section of this paper implies, we can approximate the efficiency costs of the existing tax system by measuring the efficiency losses associated with a tax of 85 per cent of net-of-tax income from capital in the corporate sector. To do this let us take as our unit of capital that amount which generated, in the period considered, $1 of annual net income. Then $K_x = \$19,547$ million, and $K_y = \$18,510$ million. Applying these figures, plus $T_x = .85$ and $S_x = -1$, to the formula $-\frac{1}{2} S_x (K_x K_y / [K_x + K_y]) T_x^2$, we obtain a measure of efficiency cost of the system of taxes on income from capital equal to approximately $3.5 billion per year. If, on the other hand, $S_x = -.5$, the efficiency cost of the same system would be around $1.75 billion per year.

To check on the plausibility of these results, we can examine the sorts of changes that would be implied by a shift to "neutral" taxation of income from capital, within the context of the model being used. Recall that in the first section, an alternative (equivalent) expression for the efficiency cost of a non-neutral tax on capital in a single sector was $-\frac{1}{2} T_x \Delta K_x$. Thus our results for an elasticity of substitution equal to unity imply a ΔK_x of approximately -8 billion units, while for an elasticity of substitution of $-.5$ they imply a ΔK_x of approximately -4 billion units. The alternative allocations of capital resources are summarized in Table 17.

Table 17

Alternative Allocations of Capital

	Corporate Sector	*Non-Corporate Sector*
Existing Tax System	19.5	18.5
Neutral Taxes ($S_x = -1$)	27.5	10.5
Neutral Taxes ($S_x = -.5$)	23.5	14.5

My own judgment is that the results for $S_x = -.5$ appear quite plausible while those for $S_x = -1$ appear rather extreme. Nonetheless, it should be recalled that there is some evidence in favor of the proposition that the elasticity of substitution between labor and capital, in manufacturing industry at least, may be in the neighborhood of unity (see Solow [4], and Minasian [3]).

ESTIMATES OF EFFICIENCY COST

Rather than elaborating the results of Table 17 which are built on the assumption that the elasticity of substitution (S_x) between labor and capital in the production of X, the elasticity of substitution (S_y) between labor and capital in the production of Y, and the elasticity of substitution (V) between the final products of X and Y are all the same, in this section of my paper I attempt to derive a general expression for the efficiency cost of non-neutral taxation of income from capital in a two-sector model.

The basic model is that developed in my paper on incidence (1), and the notation used here will be the same as in that paper.

The expression for $\dfrac{\Delta K_x}{K_x}$ obtained by solving that model is:

$$(1) \quad \frac{\Delta K_x}{K_x} = T. \frac{-Vr_y\left[g_k\, S_x \dfrac{L_x}{L_y} + f_k\, S_y\right] - S_x S_y f_L}{Vr_y\,(g_k - f_k)\left(\dfrac{K_x}{K_y} - \dfrac{L_x}{L_y}\right) - S_y - S_x\left(\dfrac{f_L K_x}{K_y} + \dfrac{f_k L_x}{L_y}\right)}.$$

where

V = elasticity of substitution between products X and Y (defined as a negative number).

S_x = elasticity of substitution between labor and capital in X (also negative).

S_y = elasticity of substitution between labor and capital in Y (also negative).

r_y = share of national income spent on Y.

Vr_y = price elasticity of demand for X (defined as a negative number).

f_k, f_L = shares of capital and labor, respectively, in the value added of industry X.

g_k, g_L = shares of capital and labor, respectively, in the value added of industry Y.

L_x, L_y = amounts of labor used in industries X and Y, respectively.

K_x, K_y = amounts of capital used in industries X and Y, respectively.

The sign of ΔK_x is unambiguously negative.

The wages bill of what is here defined as the corporate sector averaged approximately $200 billion per year in the 1953–59 period, while that for the non-corporate sector averaged about $20 billion per year. Thus we shall use 10 as the figure to be inserted for (L_x/L_y) in equation 1. The return to capital, net of tax, was about $20 billion on both sectors; thus we shall use 1 as the figure for (K_x/K_y) in equation 1. The gross-of-tax return to capital in the corporate sector was slightly over $50 billion out of a total value of product of $250 billion; hence we shall set $f_k = .2$ and $f_L = .8$. In the non-corporate sector the gross-of-tax return to capital was about $27 billion out of a total value of product of about $50 billion; hence we set $g_k = .54$. The non-corporate sector accounted for some $50 billion out of a total value of product of some $300 billion for the two sectors combined, so we set $r_y = .17$.

Substituting these values in equation 1 we obtain:

$$(2) \quad \frac{\Delta K_x}{K_x} = T\frac{-.17V\,[5.4S_x + .2S_y] - .8S_xS_y}{-.52V - S_y - 2.8S_x},$$

and for $K_x = \$20$ billion, and $T = .85$ we have:

$$(3) \quad \Delta K_x = \frac{-15.6\,S_xV - -.58\,S_yV - 13.6\,S_xS_y}{-.52\,V - S_y - 2.8\,S_x}.$$

Using this expression, Table 18 was derived.

Table 18 explores the plausible ranges for the elasticities of substitution in question. For S_x and V, the plausible range is from $-.5$ to -1. In the case of S_y, because of the importance of the housing industry and the crude oil and gas industry in this sector, the possibility of a zero elasticity of substitution is also explored. In both of these industries—recalling again that the housing industry refers to the provision of the services of housing rather than the construction of buildings—there is probably little possibility of substituting labor for capital. Nonetheless, an elasticity of zero is not very plausible for the non-corporate sector taken as a whole because of the demonstrated possibilities of substitution between labor and capital in agriculture.

Table 18

Estimates of Efficiency Cost of Existing Taxes on
Income From Capital in the United States

(1) S_x	(2) S_y	(3) V	(4) ΔK_x (billions of units)	(5) $-\frac{1}{2} T_x \Delta K_x$ ($ billions)
−1	−1	−1	−6.9	2.9
− .5	− .5	− .5	−3.5	1.5
−1	−1	− .5	−5.3	2.3
−1	− .5	−1	−5.9	2.5
− .5	−1	−1	−5.2	2.2
−1	− .5	− .5	−4.2	1.8
− .5	−1	− .5	−4.1	1.7
− .5	− .5	−1	−4.8	2.0
−1	0	−1	−4.7	2.0
− .5	0	− .5	−2.4	1.0
−1	0	− .5	−5.0	2.1
− .5	0	−1	−3.9	1.7

The general idea emerging from Table 18 is that the present pattern of taxes on income from capital in the United States probably has reduced the capital stock in the corporate sector by between ⅙ and ⅓. According to these calculations, the present capital stock of $20 billion (measured in units of net income from capital) would lie between $23 billion and $27 billion if the income from capital were equally taxed in all uses. By the same calculations, the efficiency costs of the existing pattern of taxation lie somewhere between $1 billion and $3 billion, more probably between $1.5 billion to $2.5 billion per year.[1]

[1] The results in Table 18 for the cases where $S_x = S_y = V$ are not the same as those emerging from the earlier calculations which were based on the algebraic solution of the system for this special case. The reason for the discrepancy is that the values chosen for (K_x/K_y), (L_x/L_y), f_k, etc., are derived from the tax situation rather than the pre-tax equilibrium. This is similar to the discrepancy one obtains in measuring demand elasticities over a very broad range, depending on whether one takes initial or terminal points as the basis on which percentage changes are computed.

These are probably underestimates of the true efficiency costs involved because, in the process of aggregating industries into broad sectors, distortions induced by the tax system among the industries within each broad sector were ignored. Taking these distortions into account would surely add to the estimated efficiency costs. Moreover, the calculations assume that the taxes on income from capital do not introduce any substitution-effect away from saving and toward consumption—that is, so far as the substitution effect alone is concerned, it is assumed that the elasticity of response of savings with respect to the net rate of return on capital is zero. If this substitution effect were not zero, there would be an additional efficiency cost stemming from the distortion of choices between consumption and saving. I do not wish to press this latter point too far, however, because in any taxation of the income from capital— even if such income in all industries and sectors is treated equally—some distortion of the consumption-savings choice is implicit. Only a consumption-tax of the Kaldor type would avoid this distortion altogether. My main point in presenting the cost calculations of Table 18 is to show that we could substantially improve efficiency by simply rationalizing our existing pattern of taxes on income from capital so as to ap-proach more equal tax treatment of the income generated by capital in the various industries and sectors of our economy.

BIBLIOGRAPHY

1. Harberger, A. C. "The Incidence of the Corporation Income Tax," *Journal of Political Economy*, LXX (June 1962), 215–240.
2. ____. "The Measurement of Waste," *American Economic Review, Papers and Proceeding*, volume LIV (May 1964), pp. 58–76.
3. Minasian, Jora R. "Elasticities of Substitution and Constant-Output Demand Curves for Labor," *Journal of Political Economy*, LXIX (June 1961), 261–270.
4. Solow, R. M. "Capital, Labor, and Income in Manufacturing," paper presented at National Bureau of Economic Research, Conference on Income and Wealth (April 1961).

EFFECTS OF BUSINESS TAXES UPON INTERNATIONAL COMMODITY FLOWS

Richard A. Musgrave

The purpose of this paper is to examine the effects of business taxation upon international commodity flows. From the point of view of efficiency, it is desirable to minimize such effects, and the question is what structure of international business taxation is best designed to serve this purpose. Though an important aspect of the broader problem of tax integration, this is by no means the entire story. Taxation effects on factor flows, which will be given little attention here, may be of equal or greater importance. Moreover, international business taxation poses equity problems regarding the treatment of the individual taxpayer as well as the distribution of tax bases between jurisdictions. The present discussion, therefore, covers but one aspect of a broader set of issues which arise if the principles of business taxation are reconsidered in the context of an open economy and assumes that exchange rates are fixed.

If taxes are to be neutral regarding product flows, the international price ratios of traded products at factor cost must equal those at market price. Taxes which enter into cost of production distort these ratios. Assuming the initial exchange rates to be proper, they give rise to an excess burden. Let us consider what changes in product flows result.

PRODUCTION TAXES

Consider countries A and B, producing products X and Y at pre-tax supply prices p_X^A, p_X^B, p_Y^A, p_Y^B respectively. We examine the imposition of various tax patterns, assuming fixed exchange rates to apply. It is also assumed for the time being that deficits or surplus on trade account are simply met by reduction or accumulation of reserves, without, however, affecting the money supply.

Effects on Relative Prices

We begin with production taxes which are reflected in the cost of the taxed product, e.g., a value-added, turnover or payroll tax. Such a tax may be imposed in a more or less general fashion.

1. We assume first that the tax is imposed on the production of X in A only. We then have $\hat{p}_X^A/\hat{p}_Y^A > p_X^A/p_Y^A$ where $\wedge$ indicates after tax. However, this change may involve an absolute rise in p_X^A, a decline in p_Y^A or a mixture of both.[1] As distinct from the closed economy case, this distinction is of importance. In the closed case, incidence is a matter of relative prices and absolute price changes have little importance. In the open case, what matters are relative international prices, and changes therein depend upon the movement of absolute domestic prices.

If p_X^A rises in absolute terms, we have $\hat{p}_X^A/p_X^B > \hat{p}_X^A/p_X^B$ and the result will be reduced exports or increased imports of X by A, depending on whether X was an export or import good. If p_Y^A falls in absolute terms, we have $\hat{p}_Y^A/\hat{p}_Y^B < p_Y^A/p_Y^B$, and the result will be increased exports or reduced imports of Y by A, depending on whether Y was an export or import good. Trade distortions (though at a different scale) occur in both cases, but (assuming price elasticities greater than 1) the balance of payment effects for A are unfavorable in the first and favorable in the second case.

2. Now let the production tax apply to both X^A and Y^A. If the absolute prices of the taxed products remain unchanged while factor costs fall, trade will be unaffected. If absolute prices rise, exports will decrease and imports will rise, the result being the same as that of exchange appreciation.

---

[1] To simplify, we consider throughout only the extreme cases of no price rise and price rise by the full tax. Obviously, the real situation may fall between these extremes.

3. Next, assume that similar production taxes are applied to X^A and X^B. If the absolute price adjustments are symmetrical in A and B, trade is not affected. But what if absolute price changes diverge, e.g., if p_X^A rises while p_Y^B falls? We then have $\hat{p}_X^A/\hat{p}_X^B > p_X^A/p_X^B$ and $\hat{p}_Y^A/\hat{p}_Y^B < p_Y^A/p_Y^B$. In this case, A will export less (or import more) of X and import less (or export more) of Y. Trade patterns will change, there being no assurance that even a uniform tax policy (uniform, that is, between products but not countries) will be neutral in its trade effects.

4. Similar reasoning applies if the production tax is imposed on X^A and Y^B. Now a symmetrical price response to both taxes changes relative costs for both products, i.e., $\hat{p}_X^A/\hat{p}_X^B > p_X^A/p_X^B$ and $\hat{p}_Y^A/\hat{p}_Y^B < p_Y^A/p_Y^B$. This will be the case whether the prices of taxed products rise or the prices of tax free products fall. If adjustments are asymmetrical, relative price changes are limited to one product. For instance, if p_X^A rises while p_Y^B does not, p_Y^A/p_Y^B remains unchanged, while p_X^A/p_X^B rises even more sharply. Trade changes result in both cases, but the patterns differ.

5. Finally, let the production tax apply generally between products and countries, including X_A, X_B, Y_A and Y_B. No relative price changes will occur if the adjustment in the two countries is symmetrical. Hence trade patterns will not be affected. But changes result if the price level in A rises while that in B remains unchanged. A's exports will fall and imports will rise and vice versa for B. The result (regarding both exports and imports) will be precisely the same as that of appreciation in A's or depreciation in B's currency. Again we note that even a completely uniform tax policy (uniform, that is, between countries and products) need not be neutral in its allocation effects.

Neutralizing Adjustments

So far we have assumed that the tax does not provide for differential treatment of imports or exports. Certain adjustments in the treatment of international goods may be made which neutralize tax effects on commodity flows. Returning to the above cases, we find:

1. A tax on the production of X in A may be neutralized by an export rebate ER and a compensating import tax IT on the taxed product, provided that the tax is reflected in increased price; and by a compensating import rebate IR and an export tax ET on tax-free products, where the tax is reflected in reduced factor costs.

2. For a tax on X^A and Y^A the $ER\text{-}IT$ adjustment is needed only in the case of price increase. The case of factor cost decline does not call for adjustments since there are no tax-free products.

3. For a tax on X^A and X^B, neutralizing measures are needed in the case of asymmetrical adjustment only. They take the form of $ER\text{-}IT$ adjustments to the taxed product in the country with price rise, and $IR\text{-}ET$ adjustments to the tax-free product in the country with price decline.

4. For the taxes on X^A and Y^B, neutralizing adjustment calls for application of $ER\text{-}IT$ on the taxed product in the country in which the tax leads to price rise, and application of $IR\text{-}ET$ on the tax-free product in the country in which the tax reduces factor costs.

5. For the case of asymmetrical adjustment (to a truly general tax) neutralization is obtained by applying $ER\text{-}ID$ in the country with price rise.

CONSUMPTION TAXES

We now turn to a similar analysis of consumption taxes. As before, we begin with a general view, excluding equalizing adjustments, and then consider what adjustments are called for to neutralize trade effects.

Effects on Relative Prices

Similar reasoning may now be applied to the case of consumption taxes, say a retail sales tax. By its very nature, such a tax applies to the sale of home-produced as well as imported products.

1. Suppose that the tax is imposed on the sale of X in A. If the price of X rises by the amount of tax, trade effects will be neutral. If the tax is reflected in reduced factor cost, this will not be the case. Exports of Y will increase, since $\hat{p}_Y^A/\hat{p}_Y^B < p_Y^A/p_Y^B$, the cost of producing Y in A being reduced relative to that in B. Moreover, imports of X will fall, since the reduced net price will reduce competition from B's exporters who did not share the reduction in factor costs.

2. If the tax applies to the sale of both X and Y in A, and is reflected in higher prices, trade effects will again be neutral. If it is reflected in reduced factor costs, exports will rise and imports will fall, the effect being similar to that of exchange *de*preciation. The difference with the corresponding case 2 for the cost tax is thus two-fold: In the cost-tax case the equivalence to exchange rate adjustment arose with price rise and was compared with appreciation; in the retail sales tax case it arises with factor-cost decline and is compared with depreciation.

3. Turning to a tax which applies to the sale of X in both A and B, trade distortions will result only if the adjustment for the two countries is asymmetrical, analogous to the preceding case 3 result.

4. For a tax on X in A combined with a tax on Y in B relative price changes result, as in the corresponding case for the production tax, even if the adjustment is symmetrical. But again the distortion is limited to one product in the asymmetrical case.

5. This leaves the general retail tax, applying to both countries and both products. As for the general production tax, the result is neutral for the symmetrical adjustment, but not so for the asymmetrical case. The country with rising product prices now experiences effects equivalent to depreciation, while that with falling factor costs experiences appreciation. The adjustment direction has the opposite implication as in the cost-tax case.

Neutralizing Adjustments

As in the case of cost taxes, certain adjustments may be introduced to neutralize trade effects.

1. For the case of reduced factor cost, neutralization is obtained by applying ET to all exports and by granting IR to tax-free goods.

2. If the tax on X^A and Y^A leads to reduced factor cost, ET is applied to exports but no IR is needed since there are no tax-free goods.

3. For the case of asymmetrical adjustment to a tax on the sale of X in both A and B, the country which experiences reduced factor cost proceeds as under 1. No adjustment is needed for the country with increased prices.

4. The adjustment to a sales tax on X in A and Y in B is as under 3.

5. For the case of asymmetrical adjustment to a general sales tax in both countries, IT is applied in the country which experiences price rise, while ET is applied in the country which experiences declining factor costs.

PROFITS TAX

So far we have dealt with production taxes of various sorts, and with a retail sales tax. Imposition of such taxes on product X but not on Y may be expected to raise the gross price of X relative to that of Y. This follows because variable factor inputs demand the same return in both uses, but the price of X must include the tax cost as well. The rest of the analysis follows from this initial proposition of relative price change.

In the case of the corporation tax, such a change will not come about unless there is shifting in the "short-run" sense of the term, i.e., the tax is not reflected fully in reduced profits but its effect is cushioned by administered price or wage adjustments. In the absence of such adjustments, no immediate trade effects will result. But if there is short-run shifting on domestic sales—and I am somewhat committed to this hypothesis—the situation is quite similar to that of the outright cost taxes. In this case, the profits tax qualifies for an ER-IT adjustment, provided that the shifting takes the form of absolute price rise. While determination of appropriate ER-IT rates is more complicated than in the case of a cost tax, the basic rationale is the same. At the same time, ER-IT is not called for if the adjustment operates via wage reduction. The Krzyzaniak-Musgrave results, you will recall, are silent on this point. Thus, even if the shifting hypothesis is accepted, our results do not tell us whether *ER-IT* is called for or not.

But let us assume that the tax is shifted forward on domestic sales so that the *ER-IT* adjustment is called for. If the adjustment is not made, trade effects on the import side will result at once, as imports would become cheaper relative to home products. Export effects will result with some delay to the extent that in the short run, capital previously used to produce for exports cannot be promptly used for home production, so that the return to such capital is in the nature of a rent income. Thus, the analogy to a tax on variable cost has to be qualified in this respect. But in the longer run, capital will move from production for exports to production for domestic sales so as to equalize net returns, and exports will decline.

Finally, it is conceivable (though unlikely) that the tax may be shifted on foreign as well as on domestic sales. If such is the case, no change in the domestic capital structure occurs, and *ER* is inappropriate. However, the *IT* adjustment is still called for.

NEUMARK COMMITTEE VIEW

It follows from the above that various tax patterns may give rise to a variety of results, depending on the absolute directions of the price adjustments. Matters are much simplified if one is willing to assume that (a) cost increases due to tax must be reflected in absolute price rise, and (b) the profits tax is not shifted in the short-run sense. This is the view which underlies the Neumark Report (5), GATT practices,[2] and more or less the entire discussion of tax integration in the Common Market.

Given this assumption, the underlying set of principles is very simple. Profits taxes are neutral regarding commodity flows. Production taxes upon X imposed at differential rates by A and B are non-neutral. A general production tax, imposed by

[2] No clear cut statements of these principles can be found in the GATT Articles, but practices have consistently followed these lines.

one country only, is equivalent to appreciation. Retail sales taxes, either selective or general, may be imposed at differential rates without distorting trade flows between countries. In other words, commodity taxes which are based on the "destination principle" are neutral, whereas commodity taxes based on the origin principle (unless imposed at a uniform rate) are not. Production taxes may be switched from the origin to the destination class by exempting exports or granting an export rebate, referred to as *ER* and by adding a compensating import tax or *IT*. Thus, neutral commodity taxation consists of product taxes with *ER-IT*, plus consumption taxes at the retail level. If *ER-IT* are considered undesirable because they require retention of trade controlling machinery, such need is removed by agreeing on imposition of value-added taxes at a uniform rate.

This reasoning, which also underlies current GATT practice regarding *ER-IT* is correct once the premises are granted. At the same time, *ER-IT* on cost taxes would be inappropriate if we assume factor cost is reduced—in which case cost taxes are neutral without such a correction. Similarly, it would then be necessary to supplement a retail sales tax by a compensating export tax, while exempting imports from the sales tax. Moreover, *ER-IT* for profits taxes becomes appropriate for the case of short-run forward shifting. Furthermore, if it appears that the adjustment pattern (in terms of absolute price change) differs by countries, the whole task of neutralizing the tax structure by a simple set of rules becomes impossible, and a more complex approach is called for.

TAX EQUIVALENTS OF CHANGES IN EXCHANGE RATES

So far our argument has been conducted on the assumption of fixed exchange rates. For this case, certain similarities between general tax and exchange rate changes have been observed. Assuming absence of *ER-IT*, these relationships may be noted:

1. A general cost tax, imposed in one country only, is similar to appreciation, if reflected in rising prices;
2. A general retail sales tax, imposed in one country only, is similar to depreciation, if reflected in falling factor costs;
3. A general cost tax, imposed in all countries, is similar to appreciation for countries which experience rising product prices, and to depreciation in countries which experience falling factor costs;
4. A general retail sales tax, imposed in all countries, as above is similar to depreciation in countries where product prices rise, and to appreciation in countries where factor costs fall.

Obviously, there can be no equivalence of exchange rate changes which are inherently general with tax rate changes which are applied to particular products only. Moreover, the tax changes noted under 1–4 are neutralized if the proper *ER-IT-ET-IR* are applied, so that the equivalence with exchange rate changes disappears.

"DIRECTION" OF ADJUSTMENT

Given the strategic importance which the absolute changes in product or factor prices occupy in a fixed exchange rate setting, it is well to inquire upon what factors these absolute changes depend.

To begin with, we should note that this issue must not be confused with a quite different question, traditionally considered in the closed economy context, whether a business tax is "shifted forward" in the sense of passing the real burden on to consumers; or "backward," in the sense of passing the real burden on to wage earners. Forward shifting in this real-incidence sense can come about with or without an absolute rise in product prices, just as backward shifting may occur with or without a fall in factor prices. The issue, in this traditional context of shifting analysis is one of relative prices; the issue in the present context, is one of change in absolute prices.

To illustrate, consider the case of a value-added tax of the income type, which may be expected to be reflected in a proportional reduction in factor incomes. This result may come about via an increase in product prices with factor incomes constant, or a decline in factor costs with product prices constant. Or consider a corporation profits tax and assume market forces to be such that the tax is shifted forward (in the real-burden sense) upon the consumer. Again, the adjustment may take the form of rising product prices with wages and profits after tax unchanged, or it could take the form of falling wages and profits after tax (though the latter decline would be much less than in the non-shifting case) with product prices unchanged. Similarly, backward shifting in the real burden sense could take the form of declining wages with profits after tax and prices unchanged, or of a rise in profits after tax and prices with wages unchanged. The forces which determine these relative price changes, i.e., where the real burden of the tax comes to rest, evidently depend upon the competitive (or lack thereof) market structure. There remains the question of how the absolute price changes are determined.

Obviously, the answer depends upon the macro nature of the system in which the tax change operates, not to speak of the nature of the particular tax change, e.g., whether it is accompanied by an expenditure increase, whether it is a tax substitution and so forth. To simplify, let us assume here that we deal with a tax substitution. To begin with, consider a flexible system of the classical type, in which full employment is maintained automatically, and the money supply is held constant. The absolute price adjustment, inherent in any tax change may then be said to depend upon "monetary" factors, such as effects of changes in the structure of payments upon income velocity or the operation of the real balance effects, and the extent to which the latter differentiates between holdings of transaction and asset money. However this may be, there is nothing in the operation of the pricing system which tells us what the nature of absolute price change will be. Turning now to a more realistic setting, the nature and degree of price rigidities, as well as the behavior of monetary policy becomes of paramount importance.

Consider the following five policy settings:

1. Wages flexible; monetary policy permissive.
2. Wages downward rigid; monetary policy permissive.
3. Wages flexible; monetary policy stabilizes product price level.
4. Wages downward rigid, monetary policy stabilizes product price level.
5. Wages flexible, monetary policy stabilizes factor price level.

And the possible patterns of absolute price change in response to a tax change, e.g., imposition of a value-added tax. Under 1 we are back to the general monetary forces noted in the preceding paragraph, with either adjustment pattern being possible. Under 2 the tax must either be reflected in higher product prices or be absorbed in reduced profits. Under 3 it must be either reflected in reduced money wages or be absorbed in reduced profits. Under 4 only absorption in profits is possible, while under 5 the situation is the same as under 2.

Looking at this schema, one is tempted to conclude that case 2 is the most realistic one, and that, therefore, absolute price increase is the most likely result. This conclusion, however, is qualified somewhat if the problem is looked at in a dynamic context. With economic growth, the tax change may depress money wages not in the absolute sense but in the relative sense of limiting the increase which otherwise would have occurred. This is compatible with the hypothesis of downward rigid money wages, yet for purposes of the present discussion has the same implications as would result from an actual wage decline.

EMPIRICAL ASPECTS

Let us now leave this theoretical discussion and consider to what extent the U.S. balance of payment position may have been affected by differences in the U.S. and European tax structures. The relevant comparison for our purposes is not the composition of the tax structure (per cent of total from various taxes) but the relative (or even absolute) level of tax rates. Assuming that "shifting patterns" are the same for various countries, the relevant factor (as noted before) is the different level of rates. As a first approximation, this may be looked at in terms of tax to GNP ratios, although this may be somewhat misleading since the composition of GNP (and hence the level of particular tax rates corresponding to a given tax to GNP ratio) differs among countries. Even though a number of tax comparisons have been made recently, there is no readily available table which puts matters into a form which conveniently serves present purposes. Table 19 takes a rough stab at this.

Table 19

Tax Revenue as Per Cent of GNP—1961

	U.S.[1]	Germany	U.K.	France	Italy
1. Personal Income Tax	9.2	7.6	7.1	3.9	4.9[2]
2. Employee Contr. to Soc. Sec.	1.2	4.6	1.8	3.2	0.8
3. 1 + 2	10.4	12.2	8.9	7.1	....
4. Corporation Tax	4.4	3.0	2.9	2.3	(2)
5. "Sales" Tax, etc.	11.1	17.4	9.2	14.0	15.0
6. Employer CC, Soc. Sec.	1.9	5.0	1.1	11.5	3.8
7. 5 + 6	13.0	23.4	10.3	25.5	18.8
8. Property Taxes, etc.	3.5	1.2	0.3	....	....
9. Other	0.7	−3.8	+6.6	0.1	3.5
10. Total	32.0	35.0	29.0	35.0	28.0

[1] Computed directly.

[2] Profits tax is included in line 1.

Line 1: Eckstein and Tanzi (1), cols. 1 and 4, Table 5.

Line 2: *Ibid.*, cols. 2 and 4, Table 5.

Line 4: *Ibid.*, cols. 3 and 4, Table 5.

Line 5: For Germany and U.K. the ratio of turnover excise to income tax revenue (*Ibid.*, p. 36-39) applied to the income tax to GNP ratio.

Line 6: The ratio of employer to employee contribution of Table 13, *Ibid.*, is applied to line 2.

Line 8: Based.

Line 9: Residue.

Line 10: *Ibid.*, col. 1, Table 9.

The level of *direct personal* taxes in the U.S. falls between that of the U.K. and Germany, and tends to be higher than that of continental countries. But as noted before, it may be assumed that this has no direct price effects. In comparing the income tax ratios shown in Table 19, note that the relative level of U.S. rates is greatly exaggerated by comparing rates at similar absolute income levels. A more meaningful comparison would be between equal relative (e.g., mean, limits of decile) income positions. Also, for European countries, the weight of social security contributions is higher relative to the income tax.

The *corporation profits tax* ratio as recorded in Table 19 is substantially higher for the U.S., but the more relevant indicators are the tax to profit ratios. Here we have the following picture:

Table 20

Profits Tax Rates

| | Profits Tax Rates[1] | | | | Direct Taxes on Profits and Property as Proportion of Net Profits[2] | |
| | Statutory | | Effective[3] | | | |
	Und.	Distr.	Und.	Distr.	Undistr.	Distributed
France	.50	.50	.46	.46	50	50
W. Germany	.56	.32	.53	.30	70	53
Italy	.36	.36	.32	.32	45	45
U.K.	.54	.24	.39	.18	54	24
U.S. (64)	.47	.47	.43	.43	50	50

[1] Musgrave-Richman(4), p. 74–79.

[2] Eckstein(1), Table 12.

[3] Standardized for equal depreciation.

It appears that the U.S. rate on undistributed profits is pretty well in line with, and in some cases substantially below, foreign rates. However, the U.S. rate on distributed profits is higher.

The *sales tax* pattern shows a substantially higher ratio for continental Europe than for the U.S., with a large part of the difference accounted for by turnover tax in Italy and Germany, and value-added tax in France.

Employer contributions to social security show also considerably higher ratios in continental Europe. However, it may be noted that company type contribution systems are higher here and that these should perhaps be included into the comparison.

Empirical Evaluation

The evidence of Table 19 boils down to three conclusions:

(a) The weight of personal taxes (line 3) may be somewhat higher in the U.S. than in most European countries excluding, however, Germany; (b) the corporation tax to GNP ratio (line 4) is relatively high in the U.S., but the difference is rather slight if the tax to profit ratio is considered; (c) the "cost taxes" to GNP ratio (line 7) is distinctly lower in the U.S. than in continental Europe. From what has been said before, (a) is not very relevant in this connection. The main factor is (c) and to some extent (b).

Cost Taxes. As far as the U.S. is concerned, let us assume (due to wage rigidities) that cost taxes are reflected in higher prices. The central question then is whether the higher "cost taxes" in Europe have been reflected in higher prices, lower wages, or squeezed profits. Considering European profit rates over the fifties, the latter does not seem likely. The main alternative would appear to be relatively lower wages or higher prices.

Suppose the adjustment in Europe was via wage reduction while in the U.S. it was via price increase. This would place Europe at an advantage for both the line 5 taxes where *ER-ID* applies, and the line 6 taxes where it does not apply. The advantage in the line 5 case is measured by the absolute level of European rates, while in the line 6 case it relates to the absolute level of U.S. rates. If the adjustment is towards higher prices in Europe as well, the line 5 taxes are neutral, independent of rate levels, while the line 6 taxes give an advantage to the U.S. as the lower rate country, the advantage being related to the rate differential.

One way of evaluating what happened is by general appraisal of the European scene during the fifties. With regard to *Germany* (and this is the only country on which I shall venture a general impression), the fact is that wage rates did lag during, say, the first two-thirds of the fifties, but the explanation hardly lies in the turnover tax. Other factors, such as labor influx, union attitudes, etc., seem a much more plausible explanation. This is reinforced by the fact that the tax factor did not prevent a more rapid rise in wages in recent years. As to the monetary policy restraint, it is again true that German monetary policy was on the restrictive side, although perhaps less so than usually assumed. However, the policy objective was hardly that of maintaining a fixed price level. Rather, it was one of curtailing the expansionary influence of export surplus on money supply.

Moreover, it is important to note that the high indirect tax rates were introduced even before the currency reform. This poses the question whether the price level set at the time of the currency reform was higher because of these taxes—a query impossible to answer with precision, but it seems unlikely. Beyond this, there is the question whether the existence of the given rate level was a retarding factor in wage increases. An affirmative answer would imply that the tax was absorbed into wages gradually as productivity rose by retarding corresponding wage increases—a possibility which, it seems to me, is again unlikely. While one could not say that the German situation was altogether that of our policy setting in case 1, it would be mistaken as well to interpret the situation in terms of case 3.

Apart from such general speculation about the various countries, what indices are there by which to test what has happened? Various hypotheses, not all of which are helpful, may be considered:

(1) "If countries with high indirect tax rates exhibit a low ratio of export prices to domestic prices, this is evidence that the adjustment to the tax was backward." I do not think this is correct. Whether the value-added tax raises prices or lowers wages, it will always raise the ratio of market price to factor cost. If export prices are defined net of rebate, they equal factor cost. Therefore, the tax must always lower the ratio of net export to domestic prices. Thus, a finding regarding relative prices tells us nothing about the direction of the absolute price adjustment, and it is only the latter that matters.

(2) "If net export prices in high tax rate countries are high relative to those in low tax rate countries, this suggests that the tax adjustment was favored." The trouble with this is that the comparison involves the use of exchange rates which may not be

(and indeed are not) equilibrium rates. Moreover, many other factors, e.g., productivity differences enter.

(3) If in any one country frequent tax rate changes could be observed, these might be related to wage rate or price changes. In this way, it might be possible to determine a causal influence which would solve our problem. Unfortunately, tax rate changes are usually too few (and other influences too powerful) to permit such analysis.

(4) Perhaps it might be possible to observe wage rate changes relative to productivity in various countries, and to test the hypothesis that wages have lagged more in high-rate countries. Probably the result would differ greatly for the earlier and later part of the fifties.

The general conclusion is that rigorous empirical tests would be very difficult.

Corporation Tax. With regard to the profits tax there is the further question whether it is to be considered a "cost tax," posing more or less the same problems just noted, or whether it may be expected to be absorbed in profits, leaving wages and prices unaffected.

While the traditional view has been that the profits tax does not lead to short-run changes in prices and wages, the proposition (derived from short-run profit maximization) has become dubious. Theoretically, many situations can be imagined where shifting occurs. Superficial empirical evidence shows that the net rate of return has changed little from the twenties to the fifties (which supports shifting), and that the gross profits share has remained stable (which may support non-shifting). However, these overall observations are of little value since too many factors (other than tax rates) varied as well. Recently there has been some statistical work in this area, with one study suggesting full shifting (3) and the other zero shifting (2). Having been associated with the former, I am persuaded that short-run shifting is an important factor. However, in the present context two additional questions arise.

First, it must be decided whether the absolute adjustment

was in wages or prices. The first of the above studies, though concluding that there was shifting, does not pronounce on this crucial point. However, considering the U.S. setting, let us assume that prices rose. Query: if the postwar price inflation reflected a delayed real-balance effect, was this secondary adjustment not curtailed because of the previous tax-induced price rise? And if so, which of the two was the "causal" factor?

This leaves the further question whether a symmetrical shifting assumption can be made for European profits taxes. If yes, the U.S. disadvantage (arguing as before regarding cost taxes with *ER-ID*) is measured by the relatively minor rate differential; but if the European tax was not shifted, our disadvantage relates to the absolute U.S. rate level. The observation that European firms tend to be less competitive (if correct) does not prove that they were in a better position to shift. To the extent that they are in a better position to act as pure monopolists, the opposite would follow. Quite possibly, different assumptions are in order for the U.S. and Europe—but if they are made the case for international tax integration vanishes in a morass of special situations.

Policy Conclusions

Finally a word about the policy conclusions (or questions) which this discussion implies.

1. Should a frontal attack be made on GATT rules? This could be done on two grounds:

With regard to "cost taxes," GATT policy (by permitting *ER-ID*) is based on the notion that the tax adjustment in all countries takes the form of absolute price rise. Present practice is distorting rather than neutralizing if adjustments are asymmetrical. Prevailing asymmetry is likely to be pro-Europe.

With regard to the profits tax, GATT rules (by excluding *ER-ID*) are based on the assumption that there is no wage-price adjustment. Present practice is distorting if the tax raises price. Given this assumption for the U.S. and Europe, the prevailing rate differential is slightly pro-Europe; given the assumption for the U.S. only, the situation (measured by our absolute rate level) is distinctly pro-Europe.

Some argument can be made along these lines, but one hesitates: What would be a workable alternative to GATT rules if asymmetrical adjustments are introduced? What would be done about the crediting of foreign profits taxes (presumably it would have to be replaced by deduction) if *ER-ID* is applied to the profits tax?

2. Obviously, introduction of a value-added tax per se would not help us if "over-rebating" is ruled out. Substitution of such a tax for the profits tax would help to the extent that the latter did increase price, as a "cost tax" without *ER-ID* would be replaced by one with *ER-ID*. However, one hesitates to consider such a change as long as the taxation of capital gains remains so inadequate.

3. Selective export incentives under the corporation tax may be preferable, and may stand a better chance to be applied unilaterally.

4. In addition, it may well be that tax measures aimed at the capital account would be more feasible.

BIBLIOGRAPHY

1. Klein, L. R. "Statement of L. R. Klein," *Measures of Productive Capacity*, Hearings before the Subcommittee on Economic Statistics of the Joint Economic Committee (May 14, 22, 23, and 24, 1962), p. 59.
2. Krzyzaniak, Marian, and Richard A. Musgrave. *The Shifting of the Corporation Income Tax*. Baltimore: The Johns Hopkins University Press, 1963.
3. Lerner, Eugene M., and Eldon S. Hendriksen. "Federal Taxes on Corporate Income and the Rate of Return on Investment in Manufacturing, 1927 to 1952," *National Tax Journal*, IX (September 1956), 199–202.
4. Phillips, A. "An Appraisal of Measures of Capacity," *American Economic Review*, Supplement (May 1963), p. 275.

```
CORPORATE TAX INCIDENCE:
ECONOMIC ADJUSTMENTS TO
DIFFERENTIALS UNDER A TWO-TIER
TAX STRUCTURE
```

Richard E. Slitor*

INTRODUCTION

For too long, economists have been satisfied with solemn plausibilities about the incidence of the corporate tax. In the last decade or so many have drifted towards a shifting view without really persuasive empirical evidence on magnitudes or mechanism. Discussions of matters which depend vitally on incidence have had to be routinely prefaced with schematic assumptions and intellectual hedges. Until recently, the technology which helps produce corporate profits and their tax yield has been superior to that which learns more about who pays the tax and how this result is brought about.

The traditional form of the corporate tax incidence question is threefold: Is the tax absorbed, so that corporate equity

* Grateful acknowledgment is made to Mr. Richard Goode, Mr. John A. Brittain, Mr. Gary Fromm, Mr. Edward F. Denison, Mr. Bert G. Hickman, and others on the Brookings staff for helpful advice and consultation in the preparation of this paper. I am especially indebted to Mr. Brittain for assistance on the multiple regression computations, in which Mr. Goode and I collaborated. The presentation has also benefited greatly from thoughtful comments and suggestions by Mr. Norman B. Ture of the National Bureau of Economic Research; and by Mr. J. A. Stockfisch, Mr. Gerard M. Brannon, Mr. Thomas L. Smith, Mr. Elwyn T. Bonnell, and other members of the Treasury Department's Office of Tax Analysis.

Thanks are due also to Mr. Frank de Leeuw of the Federal Reserve Board staff for helpful background discussions and to Mr. George M. Cobren and Mr. John A. Gorman of the Office of Business Economics, U.S. Commerce Department, for confirming some of my estimates.

136

capital merely works for less? Is only its differential impact within a general tax system adjusted? Or does the government merely use the corporation as a sales or wage tax collector? A more fundamental question posed is how the shifting, if any, is accomplished and what its impact is on investment, the price-wage structure, and growth.

The pioneer econometric study by Krzyzaniak and Musgrave on the short-run shifting of the corporation income tax (18) suggests that the tax, in effect, rides the coattails of corporate market power, is shifted forward almost instantaneously like an erratic sales tax, and in the process leaves the motivating forces of investment unscathed.

The present discussion has several specific objectives:

1) To comment on the arresting results of the Krzyzaniak-Musgrave study.

2) To indicate the usefulness of certain neglected empirical indicators: to test "price umbrella effects" of a shifted corporate income tax; and to compare the experience of the regulated public utility field, where the corporate tax is presumably shifted to maintain "fair rates of return," with that of other industry in recent decades.

3) To consider the tenability and implications of the view that tax can be shifted without the retardation or reallocation of investment usually associated with increasing the effective cost of equity capital as a productive factor.

4) To reassert the hypothesis that the key to the enigma of the incidence of corporate tax as part of a general system of income taxation lies in adjustments to the differentials imposed by the corporate tax as a second layer of a two-tier tax structure. In this system, the corporate levy both differentially taxes and insulates corporate profits and results in a whole range of tax differentials for different investors, varying in amount and in algebraic sign.

The Challenge of the Krzyzaniak-Musgrave Findings

Using econometric procedures designed to isolate the effect

of the corporate income tax variable among the welter of forces operating on profits and the rate of return on corporate investment, Krzyzaniak and Musgrave concluded that businessmen have been right in asserting that the corporate tax is treated like any other cost and passed immediately on to consumers when prices are determined. Moreover, they detected with some confidence what may be characterized as a "ratchet effect" in the short-run shifting process: tax increases are immediately passed forward like a sales tax, but decreases in tax are not subject to equally prompt reverse shifting so that the old tax lingers on in the form of an increase in after-tax profitability.

Apart from distributional implications, the challenge of the Krzyzaniak-Musgrave findings is obvious. They suggest not only that the corporate tax in its character as a sales tax has been essentially neutral in impact on corporate investment returns and self-financing, but also that strategically timed cycles of increases and decreases in the corporate rate can generate increased profitability and so stimulate investment. The finding of short-run shifting transcends in importance the relatively narrow question of who pays the corporate tax since it conjures up a strange new world in which neoclassical theories of the firm, the competitive structure, and the marginal cost-marginal revenue equilibrium are relegated to the scrap heap.

Current Revenue Magnitudes

At current levels (3d quarter 1965) the Federal corporate income tax absorbs some $28 billion of a $74 plus billion annual rate of corporate profits. It accounts for approximately 27 per cent of estimated administrative budget receipts for fiscal 1965. Based on estimates for the first half of 1965, the tax amounted to roughly 7 or 8 per cent of corporate gross product (GNP originating in the corporate business sector).

If the corporate tax has been fully shifted forward in sales tax fashion in the sense that after-tax profits are maintained at the level prevailing in the absence of the tax, it has increased the prices of goods and services produced in the corporate sector by nearly 8 per cent (without taking account of possible pyramiding of the tax by successive mark-ups of the cost of goods as they pass through the various production stages to the final buyer). To the extent that this hidden tax element in the corporate price structure may have been extended through "price umbrella" and price equalization effects to corporate business not paying tax and to the non-corporate sector, the total dollar impact on consumers would be greater than the amount of the tax revenue itself.

Some International Perspectives [1]

The rise in corporate tax rates since World War II has been a world-wide phenomenon. Since the early fifties, ordinary profits tax rates in the vicinity of 50 per cent, coupled with a variety of provisions for depreciation liberalization and special investment incentives have become the rule in the leading industrial countries. The following summary shows comparative corporate tax burdens, including income and equivalent direct taxes, in the United States and selected leading European countries.

Income and Other Direct Taxes Falling on a
Corporation, as a Percentage of Net Profit, September 1961
All Levels of Government

Proportion of Net Profit Distributed:	0%	40%	100%
France*	50	50	50
Germany	70	65	53
Italy	45	45	45
United Kingdom	54	45	24
United States**	55	55	55

* Figures do not include value-added taxes, which are classified as indirect taxes, although the French value-added tax levied at rates ranging up to 20 percent applies to the corporate profit component of value added and thus shares some of the characteristics of a profits tax.

** Figures include some 3 percentage points of state income tax.

Source: Foreign tax rates from *Company Taxation in Western Europe*, 3d rev. ed., R. Mees and Zoonen, Rotterdam, 1962 (published in cooperation with the International Bureau of Fiscal Documentation), p. 7.

Concern with the economic significance of this development

[1] In writing this section I benefited from a paper on European experience with direct and indirect taxes and their significance for economic growth prepared by Otto Eckstein with the assistance of Vito Tanzi for a Conference on the Role of Direct and Indirect Taxes in the Federal Revenue System sponsored by the National Bureau of Economic Research and The Brookings Institution in October, 1963.

has been largely confined to the United States, judging from the literature. Whatever the complex of forces which have moved tax structures in the direction of heavy profits levies, the preoccupation with the enigma of corporate tax incidence, the true distributional impact of the tax, and its rationale is characteristically an American specialty.

Ambiguous and Cyclically Changing Role of the Corporate Tax

For many academic economists, an unintegrated corporate-individual tax structure is an irrationality. Torn between the possibilities of double taxation and the partial insulation of retained earnings, they are further disturbed by its sales tax implications and the question whether the corporate levy is a crude instrument for absorbing some of the gains arising from imperfections in the competitive structure or merely drives administered-pricing power to new heights.

For the practical-minded, the corporate tax appears to be a productive revenue source which balances the load on different centers of economic power and eases the pressure on individual tax rates. The potentialities of shifting of the tax are frequently considered to depend on prevailing economic conditions, the phase of the business cycle, and market trends.

For many business observers, the corporate tax is inimical to growth regardless of its shifting or incidence. Unshifted, it falls on corporate savings as a source of investment expansion. Shifted, it represents an increase in the effective cost of corporate equity capital which holds back investment.

New Aspects of the Incidence Question

The question of corporate tax incidence has assumed greater importance in the past decade or so as a result of a number of economic developments. The debate over double taxation of dividends, the concern with investment levels as a component of growth, and the international payments problem—in which both the competitive position of the U.S. industry vis-à-vis producers in low direct tax countries and its attractiveness to investors here and abroad are major elements—have all contributed to the practical policy interest of the question. The effectiveness of the much discussed switch to a value-added tax, rebatable on exports, as an effective weapon in rectifying the payments imbalance, hinges to a great extent on questions of corporate tax shifting and reversibility of past shifting. The concern with increasing the rate of capital formation as a percentage of GNP in this country switched the emphasis in shifting studies to mechanisms (as distinct from distributive results per se), i.e., to re–examination of the proposition that shifting, to the extent it occurs, is effectuated by curtailing capital investment.

Response of Incidence Theory and Empirical Studies

Classic theory tended to dismiss the possibility of short-run or "price-determination" shifting of a business or capital income tax because of the assumed improbability of a non-profit maximizing equilibrium. Shifting, if it occurred, was considered to be the result of longer-run investment adjustments due to either social costs of saving and risk-bearing or non-generality of the tax and the existence of alternatives or escape hatches.

The modern tendency has been to emphasize the non-generality of the corporate tax and to stress the variety of capital transmutations and escape valves including non-corporate business, debt-intensive corporate activity, lightly taxed or regulated corporate lines, and foreign investment. At the same time, increasing attention has been given to the possibilities of short-run shifting, previously relegated to a footnote on non-profit maximizing equilibria, through such related mechanisms as:

1) Resort to an unexploited margin of market power.
2) Reaction to tax increases as a signal for higher prices in an unstable oligopolistic market situation.
3) Routine administration of prices to cover "full costs" and to maintain a target after-tax rate of return on investment.

While little attention has been given to this in the literature, certainly some have entertained the notion that the corporate tax may be shifted through automaton-like responses, imbedded rules of costing and pricing, by which business stubbornly refuses to distinguish between the announcement effects of a sales tax and a net income tax and treats any tax like any other cost to be passed on or even made subject to mark-up. Presumably, these stubborn irrationalities pay off in effective shifting. To the extent that this notion is correct, the ability of business to "stand up" to taxes with the beneficent aid of a highly inelastic demand for its product must be added to the list of forces making for shifting.

Trend of Empirical Studies

To date empirical studies of shifting and incidence have taken the following major routes:

1) Time series analysis of such major indicators as earnings rates on investment and profit shares of output.
2) The interview or questionnaire approach, inquiring of corporate management their methods of pricing and investment decision-making in relation to the tax factor.
3) The multi-variate regression, which relates tax changes among other independent variables to the prime indicators of the profit response to taxes (the Krzyzaniak-Musgrave technique).
4) Cross section analysis comparing profit characteristics of lightly and heavily taxed business sectors or regulated and non-regulated industries.
5) The "production function" approach of comparing actual output and distributive results with those provided by a model, modified to reflect alternative shifting and non-shifting assumptions and alternative directions of shifting (the method followed in a partially completed National Bureau of Economic Research study, mentioned below under *New Econometric Approaches*).

The Conflict of the Empirical Indicators

Until recently, the seeker after the secrets of corporate tax shifting has been primarily a hunter for before-tax bulges and after-tax compressions in historical earnings rates, profit shares of output, profit margins, and related prime indicators. This kind of time series analysis, associated with such names as Lerner and Hendriksen, Clendenin, Adelman, Zellner, and others, has led to the well-known "conflict" between empirical tests of shifting utilizing rate-of-return and profit-share indicators.[2] In a nutshell, the maintenance of the after-tax rate of return on invested capital between the twenties and the post-war era despite sharp tax increases suggested that the tax had been shifted. On the other hand, the relative stability of pre-tax profits as a percentage of GNP originating in the corporate sector tended to support the position that the tax had largely been absorbed by corporate earnings.

Attempts at Reconciliation of the Earnings and Profit Share Indicators

Various routes to the reconciliation of the conflicting empirical indicators have been tried. One is to assume a Cobb-Douglas production function which would result in a constant capital share of output in spite of higher pre-tax rates of return. This tends to be consistent with long-run shifting in terms of rate of return accompanied by retardation of investment. Another is to postulate some combination of capital adjustments and changes in production functions which would increase the pre-tax rate of return but keep the capital share of an increased total output constant. This tends to support long-run shifting only to the extent it assumes retardation of equity investment. To the extent that it leaves open the possibility that the tax was in effect paid out of fortuitous gains in productivity due to (1) technological progress or (2) more intensive utilization of capital based on capital shortage or favorable economic conditions, and that investment response to taxation was negligible, it suggests that the tax was absorbed by corporations and their

[2] For detailed bibliography on this point, the reader is referred to (20), pp. 310–324, and to (18), p. 8, n. 1. For an earlier excellent discussion with bibliography, see (27), pp. 300–315. The Zellner reference is to (29), pp. 444–446, with "Reply" by M. A. Adelman, *ibid.*, pp. 446–447, and "Rejoinder," p. 448.

stockholders. Adverse to the plausibility of the shifting hypothesis is its implication that in the absence of tax-caused curtailment of investment and resulting upward pressure on rates of return, the equity capital share of output would have declined substantially.

A factor which assists in the plausible reconciliation of the apparent conflict between the indicators, and incidentally tends to support the non-shifting view, is the overstatement of the rise in rates of return on book net worth due to inflation. This overstatement is largely cancelled out in the profit share indicator.

A prominent fact in the historic record is the increase in turnover (decline in the capital-output ratio) which permitted maintenance of after-tax rates of return with little or no increase in the profit margin on sales. In itself, however, this does not resolve the question whether the increase in tax from the 10–13½ per cent range prevailing in the twenties to the 52 per cent rate of the fifties absorbed gains from greater productivity otherwise accruing to labor and consumers or savings in costs which would otherwise have benefited corporations.

Various speculations have been made as to the nature of the various non-tax factors which have operated over the period of comparison (such as changes in production functions and the elasticities of substitution involved) and the extent of reallocation or curtailment of investment to effectuate shifting. Answers to these basic questions have been inconclusive even in terms of the neoclassical type of long-run shifting.

New Econometric Approaches

To meet a pressing need for the application of modern econometric procedures to the empirical problem of determining corporate tax incidence, two major assaults have been mounted: one the Krzyzaniak-Musgrave study with which this paper is chiefly concerned, the other by Professor Challis A. Hall, Jr., sponsored by the National Bureau of Economic Research, described in the next section.

Both have been concerned primarily with short-run shifting

rather than the effects associated with longer run capital adjustments. They thus concentrate on the aspect of shifting about which neoclassical theory was most firm and explicit and subordinate the saving-investment reaction mechanisms on which the neoclassic theorists tended to be more tentative.[3]

Brief Comparison of the Krzyzaniak-Musgrave and Hall-National Bureau of Economic Research Studies

As part of a broader study of corporate tax effects undertaken by Challis A. Hall, Jr. for the National Bureau of Economic Research,[4] a new technique was developed to test the traditional view that (as a corollary of the assumption that a net profits tax does not alter marginal cost at the point of profit-maximization) such a tax does not change relative inputs of labor and capital or their marginal physical or value outputs. This technique involved fitting a Cobb-Douglas type production relationship between input (of capital and labor) and output to annual data for manufacturing in the 1919-59 period. Closeness of fit was tested for adaptations of the equation reflecting three alternative hypotheses of short-run tax impact: (1) no shifting, (2) forward or sales tax shifting, and (3) backward or wage-pressure shifting. The conclusion was that the no-shifting assumption afforded a better fit, and if technical change was on balance neutral in its effect on productivities of the factors over the period studied, the results supported the traditional view of marginal profit-maximizing behavior and its tax-impact corollaries.

While the new conflict between modern empirical tests tends to add to the turmoil, the only partially unveiled Hall-National

[3] Walras states his general position: "If the tax is imposed on the interest charges on all kinds of capital goods without exception, all capitalists would be affected in proportion to their incomes, just as if there had been a reduction in the rate of income. Moreover, since a fall in the rate of income may lead either to an increase or to a decrease in savings, we cannot trace this effect any further and we may as well assume that the incidence of the tax falls on the capitalists. Granting this, I have an observation to make . . . that if the tax is imposed on the interest charges on certain kinds of capital only, such a tax on interest charges would be, in part, a consumption tax." (27), p. 454.

[4] A preliminary view of this tax shifting inquiry is contained in a paper by Professor Hall, (12). For an earlier summary of its method and results, see Norman B. Ture, "The Study of Tax Policies for Economic Growth of the National Bureau of Economic Research," *Public Finance*, Vol. XVIII, No. 2, 1963, pp. 138–139.

Bureau study is tentative to the extent that it assumes technical-progress neutrality. The Hall method does not include a calibrating procedure to permit measuring any particular degree of shifting between or beyond the extremes of zero and 100 per cent. Moreover, to date it apparently has not tested other possible alternative assumptions or constellations of assumptions as to shifting and production functions because of the excessive labor involved and the intuitive judgment of the investigator that they would not disclose better fit.[5]

The Krzyzaniak-Musgrave study on the other hand merely reasserts, at the level of the *ceteris paribus* multiple regression level, much of the old conflict and the problem of reconciliation of rate of return and profit share indicators. It assumes no particular production function, but in effect measures shifting with reference to a profit norm determined from its limited independent variables just as the older studies relied on the twenties base. Its period of observation from 1935 to 1959—skipping some but not all of the World War II years—is highly selective and its number of observations quite limited. The close similarity of its findings to those of time series studies suggests at first glance that somehow it has captured within the econometric net little more or less than the familiar results of full shifting on the rate of return basis.

Results which collide not only with accepted incidence theory but the whole marginal, profit-maximizing apparatus of economic doctrine and which discredit the existence of macro-barriers to sweeping price changes, demand special scrutiny. Conclusions which rest on multiple regressions and special assumptions as to the non-tax determinants of profits tend to call for further confirmation to the naked eye before they will support a basic reorientation of thinking on this issue.

[5] The study's reliance on a particular production function of the Cobb-Douglas variety raises the question whether the superior fit under the no-shift assumption merely reflects in more sophisticated fashion the Adelman finding of constant profit shares. In a sense the Hall method is akin to an empirical test of the applicability of Euler's theorem which would not of course hold in the case of non-marginal, non-profit maximizing equilibria. The Hall method does not depend on a profit-share or rate-of-return indicator, as such, and its proponents will argue that the particular production function used does not predetermine the results.

Econometric studies such as that by Krzyzaniak and Musgrave nevertheless mark an important new step in this phase of public finance. Whether or not we accept in literal detail its specific findings and conclusions, we must recognize the contribution their study makes (as a pilot project, if you will) in formulating the problem with greater precision and getting out of the rut of indecision which has marked discussions of the past decade.

THE KRZYZANIAK-MUSGRAVE THESIS: A CRITIQUE

The essence of the method followed by Krzyzaniak and Musgrave to test short-run shifting of the corporate tax is the familiar one of multiple regression. The rate of return on capital was selected as the indicator of shifting. Both profit return on equity and profit plus interest return on equity plus interest-bearing debt (total capital base) were tested.

Highlights of the Model

In their standard stripped down model, the indicator was expressed as a function of the tax variable, described more fully below, and three non-tax variables:

1) Last year's increase in consumption as a percentage of GNP,
2) Last year's inventory to sales ratio in manufacturing,
3) The current-year ratio of all tax receipts at all levels of government, exclusive of corporate income tax and minus transfers and grants-in-aid to the states, as a percentage of GNP.

Lagging was apparently introduced partly for reasons of economic rationale and partly to make non-exogenous variables predetermined.

The preferred tax variable was generally the total tax liability expressed as a rate of return on capital. This choice of the tax variable reflected the plausible assumption that businessmen think in terms of shifting a dollar amount of tax rather than in terms of increasing their rate of return by a given proportion of the tax rate.

Experiments using both statutory and effective rates of tax as the tax variable were also performed, and these reflected alternative behavioral assumptions as to how corporate management adjusts to the tax. Although these alternatives produced unsatisfactory and unbelievable results (shifting up to 278 per cent), tax rates were used as the "instrument" for the "negative rate of return" form of the tax variable as part of a statistical procedure mentioned later.

Measure of Shifting

The preferred shifting measure was the ratio of the increment in the rate of return before tax attributed to shifting, to the tax liability at the new shifted level, also expressed as a rate of return on investment. In this form, the measure of shifting coincided with the regression coefficient for the tax variable.

Instrumental Variable Approach

Since the tax expressed as a rate of return on capital is obviously geared via the tax rate to the rate of return itself (the dependent variable in the estimating equation) it was necessary to resort to statistical devices (the instrumental variable approach and Klein's approximation procedure) to resolve the estimating problem.[6]

Tax Variable as Negative Rate of Return on Capital

Expressed as an effective rate of return on the capital of all corporations, including those with operating losses, the tax variable will automatically tend to vary directly and with additional sensitivity with general profit levels. This results because the no-net income sector shrinks in prosperity and expands in recession, while the denominator in the ratio continues to

[6] Use of the instrumental variable approach and Klein's approximation procedure each reduced the measure of shifting on the total capital base, standard Model A, from about 142 per cent (naive least squares) to about 134 percent (see (18), Table 6–1, pp. 44–45). However, the efficacy of this type of procedure is doubtful, particularly where the sample is small. See, for example, (15), pp. 165–168.

represent all corporate industry.[7] The graduation of rates for small companies has a similar effect.

The Basic Findings

As we have seen, the authors' basic finding that there is shifting in terms of maintaining the after-tax rate of return echoes the decade-old finding of the rate-of-return school which was based on a comparison of the twenties and the fifties. In lieu of the profit norm of the twenties relied on by the time-series investigators, they have substituted a profits equation which estimates profits in the absence of tax on the basis of a simplified economic model. But the Krzyzaniak-Musgrave findings on short term shifting (as distinguished from the mixture of long and short term effects presumably embodied in the time series results) lead to a remarkable series of half-conclusions, half-policy implications.

The basic thrust of the Krzyzaniak-Musgrave findings is that a large part of the corporate tax is shifted forward like a sales tax within the current tax year, by a mechanism or combination of business behavior rules which substantially eliminate the curtailment of investment as a means for effecting the shift. In fact, if one accepts the undiluted numerical findings of their standard model, there is substantial overshifting. Prior to qualification of the "overshifting" position to adjust for inflation and to allow for correlations between the tax and rate of return variables via expenditures, the regressions indicated that some 123 to 134 per cent or more of the tax was shifted (depending on the capital base used and other variations). Prior to these retreats the authors in fact defended the possibility of more than 100 per cent shifting on the basis of various forms of "overshooting the mark."

The shifting disclosed by the Krzyzaniak-Musgrave findings, as they interpret it, is effectuated by conscious decisions of management in setting prices and not by impersonal market

[7] The actual effective tax rate (tax liability expressed as a percentage of corporate earnings) whether computed on the net income of profitable corporations only or on the total net income after losses of deficit companies would behave differently: the numerator (taxes) and the denominator (earnings) would tend to move together.

forces such as the flow of investment. The wedge driven between factor costs and prices by the corporate tax is apparently conceived to be based on resistant wage rates (although wages may at some later time be pressed upwards to recoup some of the initial price increase due to shifting). It is apparently because of this and the nature of the shifting mechanism that the direction of shifting is forward.

The related findings that (1) the shifting is not a two-way proposition, (2) the tax once embodied in higher prices is not quickly or consciously unshifted in the event of tax reduction, and (3) short-run effects persist to merge into the long-run picture, add to the startling image of the corporate tax in the manufacturing sector invoked by the study.[8]

The tax element which Krzyzaniak and Musgrave find to be subject to shifting is the entire corporate tax, not the differential burden on corporate earnings as against other forms of business and investment income within the setting of a general income tax embracing an unintegrated two-tier structure of corporate and individual income taxes.[9]

Collision with Prevailing Views

From this brief resumé it is apparent that the Krzyzaniak-Musgrave thesis is iconoclastic in the extreme. It may be helpful to list some of the effigies which their findings tend to demolish. In addition to the obvious policy implications which Krzyzaniak and Musgrave are quick to point out (absence of substantive double taxation of dividends, worse than failure of the corporate tax as a rough instrument for bringing retained earnings to account, and innocuousness of the tax in its impact on profitability and sources of self-financing), the findings tend to collide with or reject:

[8] Conclusion reached by a differencing procedure and formulation of separate relationships between earnings rates and positive and negative changes in the tax variable. (18), p. 58. See also p. 64.

[9] This conclusion is based on a somewhat higher correlation coefficient R obtained when the entire corporate liability variable is used and the insignificant regression coefficient for the lagged differential (where the relationship would be expected to be greater because of the longer-run capital diversion mechanism presumably responsible for shifting the differential). *Ibid.*, pp. 57–58.

1) The traditional view of generally prevalent profit-maximizing behavior, much of the whole apparatus of marginality in pricing and output determination and, to a considerable extent, the principle of proportionality and minimum-cost combination of factors insofar as corporate capital is concerned.

2) The Harberger theory (a modernized version of the Walrasian analysis of the impact and incidence of a non-general tax on capital rewards) which postulates absorption of the corporate tax by capital in general (the familiar dichotomy between business and consumers as such being treated as irrelevant) with "structural" or intra-capitalist shifting between corporate and non-corporate or debt-intensive investment involving capital flows, distortions of relative prices, and underallocation of investment to corporate equity lines ([13], pp. 231–250, and [14], pp. 215–240).

3) The Rolph-Stockfisch view that taxes, whether imposed as sales-excise levies or levied on the rewards of the productive factors, are shifted backwards or absorbed by the productive factors in the absence of an accommodating monetary policy which in effect would place the whole shifting process in the hands of non-tax forces. (See [24], especially pp. 139–140.)

4) The Goode analysis of macro-obstacles to shifting of the corporate tax via more or less arbitrary price mark–ups because of aggregate demand limitations and the hazard that curtailment of output and investment to enforce general price increases will send the economy into a tailspin. (See [11], pp. 61–62.)

5) The view held by important sectors of the business community that the corporate tax, even though shifted, can be passed on only through a mechanism involving cuts in output and investment. In this view as more precisely formulated, there are undesirable repercussions on investment whether the tax is shifted immediately or in the longer run since the shifted tax

nevertheless increases the cost of equity capital investment (and possibly total corporate investment by changing the quality of a higher debt component) relative to other factors of production. This is considered a form of unneutrality which reduces the employment of the more efficient capital-intensive methods of production generally requiring the corporate form of legal organization. (See [3], pp. 60–62, and [21], especially pp. 8–21.)

6) The generally held view that shiftability depends on non-generality, alternatives, or irrationality or instability in the starting position, that business generally cannot "stand its ground" and pass on the tax with a magic wand of reserve market power.

A Tribute

No one approaches the subject of corporate tax incidence without bias and preconception or without giving hostages to fortune.

In appraising the impact of the corporate tax as part of a general system of income taxation, the economist is confronted with an exceedingly complex theoretical problem in which the unintegrated corporate layer both brings retained earnings to a rough accounting and insulates them from the full graduated individual scale. The shape of the economy on which he must rest his analysis contains an undeniable but not fully measured element of market power and administered pricing. This complicates the problem compared with the simplified competitive structure and profit-maximization assumed by the neoclassic theorist. The task of empirical analysis is easily influenced by the investigator's attitudes and value judgments respecting the corporate enterprise system and indeed the economic power structure.

The business interest group must legitimately thread its way with caution between claiming its own relief will spur investment, taking credit for bearing a large share of the fiscal load, and relinquishing the Machiavellian argument that the tax is borne by those who labor or consume. Labor has been committed to substantial taxation of corporate profits but rejects the double taxation theory and must be reserved in turning its back on credit for absorbing some of the load. Government is bound to the yield of this second largest revenue producer which has long been embedded in its fiscal structure.

The typical reaction to the unexpected and disturbing model of the economy and its responses to the tax structure disclosed by the Krzyzaniak-Musgrave study tends to be resistance and incredulity. This is true even if the econometric results showing shifting of 100 per cent, 134 per cent, or more are tempered to take account of the failure of the regression to isolate the inevitable correlation between government expenditure effects plus tax legislative policy and the level of profits. But no one can afford to be cavalier in dismissing the challenge of this valuable application of modern econometric procedures.

Krzyzaniak and Musgrave have not hesitated to clamber out on a limb or to produce answers without equivocation and pussyfooting. It is for us to judge whether the product of their multiple regression procedure makes *ceteris paribus* a substantial reality and whether it is sufficiently firm to sustain the new view of the corporate tax and the economic world which the bald findings appear to call for.

Hint of New Laws of the Firm

It is possible to interpret the Krzyzaniak-Musgrave results merely as a finding of fact that (1) the administered price-restrained monopoly area covers a large part of manufacturing, and (2) the reserve margin of market power which permits shifting is deep. But a more intriguing possibility is raised by the fact that it contains a hint of mysterious new laws of business behavior. If the results reflect not merely market power but the sheer generality of full-cost pricing even in industries which substantially meet the criteria of competition (subject to some minor tilting of the individual firm's demand curve), we are in a new and disconcerting world. In this novel concept of the economic environment, static elasticities and marginal cost-marginal revenue equilibria give way to more complex, fluid, and dynamic concepts in which micro and macro economics interact. If the factual results really support this glimpse of new vistas, the study may jolt price and incidence theory out of the established groove of marginal rationalities.

Plan of Discussion

No attempt is made here to describe in any detail the various procedures, formulations, experimental trials, behavioral assumptions, and special statistical techniques employed in the Krzyzaniak-Musgrave study. Indeed, one of the more obvious criticisms of the study is that such a variety of alternative formulations and measures are offered, giving a wide range of answers as to the degree of shifting, that the exact result becomes almost a matter of "you pays your money and you takes your chances." In the end, econometric quantification yields to judgment.

The following discussion touches on what appear to be the highlights of an evaluation of the Krzyzaniak-Musgrave investigation.

The Profit-Predicting Model

The major role in the effort to isolate the effect of tax changes on rate of return must be assigned to the model or profit equation used. This Hamlet in the drama of multiple regression is introduced by Krzyzaniak and Musgrave with the austere statement: "Experimentation led to the following formulation: . . . ." ([18], p. 33).

In its general form, the profit estimating equation was formulated as follows:

$$Y_{g,t} = a_0 + a_1 \text{ Delta } C_{t-1} + a_2 V_{t-1} + a_3 J_t + a_4 X_t + a_5 G_t + a_6 X_{t-1} + U_t,$$

where

$Y_{g,t}$ = gross rate of return on investment, before tax, for the current year

Delta C_{t-1} = prior-year change in the ratio of total consumption expenditure to GNP in 1959 prices

V_{t-1} = prior-year inventory to sales ratio in manufacturing (apparently converted to an index form)

$\mathcal{J}_t$ = current-year ratio of federal, state, and local tax receipts, exclusive of corporate tax accruals, minus domestic transfers and grants-in-aid to state and local governments to GNP

G_t = current-year ratio of federal purchases to GNP

X = the corporate tax variable in its generic form, lagged and unlagged according to the subscript: for the bulk of the analysis the tax variable takes the form of L, the tax liability expressed as a rate of return on capital, giving what is characterized as Model A; for other applications, it is Z, the statutory tax rate, or Z*, the effective tax rate, giving Model B.

U_t = stochastic variable

The authors recognized the limited number of variables permissible in line with the number of observations and the desideratum that the variables be correlated with rate of return but not with each other. As previously indicated, when the chips were down, the study relied essentially on only three independent variables other than the corporate tax factor:

1) Delta C_{t-1}: The consumption variable (a "bullish" pseudo-accelerator factor, with a positive regression coefficient)
2) V_{t-1}: The inventory-to-sales ratio factor (which may be identified as the involuntary inventory accumulation variable, with a negative coefficient)
3) $\mathcal{J}_t$: The aggregate tax factor (which may be thought of variously as reflecting the size of the government sector, the overall budgetary position of government, and the deflationary impact of taxes generally on profits, with a negative coefficient).

As background, the authors sketch out a more complex macro model (pp. 35–36) with an impracticably large number of variables for which the basic models used are a kind of shorthand. However, the relationship between it and Models A and B seems tenuous. What is the economic rationale for the three basic variables other than the germinal ideas suggested by the accelerator, involuntary inventory accumulation, and profit-deflating labels I have, perhaps mistakenly, attached to them? [10] What general acceptance do these particular variables or combination of bullish or bearish signals have as predictors of earnings rates? What experimentation went into their formulation? What other equally reasonable formulas were tested and how would the results vary with the different alternative models?

The Krzyzaniak-Musgrave model bears little resemblance to the profit equations used in such well-known econometric models as those of Klein (Wharton School), Kuh, Suits, Fromm, Liu and others. (See [10], pp. 84–85.) While consumer spending, inventory behavior, and general tax levels are all recognized indicators of the economic outlook, the particular formulation and lagging employed by Krzyzaniak and Musgrave would seem to be regarded as an unusual profit model by most experts in or on the outskirts of this highly specialized field. [11] I speak with some reticence on this point since there are at least as many opinions as there are experts on the prime determinants of profits. However, since the model in effect defines *ceteris paribus* and predetermines the answer to the shifting question

[10] The possibility of confusion is readily illustrated by the case of the Delta C variable. It has a positive multiple regression coefficient, indicating that it signals higher rates of return *ceteris paribus*. Its simple correlation coefficient with the dependent variable, while low, is negative (see (18), Table 6–2, p. 46, and Appendix II-A of this paper). The initial reaction of some model experts I have consulted, however, is that C as a percentage of GNP would be expected to increase in depression when profits declined, also to decrease in certain war periods when government requirements compressed private consumption.

[11] In line with widely held views, one important difference is that the Krzyzaniak-Musgrave equation generally ignores the implications of the fact that previous experience indicates a Cobb-Douglas function does a reasonably good job of explaining the shares of capital and labor in output. If this is correct, it would imply that the rate of return on capital is not a basic variable. It should be expected to rise in a period in which the ratio of capital to output changes as much as it has over the last 30 years. Some believe there is an appearance of capital shortage now relative to the capital-output ratio of the twenties, perhaps not due so much to the corporate tax itself as to the low investment associated with depression and war from 1930 to 1946. This factor, left out of the Krzyzaniak-Musgrave equation, would help account for higher rates of return in the high-tax periods.

posed, either the sanction of wide acceptance or a detailed justification seems in order.

The major suspicion raised by the Krzyzaniak-Musgrave model in the light of its surprising results is that it provides an inadequate or incorrect specification of corporate earnings rates in the absence of tax. As a consequence, the burden of explaining earnings is thrust upon the corporate tax variable, itself collinear with "economic pressure" levels which are important determinants of corporate profits. To the extent that this suspicion is correct, the apparent measure reached by Krzyzaniak and Musgrave overstates shifting and merely reflects the correlation between corporate earnings rates and the general pressure in the economic boiler with which corporate tax levels have historically been linked. This linkage is particularly close if the corporate tax variable is measured, as it is by Krzyzaniak and Musgrave, to include excess profits tax and to reflect the effect of loss companies and rate graduation to aid small firms.

While this suspicion is akin to the concern expressed by Krzyzaniak and Musgrave that they have not fully separated out government expenditure effects, it is directed more basically to the specific formulation of their multiple regression. Just as the answer to the question of shifting posed by the time series investigators is predetermined by, and is no better than, their selection of historic base period and indicator, so the Krzyzaniak-Musgrave thesis rests in large part on their selection of data and their profits equation.

Empirical Test of the Krzyzaniak-Musgrave Profits Equation

To test the validity of this skepticism, I arranged to have the Krzyzaniak-Musgrave data run through a series of alternative computations, using an "economic pressure" variable to supplant or supplement the independent variables of their standard Model A. The pressure variable selected is the Knowles ratio of actual to potential GNP, published in 1960 for the Joint Economic Committee. (See [17], p. 37.) To avoid resort to the instrumental variable approach, the naive least squares technique was used. The computations were confined to the total capital base, affording a basis for direct comparison with the 142 per cent measure of shifting reached by Krzyzaniak and Musgrave with the same method. ([18], Table 6–1, pp. 44–45.)

The results of this experimentation are here represented in Table 1. The pressure variable is denoted by the symbol P_t; other terms are as defined by Krzyzaniak and Musgrave. Line 2 of the table shows the results of a re-run of the Krzyzaniak-Musgrave model, with some rounding of the data to facilitate processing. This confirms their computation of between 141 and 142 per cent shifting, although somewhat different values were obtained for the other variables and tests of significance.

Effects of Introducing an Economic Pressure Variable

Substitution of the pressure variable P_t for the consumption variable Delta C_{t-1} shown in line 3, reduced the measure of shifting from 141 to 87 per cent, a reduction of 54 percentage points in the measure itself, or about 38 per cent of the original estimate. The standard error of the shifting measure increased somewhat and its significance decreased, although it remained highly significant. However, the new pressure variable itself was not quite significant at the 5 per cent level. The inventory-sales ratio variable became insignificant.

A Caveat

I hasten to warn that the 87 per cent figure reached here and similar figures in the subsequent trials should not be interpreted as my revised measure of shifting. Rather, they are designed to point up the fact that, apart from inadequacies of their data, the Krzyzaniak-Musgrave results depend in large part on their profits model and, even on the basis of their data, sustain sharp cutbacks as a more adequate economic explanation of earnings rates is built into the model.

The pressure variable P_t used in the experimentation outlined here is itself not fully adequate, and "better" non-tax variables reflecting the profit-level temperature of the economy would in my opinion result in further reduction in the shifting measure.

Table 21

Revised estimates for all manufacturing, total capital base, Model A, with alternative "profit equations" (20 Observations, 1935–42, 1948–59, Naive Least Squares)

| No. | Description | Regression Coefficients, [ ] error* | | | | | | $\bar{R}^2$ Corrected for the Number of Degrees of Freedom | $\bar{R}$ | d Stat. | Shifting Measure, ( ) Its Standard Error |
		Intercept	$DeltaC_{t-1}$	V_{t-1}	Variables J_t	as fractions of standard L_t	P_t				
1.	Krzyzaniak-Musgrave #6 Table 6-1	n.c.	.4966 [3.5440]	−.4681 [−3.0253]	−.8967 [−5.4347]	1.4199 [15.3468]		(.961)**	.9805	2.6526	1.4199 (.0925)
2.	No. 1 above, Rounded Data	.2683 [5.1985]	.4338 [2.9333]	−.4556 [−2.7140]	−.8355 [−4.8100]	1.410 [14.1051]		.955	.977	2.660	1.410 (.0999)
3.	Substitute P_t for Delta C_{t-1}	.005173 [.0341]		−.3238 [−1.4808]	−.6841 [−3.6690]	.8707 [3.1658]	.2590 [1.8039]	.942	.971	2.591	.8707 (.2750)
4.	Substitute P_t for V_{t-1}	−.1242 [−1.6000]	.4648 [3.5121]		−.7778 [−5.3008]	.8653 [4.0706]	.3487 [3.5355]	.963	.982	1.980	.8653 (.2126)
5.	Substitute P_t for J_t	−.1509 [−.7641]	.1965 [.9254]	.0886 [.3189]		.9950 [2.6897]	.2297 [1.1960]	.896	.945	1.125	.9950 (.3699)
6.	Add P_t Variable to Model	.007878 [.0680]	.4405 [3.4339]	−.2506 [−1.4907]	−.8576 [−5.6829]	.9420 [4.4690]	.2670 [2.4384]	.966	.983	2.355	.9420 (.2108)
7.	Substitute P_t for All Independent Variables except L_t	−.1266 [−1.0218]				.9615 [2.8679]	.2223 [1.4729]	.903	.950	1.457	.9615 (.3353)

* Consistent with the convention followed by Krzyzaniak and Musgrave, this value (usually referred to as the T-ratio) is given a negative sign where the regression coefficient is negative.

** Figure supplied.

Note: Subject to minor rounding of data, variables other than P_t are as set forth in K&M, Appendix A, pp. 72–75. The P_t variable values are from the Joint Committee Print, *Potential Economic Growth, op. cit.*, p. 37.

Replacing the inventory-sales ratio variable V_{t-1} with the pressure variable, shown in line 4 of Table 21, reduced the measure of shifting slightly further to about 86½ per cent. In this case, the tax variable is significant, the pressure variable itself is fully significant at even the 1 per cent level, and the significance of the other variables increased compared with their T-ratios in the rounded-data re-run of the original Krzyzaniak-Musgrave model.

With the Durbin-Watson statistic at slightly less than 2, this series, unlike the great majority of the Krzyzaniak-Musgrave runs, passes the test for serial auto-correlation.[12]

A smaller but still substantial reduction in the measure of shifting (47 percentage points) occurred with the insertion of P_t as an additional independent variable, as shown in line 6, Table 21. The standard error of estimate for the shifting measure is moderate, and the pressure is fully significant. The reader will note the contrast between these results and those obtained by Krzyzaniak and Musgrave when they introduced a federal purchases variable (G_t) into the standard model. Their addition of G_t increased the measure of shifting from 134 per cent to 151 per cent ([18], Table 6–1, ll. 2–3, pp. 44–45).

Substitution of the pressure variable for the general tax collection variable V_t and for all the independent variables (other than L_t) respectively (lines 5 and 7, Table 21) produce less reduction in the shifting measure, larger standard errors, and inadequate tests of significance for the P_t variable. It is noteworthy that with the substitution of P_t for $\mathcal{J}_t$ (Table 21, line 5) the coefficient for V_{t-1} changes its usual sign and becomes completely insignificant. This may suggest a defect in the Krzyzaniak-Musgrave model.

The simple correlation matrix for the above computations is presented with a brief comment in Appendix II–A. This confirms the correlation between the economic pressure variable P_t and the dependent earnings rate variable $Y_{g,t}$ suggested by

[12] The importance of the various failures to pass the Durbin-Watson test for negative serial auto-correlation would seem to be a matter of opinion. Even if no bias in the measure of shifting per se results, R tends to be overestimated, errors understated, significance overstated. There is also the implication that either the model incorrectly explains earnings rates or a significant variable is omitted.

the preceding discussion. It also shows the collinearity between P_t and L_t which apparently reduces the shifting measure when P_t is introduced.

It is recognized that some would contend that where independent variables are collinear, as are P_t and L_t, it is difficult to quantify their relative importance in the manner suggested by the experimentation shown in Table 21 above, and some indeterminacy of relative causal effect exists. For whatever further light it may throw on this point, a summary analysis of the relative contribution and the individual importance (Beta coefficient) of the different independent variables is presented in Appendix II–B.

All in all, it seems fair to conclude that defects and idiosyncracies of the Krzyzaniak-Musgrave profit equation account for a considerable part of their measure of shifting. As will be seen later, if the reduced measure of shifting is further adjusted to take account of (1) overstatement due to use of the naive least squares method, (2) adjustment for inflation, and (3) correlation between the corporate tax variable and rate of return via public expenditures not reflected by the contribution of the pressure variable alone, the resulting adjusted measure of shifting even on the basis of the Krzyzaniak-Musgrave data would seem to be moderate at best.

Basic Data and Time Period Coverages

The study is confined to manufacturing corporations on a time series basis. The study thus overlooks opportunities to compare manufacturing with total corporate enterprise for a clue to the extent that the special competitive structure in manufacturing may account for the high degree of shifting recorded.

While the basic results relate to manufacturing industry as a whole, the Krzyzaniak-Musgrave model was also applied to selected manufacturing sub-groups, to some asset size classifications, to selected groups of "price leaders" and "price followers," and to certain individual companies ([18], pp. 58–62). The shifting measures for the sub-groups were similar to the over-all results; the measures varied (not always in the way one would expect from market structures) and ranged as high as 175 per cent.[13]

The study neglects comparison with the regulated public utility field to ascertain similarities or differences of shifting results in relation to a form of industry in which shifting is effectuated by adjustments in consumer charges. Similarly, it is silent on the comparative tax experience of the mineral industries. The well-known fact that after-tax returns are not generally higher in the mineral industries than in manufacturing or industry as a whole and the findings of the Krzyzaniak-Musgrave study taken at face value thus pose the intriguing question of the ultimate destination of depletion, liberalized depreciation, and other tax incentive benefits.

The rejection by Krzyzaniak and Musgrave of cross section analysis by manufacturing sub-groups is somewhat puzzling, as is their statement that they abandoned an original intent to combine time and cross section analysis by using firm data because "it turned out that the tax variable does not differ sufficiently between firms to permit cross section analysis" ([18], p. 22). It is a matter of everyday observation that wide variations in earnings rates exist.[14]

Basic data used in the study for manufacturing and its sub-groups are from *Statistics of Income*.[15] The period covered is from 1935 to 1959, excluding the war and postwar years 1943–1947. Part of the World War II period and prior defense recovery years are included, as is the Korean period. The Great Depression years of the early thirties are excluded for understandable reasons but the twenties, which provide the standard basis of

[13] For twelve textile companies and also for fifteen "price followers" in the post-war era.

[14] In 1958, for example, the after-tax rates of return on stockholders' investment for the three largest companies in motor vehicle manufacturing ranged from −4.2 per cent to 12.6 per cent; for the four largest office and store machine manufacturers, from 6.3 per cent to 18.8 per cent; for the four largest turbine and engine manufacturers, from 1.7 per cent to 13.2 per cent; and so forth. See (9).

[15] Like all *Statistics of Income*, their figures therefore represent pre-audit tabulations; they do not reflect the effect of renegotiation on profits and taxes; they also do not reflect the effect of subsequent loss carrybacks to the particular tax year or excess profits tax relief adjustments. The problem of consistency of data over time is of course perennial in a coverage from 1935 through 1959.

comparison for time period studies were rejected because of difficulties in securing comparable data. Tax liabilities are defined to include excess profits tax. Rates of return are computed by relating net income of profitable companies less losses of deficit firms to the capital investment of all.

This selection must have governed the results to a considerable degree since, with the exception of the late fifties, the periods included were consistently characterized by rising trends of profits and tax rates. A time series analysis through the fifties with the thirties as a comparison period would show substantially greater shifting than one with the usual twenties as standard.[16]

The major events in the period covered which might tend, on the shifting hypothesis, to initiate perceptible changes in price-cost-output relationships and pre-tax profits boil down to three:

1) The creeping rise in profits tax rates in the thirties.
2) The sharper rise in the early World War II period.
3) The abrupt rise of the general corporate rate to a 52 per cent plateau plus the temporary excess profits tax beginning in 1950.

These separate tax episodes each coincided with rising movements in earnings. Surely this relationship dominated the Krzyzaniak-Musgrave regressions, but its indication as to the causal relationship between taxes and profits is subject to different interpretations.

On the other hand, tax-reducing changes such as the build-up of depreciation deductions under the faster 1954 code methods tended to coincide with subsiding levels of earnings rates as previously suggested. In view of the apparent sensitivity of the Krzyzaniak-Musgrave model to relatively small differences in data, decreases in the deficit company group in boom periods and increases such as occurred in the fifties may also have had significant effects on the correlation between earnings rates on

[16] The tax increase was proportionately smaller and the rate of return increase proportionately greater between the thirties and the fifties than between the twenties and the fifties. This is supported by the time series data given a "preliminary view" in (18), p. 17.

the investment of all manufacturing companies and the L_t corporate tax variable. This source of correlation is misleading as an indication of shifting since it is purely statistical and there is little reason to suppose that the behavioral assumption underlying the model calls for profitable companies to unshift the tax reduction received by loss companies as a result of their not making money or for the loss companies themselves to lower prices further in a loss situation merely because their current tax liabilities disappeared (or gave way to carryback refunds).

Plotting the Krzyzaniak-Musgrave data for pre-tax earnings rates against their preferred tax variable (negative rate of return on capital) and giving a linear fit to the scatter by visual methods, I derived the following approximate relationships:

1. Total capital base

$$Y_{o,t} = 5 \text{ per cent plus } 1\frac{1}{2} L_t$$
or
$$L_t = .67 \ (Y_{o,t} \text{ minus 5 per cent})$$

2. Equity base

$$Y_{o,t} = 5 \text{ per cent plus } 1\frac{3}{7} L_t$$
or
$$L_t = .7 \ (Y_{o,t} \text{ minus 5 per cent})$$

3. Equity Base Corrected for Inflation

$$Y_{o,t} = 5 \text{ per cent plus } \frac{5}{4} L_t$$
or
$$L_t = .8 \ (Y_{o,t} \text{ minus 5 per cent})$$

What do these rough results suggest? On the total capital base, for example, they may be interpreted alternatively as showing that in the historic period under survey corporate income and profits taxes were (1) shifted in the sense that rates of return were pushed above 5 per cent as high as 150 per cent of the tax or (2) absorbed two-thirds of earnings in excess of 5 per cent. No firm conclusions about shifting could be drawn from such data, of course. Nevertheless, they suggest the nature of the collinearity between earnings rates and taxes as rates of return in the observation periods.

While Krzyzaniak and Musgrave dispose of the argument of possible collinear time trends for $Y_{g,t}$ and L_t by the conventional technique of differencing the model and demonstrating that the shifting measure is not substantially altered ([18], pp. 48–49 and Table 6–1; line 11, pp. 44–45), it seems apparent that the historical relationship (not a matter of single collinear time trends but several major episodes) dominates their results and is subject to alternative interpretations. The excess profits tax, for example, was levied in high profits years to absorb profits arising from the nation's defense effort. To interpret the situation as one in which the excess profits tax was added to prices and pushed up pre-tax earnings seems to distort reality.

Krzyzaniak and Musgrave make no mention of the problem of the timing of tax legislation in relation to their behavioral assumption although in some cases corporate tax changes enacted prior to the filing of returns could not have been known to business throughout the tax year. Neither do they discuss the possible implications of the two episodes of transition to a more current tax payment system for corporations.

Credibility of Results

Nowhere in the Krzyzaniak-Musgrave study is any attempt made to translate the numerical measures of shifting turned out by the regressions into rate-of-return or profit-share effects in a way which permits common sense appraisal of the implied pushing up of profit levels. This section explores some of these implications in an effort to test the credibility of the results.

On the total capital base (profits plus interest related to equity capital plus interest-bearing debt) using their preferred Model A (tax variable expressed as a negative rate of return on capital) the Krzyzaniak-Musgrave study disclosed measures of shifting for different periods, lagging, and model variations ranging from about 103 per cent to about 162 per cent ([18], Table 6–1, pp. 44–45). Using only the preferred "standard"

Model A (eliminating government purchases as an independent variable and lagging of the tax variable) but experimenting with the equity as well as the total capital base, the study produced shifting measures ranging from about 78 per cent to about 146 per cent ([18], ll. 1–10, Table 7–1, pp. 54–55). The standard Model A for all 20 observation years reflected shifting of about 134 per cent on the total capital base and about 123 per cent on the equity base. Half the trials shown for Model A showed shifting of 134 per cent or more.

As previously noted, Model B (tax variable the statutory or effective rate of tax) gave answers showing shifting as high as about 278 per cent ([18], Table 6–3, pp. 50–51).

It seems fair to say that the authors' best numerical answers to the degree of shifting prior to adjustment for inflation and the retreat for intercorrelation of tax rates and government expenditures were 134 per cent on the total capital base and 123 per cent on the equity base ([18], Summary, Table 8–1, p. 64).

What does this shifting of 123 or 134 per cent mean in practical terms? Since the preferred "gross formulation" measure of shifting used is the ratio of the increase in the pre-war rate of return (ascribed to shifting) to the tax liability in the new "shifted position" (expressed as a rate of return on capital), it is almost immediately evident that while 100 per cent shifting with a 50 per cent tax rate means pushing a pre-tax rate of return of 10 per cent to 20 per cent (or doubling), 133 per cent shifting would mean driving a 10 per cent return to 30 per cent (or tripling).[17] Shifting of 125 per cent would involve multiplying the pre-tax return by 2.67. Under a 50 per cent corporate tax rate, the multiple or snowballing effect of shifting approaches infinity and the system becomes explosive as the value of the shifting measures approaches 2. These multiples would be higher for a tax rate above 50 per cent and lower for tax rates below 50 per cent.

With an effective corporate tax rate of 67 per cent, one which was approached but not reached in the excess profits tax years

[17] The derivation of the equation for the multiples involved in the snowballing effect and additional illustrative figures are presented in Appendix II-C.

1942–44, a 125 per cent measure of shifting implies sextupling of pre-war earnings rates, and the system becomes explosive as the measure approaches 1.5.

Exploring the point a little further, it becomes evident that if 133 per cent shifting implies a tripling of pre-tax rates of return under a 50 per cent corporate tax rate, it also implies an increase in the after-tax return by one-half. Similarly, 125 per cent shifting would involve increasing the after-tax return by one-third.

Conversely, a 133 per cent shifting measure implies that a 20 per cent observed rate of return would have been only $6\frac{2}{3}$ per cent in the absence of tax. This suggests that a profit share of corporate GNP amounting to 20 per cent, developed under the pressure of a shifted 50 per cent corporate tax, would have been only $6\frac{2}{3}$ per cent in the absence of tax; and that a profit share of 16 per cent (roughly the current level) would have been only a little over 5 per cent. This would implicitly "downgrade" the importance of the substantive contribution of capital to GNP and growth below the most conservative estimates.

In my opinion, shifting on this scale, long- or short-run, defies credulity. The corporate tax has not been that "profitable" to corporate enterprise, and profits would not be so low in the absence of the alleged tax "blow-up."

Implications as to Profits Pattern with Zero Tax

Implicit in the Krzyzaniak-Musgrave theory is the rule that, with 100 per cent shifting (or some approximation thereto) operative year in and year out, the after-tax profits series tends to reflect the pre-tax series pattern which would have prevailed in the absence of the corporate income tax. This thesis implies that a lower, flatter, less jagged curve of profits would have developed in the absence of the tax or with consistently lower taxes. On the basis of shifting of 125 per cent, 134 per cent or more as indicated in some of the numerical results of the Krzyzaniak-Musgrave study, and in combination with the rising trend of tax rates 1935–1959, the implied trend of profitability is not only substantially lower but also downward.

As a simple test of plausibility, the table below compares the actual rates of return on equity capital in manufacturing (uncorrected for inflation) as tabulated by Krzyzaniak and Musgrave for 1936 and 1957 ([18], Table A–2, Appendix A, p. 74), and the rates of return with zero tax in those years implied by shifting measures of 100 per cent, 125 per cent, 133 per cent, and 150 per cent, respectively.

Equity Capital — all Manufacturing

	1936	1957
Rate of Return before Tax	9.6%	16.3%
Effective Tax Rate	16.2	50.7
Rate of Return after Tax	8.0	8.0
Implied Rates of Return with Zero Tax:*		
100 Per Cent Shifting	8.0	8.0
125 Per Cent Shifting	7.6	5.9
133 Per Cent Shifting	7.5	5.3
150 Per Cent Shifting	7.2	3.8
(75 Per Cent Shifting	8.4	10.1)

* Implied rate of return with zero tax ($Y'_{g,t}$) computed from the equation
$$\frac{Y_{g,t} - Y'_{g,t}}{Z^* \, Y_{g,t}} = \text{measure of shifting.}$$

Inasmuch as 1957 was on almost all counts a "stronger" economic year than 1936, it is especially difficult to accept the implication that rates of return on equity capital would have declined with zero tax as implied by a shifting measure of 125 per cent on the equity base. Even a 75 per cent shifting assumption (shown in parenthesis in the table above) implies that even between the dark days of the middle thirties and the peak peacetime boom of 1957, rates of return, including a significant overstatement due to inflation, would have increased only 20 per cent with zero tax.

Retreat from Initial Numerical Results

One must point out that Krzyzaniak and Musgrave modify their basic numerical results by adjusting for inflation, which brings their measure down to about 100 per cent. They then make a further withdrawal based on judgment reducing the measure for the impact of government expenditures without attaching any specific figure to this additional downward adjustment. Nevertheless, the exact quantitative results of their procedure prior to the ambiguous inflation adjustment [18] and prior to semi-subjective and non-quantitative correction for the contaminating influence of "budget incidence" collinearity of profitability ([18], p. 47) expenditures (G_t), and tax levels (L_t) are difficult to reconcile with the changes in earnings rates and profit shares which have occurred. Exactly how difficult will depend to some extent on the interpretation of the adjustment for inflation discussed later.

It is true that Krzyzaniak and Musgrave are measuring short-run shifting, and amounts of shifting which appear unrealistically high for the long run may ebb away in subsequent years. Moreover, the shifting of any one year may be thought of as the response to the increase in the tax over the level to which a long-run accommodation has been previously made. However, the general models do not estimate shifting of the increment of tax but estimate "what the rate of return in any one year would have been had the tax rate been zero" ([18], p. 39). A differencing procedure which related increments in the corporate tax variable and other independent variables to increments in the rate of return showed 142 per cent shifting, only slightly higher than the basic model (pp. 48–49 and line 11; Table 6–1, pp. 44–45). Moreover, there are clear suggestions at various points in the study that the short-run effect persists and merges with the long-run, thus avoiding adverse incentive and business savings effects (e.g., pp. 64–65).

The Inflation Adjustment

To what extent is the finding of shifting of 123 to 134 per cent (depending on the capital base), which implies a snowballing or multiple effect on pre-tax rates of return of roughly 2.67 to 3 under a 50 per cent tax rate made more credible by adjustment for inflation?

Running the regressions again with income and balance sheet data adjusted to correct for inflation, Krzyzaniak and Musgrave

[18] The ambiguity involved here is whether the reduced measure implies that there was overshifting but inflation filched from business some nominal "overshooting of the mark" or whether business was able to isolate the amount of real profits after inflation adjustment and pass sufficient amounts on to consumers to neutralize inflation distortions and cover taxes.

reduce the equity-base shifting measure to a little over 100 per cent. Taken at face value, this more conservative measure would eliminate the paradox of "overshooting the mark" and making a profit out of taxation. However, it poses a problem of interpretation, which the authors recognize but do not resolve, leaving a range of between about 101 per cent and 123 per cent for shifting on the equity base for the period as a whole (ll. 7 and 3, Table 7–1, pp. 54–55).

One possible interpretation of the interaction of tax shifting and inflation distortion is that business actually overshot the mark pushing pre-tax rates of return up far more than necessary to shift the tax, but that these profits of overshifting were offset by the illusory return due to inflation. This assumes that overshooting the mark was exactly but coincidentally offset by overstatement of earnings rates due to such factors as inflationary inventory profits, understatement of the current erosion of depreciable assets, and understatement of equity on the books.

The other alternative is to assume that corporate management accurately looked through the money illusion, either created or accepted from the market sufficient nominal profits to make up for the shortfall caused by inflationary overstatement of real earnings, and then passed forward only enough tax to keep their adjusted earnings on target.

The first interpretation implies that shifting substantially in excess of 100 per cent actually occurred but was fortuitously cancelled by inflation. The second implies not only that manufacturing enterprise, in its collective wisdom, was extraordinarily accurate in passing on the amount of the tax—no more, no less—but also that it was extraordinarily penetrating in discerning what the real profit "norm" was in each situation, diligent in gauging the impact of inflation, and dexterous in handling the tax shifting so as to maintain after-tax real earnings at the implicit standard of the Krzyzaniak-Musgrave model.

I find either alternative difficult to believe. In any event, this complication leaves an area of doubt in the precise numerical measure of shifting forces per se.

Blurred Image of Management Behavior

The image of the economy and of the way business management responds to taxation conveyed by the Krzyzaniak-Musgrave study is also correspondingly blurred by the treatment of
inflation effects. On the one hand, overshooting the mark
conveys the impression of an unstable group of over-anxious
oligopolists, concentrating on making sure that their tax liability
is passed on, but unskillful in insulating themselves against
attrition of nominal profits by inflation. On the other, we are
treated to a picture of restrained, statesmanlike, and efficient
economic calculators, in full command of the situation but
prepared to utilize their market power only to the extent necessary to protect their normal earnings position from the inroads
of either inflation or taxation.

The Ratchet Effect

The Krzyzaniak-Musgrave finding that there is no speedy
unshifting of the corporate tax in consequence of a tax rate
decrease, so that short-run shiftability is a one-way street,
hangs by a statistical thread. Yet its policy implications are
spelled out in greater detail than those of any other single item
in the list of unorthodox policy conclusions drawn from the
regressions ([18], pp. 65–66). The authors recognize it as a very
tentative hypothesis, but suggest the conclusion which normally
follows from the view that the corporate tax is not shifted:
"A reduction in the tax increases profitability, initially at least,
and hence may encourage capital formation via the incentive
arguments. The distributive gain is to profits rather than wage
earners or consumers. These consequences of rate reduction may
be significant, even if failure to unshift is only temporary"
([18], p. 66). In short, the corporate income tax is viewed as a
sales tax without adverse effects on business savings or profitability on the way up, and as a kind of "unjust enrichment"
on the way down with an accompanying abnormal stimulus (of
uncertain or indefinite duration) to investment.

This result was arrived at statistically by differencing the
model and introducing two tax variables, one the increment in

tax as a negative rate of return in years of a tax rate increase (set at zero in other years), the other the decrease in tax as a negative rate of return in years of a tax rate decrease (set at zero in other years). The estimated degree of shifting was 170 per cent for the positive change and only 7 per cent for the negative change (p. 58).

It will be recalled, however, that only one of the maximum of 20 observation years (1935–42, 1948–59) covered by the study involved a statutory rate decrease; and that was not a general corporate tax rate cut but the termination of the Korean excess profits tax effective in 1954. The observed "ratchet effect" therefore is based on only one instance of a statutory tax rate cut, one which was known in advance, and the effect of which by its special nature would be, other things being equal, to enlarge rather than to depress profits. In addition to the 1954 change which affected both statutory and effective rates, the effective rate of tax as measured by Krzyzaniak and Musgrave (Table 3–1, p. 28) decreased in 1935, 1936, 1939, 1948, 1952, 1955, 1956, and 1959—usually by minor amounts reflecting such things as loss companies.

The statistical exercise which led to the "ratchet effect" demonstrates the dominating importance of rate increases in the correlation between taxes and earnings rates, much of which is accounted for by the fact that rate increases in the period covered, generally coincided with increases in profitability. When this collinearity is separated out, the remaining data, which include relatively minor instances of effective rate reduction, naturally show little correlation between corporate taxes and profits.[19] I suspect that this indicates not so much a uni-

[19] In 1959, for example, the effective rate of tax in manufacturing as observed by Krzyzaniak and Musgrave, decreased from 50.96 per cent to 49.77 per cent, although the general statutory rate of 52 per cent was unchanged (Table 3–1, p. 28). This decrease was due primarily to shrinkage of the deficit company area in 1959. At the same time, the current year tax as a rate of return on net worth rose from over 6 per cent to over 8 per cent, reflecting the sharp recovery in corporate earnings. Without trying to unravel the multiple regression verbally, it is obvious why 1959, treated as a year the effective tax rate decreased, would probably not contribute to any correlation on the downside between the tax variable and the earnings rate. It seems likely that further detailed analysis of the events behind the data would throw additional light on the causes of the ratchet effect.

directional behavioral reaction to tax changes as the previously suggested defects in the statistical basis for the finding of shifting.

The reader will, of course, note the inconsistency between the ratchet effect and the assumed mechanism of target-return pricing. While I will not attempt a detailed discussion of this point here, it would seem that any deliberate pursuit of a particular after-tax rate of return goal would quickly become confused as effective tax rates changed if management applied a "double standard" to tax increases and tax decreases. Suppose effective rates drop from 60 to 40 per cent, as they did between 1945 and 1946, then rise again to 45 per cent, as they did in 1950. The ratchet effect for the 20 percentage point drop must quickly discontinue (or be offset against the subsequent rise) or the price policy of business management will have to assume the task of shifting a cumulatively greater load.

Benign Effect of Current-Year Shifting on Investment

The degree of shifting measured by Krzyzaniak and Musgrave is essentially similar to that estimated by the time series investigators using the rate-of-return indicator. The uniqueness of their results relates to the timing, the presumptive mechanism, and perhaps the direction of shifting.

The first and perhaps most challenging of the policy conclusions which the authors draw from the finding of current, forward shifting is: "An increase in the corporate tax rate does not depress growth via the rate-of-return or available-funds type of responses" (p. 66). Presumably the careful wording of this conclusion leaves the door open to possible adverse effects on investment and growth via the supposed erratic sales tax effect on consumption. The compression of personal savings or other personal expenditures which might result from a heavy sales tax impact if overall demand for manufactured products is inelastic (as the authors seem to regard it) is not fully considered.

The authors indicate that ideally, they would seek "differential" effects of the corporation income tax versus a fiscal substitute, but they recognize that this would be impossible. As second choice, they aim at "absolute" effects which involve aggregate demand changes. They finally settle for a mixture of "budget" incidence (tax accompanied by increased public expenditure) and "absolute" effects (pp. 6–7). Under a "budget" concept, government expenditures supplant private savings or consumption taken up by the tax. Whatever the concept (and particularly if it is not solely a matter of "budget incidence" in a less than fully employed economy) there remains a question whether and how the impact of the short-run sales tax shifting might affect growth and investment even if it leaves business investment returns and ability to self-finance intact. This in turn depends to a great extent on (1) whether the supposed sales tax effect cuts down on consumer spending or personal saving or merely triggers a diffused inflationary effect on the wage-price structure and (2) whether the underlying problem of achieving savings = investment with high employment and growth is one of pruning surplus *ex ante* savings or bolstering the level of savings = investment. Since the authors' model is not explicit in this respect, for the period of observation as a whole or any part thereof, we are left in a quandary as to the overall interpretation of the result beyond preservation of corporate investment returns and *ex ante* savings.

Granted that the authors are not under heavy obligation to go into interpretive matters in this type of empirical study; granted that empirical models may be chosen which avoid a commitment to a Keynesian or neoclassical system or to a particular type of competitive structure; still, when policy implications are drawn or causal mechanisms read into the results, the bland simplicity of the regression construct handicaps policy generalizations.

Conflict with Prevailing Views of How Shifting is Accomplished

In any event, the important point which I wish to discuss here is the sharp and quite explicit conflict between the authors and others who accept the possibility or probability of full shifting of the corporate tax on its implications for capital formation.

Generally speaking, economists and business groups who recognize the possibility of shifting consider the basic mechanism to be curtailment of investment. Their typical view is that while the corporation income tax has been substantially equivalent to a sales tax, it has been shifted by a hidden restraint on the increase in production, imposed in turn by the fact that investment is sensitive to rates of return after payment of tax and is curtailed, at least relative to the rate of expansion otherwise possible. Accordingly, the corporate income tax is deemed to be a cause of a slower rate of economic growth and smaller gains in productivity. One symptom of this is believed to be the relative weakness of business investment in plant and equipment as a component of total investment and of GNP, e.g., (8). The question is also raised whether tax effects may not have supplemented technological factors in bringing about the decline of roughly one-sixth in the manufacturers' inventory-sales ratio during the past twenty-five years.

A number of analysts, including Shoup, Beck, Bodenhorn, and Brown, have dealt with the possibilities of facilitating and speeding up the essentially long-run mechanism of capital adjustment, through favorable turnover ratios, economized use of working capital, or leverage of adjustments in the rate of expansion of capital in a growing economy.[20]

The business-oriented economist in particular is likely to assert that (1) there is nothing instantaneous or automatic about the process of shifting, (2) a competitive enterprise (sometimes defined as any other than a regulated utility which can pass tax on to customers as part of the regulated service charge) cannot simply mark up its prices to pass the tax along unless its competitors can be counted on to do likewise—which they cannot, (3) exceptional situations may exist where concurrent efforts to raise prices to cover tax are effective in shifting tax without serious disturbance of relative market positions, but this is not general, and (4) consequently, the sales-tax type of shift is not widely feasible or prevalent. (See [21], pp. 8–10.) Rather, this type of observer is likely to hold the neoclassical

[20] For a summary and specific references, see (20), pp. 314 and 317.

view that corporate shifting occurs only gradually, perhaps with help from favorable aggregate demand situations, through constriction or diversion of the flow of investment, limiting the supply of goods produced by corporate enterprise. The result according to this kind of thinking is to raise prices relative to other-than-equity-capital costs, capital-output ratios being taken into account.

Mystique of Timing

Krzyzaniak and Musgrave specifically take to task the view that if the corporate tax is passed on through immediate administered-price adjustments it deters investment as much as if it were shifted by the slower process of reducing the use of equity capital.[21] They further suggest that the Harberger thesis of equalizing inter-sector capital flows is diminished in practical importance if "there is a quick and persistent recoupment of the tax prior to capital adjustment" (p. 5, n.). This point is further developed as their analysis unfolds. The authors reiterate the position that if short-run depressing effects on the rate of return are immediately recouped (1) there will be no long-run cutback of the capital supply, whatever its elasticity, and (2) Harberger-type capital flows out of corporate equity-intensive lines will be less than if there was no initial price rise in that sector to shift the tax (p. 64, including n. 2).

What is the unstated rationale of this interpretation? It would seem to be simply this: The inter-sector capital flows in response to tax differentials are normally due to two separate but interrelated forces, one the disparity in after-tax rates of return which impel capital owners to switch, the other the shift in consumer demand in response to relative price changes which expands the scope of some and contracts the scope of other opportunities for investment by the final demand mechanism. The motivating force of this carrot-stick process is considered less if the stick side of the arrangement is removed by the immediate price increase which maintains the after-tax rate of

[21] This view is expressed in (3), pp. 20–22. It receives critical comment in (18), pp. 4–5, n.

return on an otherwise redundant capital investment and thus prevents adverse effects on total capital formation.

Final demand and least cost combination rules are the traditional determinants of factor use and allocation. From this standpoint, it is not clear how the final equilibrium will be significantly different, regardless of the timing of the price changes, if the cost of capital in the equity lines remains unchanged. On the assumption that the corporate tax increases the cost of equity capital, long-run products prices will be increased to the extent the corporate tax is a necessary input in their production.

We must remember, however, that Krzyzaniak and Musgrave seem to believe that the immediate price increase in the equity intensive sector represents the utilization of reserve market power. This would increase the total amount spent by consumers and government on corporate manufactured products, the increase presumably representing some combination of inelastic consumer demand, balanced budget multiplier, and monetary complaisance. The implicit inelasticity of consumer demand in combination with higher prices for manufacturing output would seem almost necessarily to result in reduced relative demand for the goods and services of non-corporate and debt-intensive lines. Under these assumptions, it is difficult to see how there could be an associated shift on net balance of either money demand or investment to the non-corporate sector in response to relative price changes. Indeed, the non-corporate or elastic-demand sectors might be expected to suffer some attrition unless the tax is a burden to no one.

What appears at first inspection to be a mysterious effect of timing is in reality the authors' reliance on unexploited market power and compressibility of expenditures in other directions, to explain their 100 per cent shifting.

The above reasoning would not be altered in substance by the possibility of a monetary accommodation to finance the larger money value of output due to forward shifting. With a general increase in the monetary value of output, the use of reserve market power by the corporate manufacturing sector would still prevent the shift in relative demand elsewhere in much the same way as in the case of a constant aggregate dollar demand.

Paradox of Instant Shiftability: A Tax Cost which Is Not a Cost

The shifting process which Krzyzaniak and Musgrave read into their regressions presents a paradox. The corporate tax is a cost or is treated as a cost—that is why it is shifted. Added to price, it is an element of cost to the consumer. But, in the Krzyzaniak-Musgrave view, to corporate management in position to shift this amount almost without effort, it is a cost which is not a cost. It can be passed forward with lightning speed. Its weight is as gossamer. In familiar economic metaphor, it can be paid out of a widow's cruse of "unliquidated gains" of market power.

How broad is this front of market power? What is the depth of its reserve? [22] Does it have no limitations? How can the corporate tax so easily exploit market power without interference from an alert union movement? To what extent does instant shifting depend on flexibility in the monetary system or the cooperation of the monetary authorities? How much do the results depend on the increasing level of utilization of resources in the period 1935–59? Are the rules applicable to a 15 per cent tax also good under a 50 per cent tax and equally valid for still higher rates? Is the phenomenon of tax snowballing no significant impediment to the shifting process? These queries express my skepticism of a 100 per cent instant shifting rule.

SOME NEGLECTED EMPIRICAL INDICATORS

Several sources of light on the corporate tax incidence question have received strangely little attention and will be touched on in this section.

Price Umbrella Effects

One of the frequently cited "undesirable consequences" of a shifted corporation income tax is what may be generically de-

[22] Incidentally, what of the firm which restrains profit maximization by a "live and let live" policy—not reducing prices as much as possible to make more profits, so that it can keep its share of the market within traditional bounds.

scribed as its "price umbrella" effect. By its nature, the corporate tax is paid only by the profitable and therefore the more efficient firms. It costs the marginal producer little or nothing. It is contended, therefore, that shifting of the tax by the more profitable corporations raises a price umbrella over both the inefficient firm and the obsolete machine. As Clendenin put it, the "widening of the margin between costs and selling prices by successful corporations . . . must afford new firms, small firms, inefficient firms, and unincorporated firms a better competitive chance than they would otherwise have" ([2], p. 396). These potential effects are sometimes cited in behalf of the replacement of part or all of the corporation income tax with a value-added tax. Proponents of the value-added tax believe that the present system leaves too many resources in the hands of those least able to use them, artificially extends service lives of depreciable assets, and holds back the pace of modernization. They point out that the value-added tax, by contrast, though shifted, would be a cost of operation for all competitors in proportion to their use of productive factors.

Our immediate concern with price umbrella effects is not their validity as arguments for restructuring the corporate tax but as possible symptoms of shifting. The greater the price umbrella reflecting the increased spread between costs and prices due to shifting, the narrower should be the sector of firms operating at a loss. If the price umbrella effect is present, one would expect that as tax rates rose in recent decades the scope of no-net income operations would be curtailed.

Margin of No-Net Income Operations

The salient results of a study of changes in the relative importance of corporations with no net income (deficit corporations) in the manufacturing and utility fields in recent decades are summarized in Table 22. The scope of the deficit corporation group has been measured in terms of numbers of firms, total receipts, assets, and the amount of the deficit. The magnitude of deficit operations is, of course, dependent in part on economic conditions, pressure of demand, and similar non-tax circum-

Table 22

Summary analysis of price umbrella effect

Period	Applicable General Corporate Tax Rate (Per Cent)	Deficit Corporation Group as Per Cent of Total[1]							
		Numbers		Total Compiled Receipts		Assets		Net Deficit[2]	
		Mfg.	Reg. Util.[3]	Mfg.	Reg. Util.[3]	Mfg.	Reg. Util.[3]	Mfg.	Reg. Util.[3]
1926-29	11–13½%	40.2%	29.4%	17.1%	6.3%	19.0%	n.a.	18.2%	6.6%
1936-39	15–19	54.0	48.3	20.1	11.8	21.1	13.8%	15.9	6.3
1946-49	38	34.6	37.8	7.5	5.2	7.4	3.7	6.0	1.7
1957-60	52	39.1	38.3	10.3	2.0	9.5	2.8	7.3	1.3[4]

Source: Computed from *Statistics of Income.*

[1] Data for corporations with no net income as percentage of total for all active corporations in corresponding classification, except in case of the amount of the net deficit as explained in footnote 2. Percentage for each period is unweighted arithmetic mean of component years of period.

[2] Net deficit of corporations with no net income as per cent of net income of corporations with net income.

[3] "Individually" regulated public utilities, i.e., total utility group, excluding transportation.

[4] Average excludes 1960 (when deficits were 7 per cent of net income of companies with net income) because of distortion in that year surmised to reflect foreign expropriation losses.

stances and therefore does not meet the *ceteris paribus* condition. Nevertheless, the pattern of changes in this indicator—particularly on the basis of a comparative analysis of manufacturing and the individually regulated utilities—suggests some interesting generalizations.

In terms of receipts, assets, and the amount of the net deficit, the no-net income portion of the corporate sector has shrunk markedly in the postwar period as compared with the twenties and thirties. There has been a perceptible increase in the scope of the deficit group for manufacturing in the fifties over the forties, but the no-net sector generally remains only a fraction of its pre-war magnitude. For the utility group, however, receipts and assets of the deficit firms were relatively smaller in the fifties than in the forties. Changes in the relative number of deficit firms have followed a faintly similar pattern, but the swings have been much smaller in magnitude.

From the over-all picture the impression is inescapable that there has been a marked change in the economic environment as between the prewar and the postwar decades and that it has decreased the chances of deficit operation. This is consistent with the hypothesis of a price umbrella effect: an increase in the normal spread between costs and prices relative to what in combination with representative output levels produces a net profit.

To the extent the prewar and postwar years, or more specifically the late twenties and the late fifties, are comparable in other essential respects (pressure of aggregate demand on capacity, "temperature" of the economy, wage-price relationships, competitive structure, and other factors affecting opportunities for making profit and avoiding loss), one may suspect that an important cause of the greater cost-price spread relative to output may be shifting of the higher corporate tax in the latter period. However, in view of the contribution of national policy under the Employment Act of 1946 and the sustaining force of higher defense expenditures, it would seem reasonable to attribute a considerable part of the reduction in the no-net margin to non-tax factors. It is a matter of judgment whether

Table 23

Summary comparative analysis of net income as percentage of
receipts and net worth, for manufacturing and individually
regulated public utilities, selected periods 1926–1960

Period[1]	Applicable General Tax Rate	All Manufacturing				Public utilities excluding transportation			
		Net Income Before Taxes, as % of:		Net Income After Taxes, as % of:		Net Income Before Taxes, as % of:		Net Income After Taxes, as % of:	
		Total Compiled Receipts	Net Worth	Total Compiled Receipts	Net Worth	Total Compiled Receipts	Net Worth	Total Compiled Receipts	Net Worth
1926–29	11–13½%	5.7%	7.7%	4.8%	6.6%	13.1%	n.a.	11.3%	n.a.
1936–39	15–19	5.4	7.7	4.4	6.3	16.8	6.2%	14.5	5.4%
1946–49	38	8.6	19.1	5.3	11.8	17.1	9.1	11.4	6.1
1957–60	52	6.3	14.0	3.1	6.9	16.5	12.6	7.9	6.0
Change 1957–60 over:									
1926–29									
Amount: % Pts.		+.6	+6.3	–1.7	+.3	+3.4	n.a.	–3.4	n.a.
Percentage		+10.5	+81.8	–35.4	+4.5	+26.0		–30.1	
1936–39									
Amount: % Pts.		+.9	+6.3	–1.3	+.6	–.3	+6.4	–6.6	+.6
Percentage		+16.7	–81.8	–29.5	+9.5	–1.8	–103.2	–45.5	+11.1
1946–49									
Amount: % Pts.		–2.3	–5.1	–2.2	–4.9	–.6	+3.5	–3.5	–.1
Percentage		–26.7	–26.7	–41.7	–41.5	–3.5	+38.5	–30.7	–1.6

[1] Figures shown for periods are unweighted arithmetic means of percentages for component years.

Source: Computed from *Statistics of Income*.

the remaining relatively modest reduction in the scope of loss operations in manufacturing is reasonably proportionate to the substantial additional wedge of 38½ to 41 percentage points of corporate tax inserted between prices and costs in the interval. In making this judgment, it is important to bear in mind that 40 percentage points of tax translates into only about 2 or 3 per cent of sales and roughly 6 or 7 per cent of value added in manufacturing for the late fifties.

As has been repeatedly demonstrated, while the ratio of profits before tax to sales has varied and has risen sharply in war and boom periods, it was relatively constant as between the late twenties and the late fifties.[23] Calculations based on *Statistics of Income*, presented in Table 23, show, for example, that net income before tax was about 5.7 per cent of total compiled receipts of manufacturing corporations in the 1926–29 period and about 6.3 per cent in 1957–60, an increase of only about 11 per cent. Turnover or the ratio of receipts to equity capital in manufacturing increased by about two-thirds over the same time span.

Price versus Physical Volume

To what extent can changes in the size of the no-net sector reflecting price umbrella effects be attributed to short-run price decisions of management rather than to longer-run capital adjustments? To throw some light on this question it may be helpful to examine some of the year-to-year changes in the scope of no-net operations, profit margins, and rates of return. A brief illustrative analysis of these and related changes in production, prices, and wage rates for 1949–54 is shown below:

In 1950, the receipts of the no-net group in manufacturing dropped to 4.7 per cent of the total, compared with 10.6 per cent in 1949. The percentage then rose to 5 or 6 per cent in each of the following 3 years (1951–53). The sharp rise in rate of profit on receipts and net worth from 1949 to 1950 was associated with an 11 percentage point or 17 per cent rise in manufacturing production but only a 3 percentage point or less

[23] See, for example, the summary analysis in (5), pp. 1584–1585.

Manufacturing corporations

	Receipts of No-Net Income Corporations as Per Cent of Total	Net Income before Tax as Per Cent of: Total Compiled Net Worth	Net Income before Tax as Per Cent of: Receipts	Manufacturing Industrial Production Index	Industrial Wholesale Price Index 1957–59 = 100	Index of Adjusted Hourly Earnings, Mfg.
1949	10.6%	16.0%	7.6%	65	80.0	66.1
1950	4.7	24.4	10.8	76	82.9	68.2
1951	5.3	23.7	9.7	82	91.5	73.6
1952	6.4	18.6	7.8	85	89.4	77.4
1953	6.1	19.6	7.6	93	90.1	81.6
1954	10.5	15.3	6.8	86	90.4	84.3

Sources: Manufacturing Production Index (Board of Governors of the Federal Reserve System), Industrial Wholesale Price Index (Department of Labor), and Index of Adjusted Hourly Earnings in Manufacturing Industries (Department of Labor) from 1962 Supplement to Economic Indicators, Joint Economic Committee, 87th Cong, 2nd Sess., pp. 53, 92, and 48, respectively. Other data computed from *Statistics of Income*.

than 4 per cent rise in the industrial wholesale price index. While the rise in profit margins coincided closely with the price rise, it must be noted that the average hourly wage index also increased 2.1 percentage points or over 3 per cent.

In 1951, the wholesale industrial price index rose about 9 percentage points or 11 per cent as against an increase in the manufacturing production index of only 6 points or less than 8 per cent, but profitability decreased and the no-net sector increased.

Profitability is the resultant of both physical volume and prices. Profits in the short run seem to have been more closely correlated with volume of physical output than with prices. In the short run, wage changes seem to be an important factor. It is my tentative conclusion, advanced here without the elaborate empirical backing which it obviously requires, that the observed short-run variations in the no-net group which may be attributed to some kind of price umbrella effect is not the result of arbitrary year-to-year price changes but to a constellation of price-output-cost changes reflecting economic conditions not entirely under the conscious control of management.[24]

Price Umbrella Effect More Clearcut in Regulated Utility Field

As shown in Table 22 above, the price umbrella effect seems to have been relatively greater for the regulated public utilities than for manufacturing. Between 1926–29 and 1957–60, the deficit corporation share of total compiled receipts dropped from 17.1 per cent to 10.3 per cent for all manufacturing (a decrease of about 40 per cent); for the utility group (excluding transportation) the deficit group share of receipts declined from 6.3 per cent to 2.0 per cent (a decrease of nearly 70 per cent). Moreover, the decline in the deficit group continued in the utility industry between 1946–49 and 1957–60, presumably reflecting the Korean rate increase. In manufacturing, the trend

[24] In a non-profit maximizing situation management may plan both price and output. However, the actual earnings outcome for the year as a whole will be uncertain, if for no other reason, because of macroeconomic factors.

was reversed in the late fifties. Granting the pitfalls of the implicit *ceteris paribus* assumption, it would seem that any shifting or price umbrella effect which can be deduced from the shrinkage of the no-net category was more complete and effective in the utility area where it may be presumed to take place by relatively specific adjustments of consumer service charges.

Secondary Price Umbrella Effects on Unincorporated Enterprise

It might be expected that a tax shifting price umbrella effect in the corporate sector would communicate itself to the non-corporate sector in two ways: (1) by creating a more favorable cost-price-output constellation which would tend to reduce the scope of deficit operations within the non-corporate sector and (2) by improving the competitive situation for non-corporate enterprise as a whole, which would benefit from a higher price structure without being subject to the corporate tax, this being reflected in relative expansion of the non-corporate sector itself.[25]

Table 24 presents a summary comparison of the deficit area of manufacturing operations, measured in terms of receipts, for corporations, sole proprietorships, and partnerships for selected years 1939–60. While there are superficial similarities in the pattern of variation for the three sectors, the partnership sector developments seem more similar to the corporate than those shown for sole proprietorships. However, unlike the corporate deficit area which has shrunk in the postwar period compared with 1939, the deficit group of sole proprietorships and partnerships has expanded, measured in terms of receipts.

There has been no relative expansion of the non-corporate business sector in the postwar period at least. On the contrary,

[25] If the previous interpretation of Krzyzaniak and Musgrave is correct that the important manufacturing firms face very inelastic demand curves, it follows that because of aggregate demand constraints the unincorporated sector may lose sales when the stronger corporate sector raises prices. If this is the case, the price umbrella effect would work in just the opposite direction from that suggested by the conventional argument. I am indebted to Mr. Gerard M. Brannon and Mr. George E. Lent for comments and suggestions on this point.

Table 24
Receipts of firms without net profit as a percentage of the total, for manufacturing

	Corporations	Sole Proprietorships	Partnerships
1939	14.3%	9.6%	4.5%
1945	5.6	6.9	2.8
1947	4.9	11.2	5.8
1949	10.6	14.2	n.a.
1951	5.3	9.8	n.a.
1953	6.1	9.1	7.8
1955	5.9	9.3	n.a.
1957	9.7	19.1	11.9
1958	11.1	12.4	12.4
1959	9.1	9.0	9.2
1960	11.4	11.3	10.9

Source: Computed from *Statistics of Income.*

corporate growth has outstripped that of unincorporated enterprise. As shown in Table 25, while total corporate receipts more than tripled between 1945 and 1960, those of sole proprietorships only a little more than doubled; in the same period, corporate net income doubled while that of the sole proprietorships increased about 75 per cent. Partnership growth has been still smaller.[26]

Table 25
Comparative growth of corporate and non-corporate sectors
All industrial divisions
($ Billions)

Year	Sole Proprietorships		Active Partnerships		Active Corporations	
	Business Receipts	Net Profit[1]	Business Receipts	Net Profit[1]	Total Compiled Receipts	Net Income[1]
1945	$ 79.0	$12.1	$47.5	$6.8	$255.4	$21.1
1951	131.9	16.6	n.a.	n.a.	517.0	43.5
1960	171.3	21.1	72.8	8.4	849.1	43.5

[1] Less net loss or net deficit.

Sources: *Statistics of Income.* Proprietorship and Partnership data from *U.S. Business Tax Returns,* 1960–61, U.S. Treasury Department, Internal Revenue Service, pp. 130 and 135.

[26] In order to save taxes there was apparently a fairly large flight from the corporate to the partnership form during World War II, which may affect comparisons with 1945.

Our findings with respect to secondary price umbrella effects on non-corporate enterprise therefore tend to be negative.

Comparative Earnings Experience of Manufacturing and "Individually Regulated" Public Utilities

The comparative earnings experience of the regulated public utilities presents intriguing possibilities for the incidence investigator. (E.g., [11], pp. 51–52.) The reasonable rate of return on investment which they are allowed to earn (usually 6 per cent or so on equity) is determined net after taxes. While earnings may rise slightly above or fall below the standard level because the regulatory commissions may not adjust rates promptly or precisely, or because utilities may be unable to earn a specified return at profit-maximizing rates of service charge, they nevertheless represent a substantial area of industry in which the corporate tax is quite effectively shifted. This is particularly true of the utilities whose rates are regulated on an individual company basis: the electric, gas, telephone, water, and similar service corporations, as distinct from the transportation industry.

Some observers have been interested in the regulated utilities as an alternative investment outlet which along with other escape hatches would afford a shifting mechanism for the corporate tax generally. (See [20], p. 320.) Our present interest is in the behavior of their earnings position compared with other fields, particularly manufacturing, in periods of substantial tax increases, as a benchmark for shifting processes in ordinary industry.

Looking at the earnings experience of the regulated public utilities over the past three decades, summarized in Table 23 and shown on an annual basis in Appendix II–D, it is apparent that the pre-tax earnings rates on equity investment have almost steadily risen with the increases in corporate income tax so that the after-tax earnings rate has been substantially preserved. This is clearly shown for the rise in the general corporate rate from 38 per cent to 52 per cent between the forties and the fifties, as well as in the previous rise in tax between the thirties and the forties.

Rates of return in manufacturing rose in the forties over the twenties and thirties by more than enough to shift the tax involved in the historic rates of return. As a consequence, after-tax rates of return rose to nearly 12 per cent in the computations shown in Table 23, as compared with the 6½ per cent standard of the prior two benchmark periods. However, when tax rates were increased in the fifties, pre-tax returns declined, so that after-tax returns were reduced to a level only slightly above the twenties and thirties.

Manufacturing thus does not show the clear and consistent pattern of tax shifting (or regulation in peak earnings periods) disclosed by the regulated utility experience. There has not been demonstrated a clear pushing up of the gross rate of return manufacturing to preserve after-tax norms such as occurred in the case of the utilities. It is true that the after-tax rate of return of manufacturing corporations may be interpreted as showing resistance to compression below historic norms which in turn may be regarded as some kind of target or investment-limiting figure. But there has not been sufficient time to test the resistance of such a norm, and there may never be a real test in the laboratory of history since conditions have changed, investment incentives were introduced in 1962 to partially neutralize the 52 per cent corporate tax rate, and reductions in the general tax rate to 48 per cent have now been adopted by the Congress.

Use of Turnover rather than Price Increases to Pay Tax: Manufacturing vs. Utilities

As shown in Table 23, both manufacturing and the regulated utilities have maintained after-tax rates of return on net worth with relatively small increases in pre-tax profit margins on receipts and appreciable decreases in after-tax margins. While some of this may be a money illusion phenomenon, reflecting, among other things, the lag in the adjustment of book capital to current prices, much of it reflects increased turnover and the well-known decline in the capital-output ratio.[27]

[27] A perceptible contributing factor to the increase in the ratio of receipts to net worth has been the rise in the ratio of long-term debt to equity, illustrated in the following tabulation:

Ratio of long-term debt to net worth

	1950	1959
All Industries	29.3%	36.7%
Manufacturing	12.7	19.8
Utilities, excluding Transportation	82.4	87.4

Source: Computed from data in *Statistics of Income*

Both manufacturing and utilities displayed a somewhat similar overall pattern of adjustment, as shown in Table 23. However, with the exception of the comparison of 1957–60 margins with 1936–39, the utilities displayed appreciably smaller proportionate cuts in their after-tax margins on receipts and greater proportionate increases in their before-tax margins (see percentage change analysis, lower half of Table 23). The implication would seem to be that in the utilities case greater reliance was placed on overt price changes to meet increased taxes and less reliance on more intensive utilization of capital or reduction in capital inputs relative to other factors, than in the case of the manufacturing industries.

Undoubtedly, the general trend towards higher receipts relative to capital facilitated the task of the regulatory agencies in enabling the utilities to earn a reasonable after-tax return on capital. The same condition made it easier for manufacturing corporations to absorb higher taxes from increased turnover, without specific price increases which increased the profit margin or sales, for that purpose. Nevertheless, when deflationary forces gripped the economy, the utilities' greater ability to rely on controlled consumer rates specifically designed to pass on the corporate tax and leave a specified rate of return on investment made itself felt even in the short run. A year-to-year comparison of manufacturing and utility earnings rates is presented in Appendix II–D. In the recession of 1958, for example, after-tax rates of return on equity for the utilities dropped only from 6.0 to 5.8 per cent; in manufacturing, the decline was from 7.7 to 5.8 per cent. The same phenomenon appears in the 1938 recession and in other periods. This is due in part to the greater cyclical stability of demand for utility services. Nevertheless, a certain proportion of utility rates are in process of review and adjustment each year, and the chances that the decision will be made in the utility's favor would be greater if its earnings were currently unfavorable.

DIFFERENTIAL BURDEN ON CORPORATE EARNINGS: KEY TO THE ENIGMA OF CORPORATE TAX INCIDENCE

Past attempts to ascertain shifting and incidence of the corporate income tax have been conceptually directed at the wrong thing. This may not have affected the empirical results but it has affected their interpretation. Generally speaking, the time series investigations that led to the conflict of the earnings rate and profit share indicators implicitly assumed that shifting of the tax called for an increase in the pre-tax earnings rate or profit share which would leave the after-tax earnings position intact at the corporate level. In this over-simplified view, an investment by the corporation which would normally require an 8 per cent return would, assuming full shifting, be made only if it promised to yield 16 per cent subject to approximately a 50 per cent tax. In fact, however, the corporate tax must be viewed in the context of a general system of income taxation. Harberger, Stockfisch, and others have called attention to the fact that if shifting of the corporate tax occurs as an investment response to equalize the rate of return to capital in various alternative uses (with proper allowance for risk and tax differentials), only a fraction of the corporate tax itself would have to be shifted in order to eliminate any substantive differential burden on corporate equity earnings (as against non-corporate business profits, interest on debt, rent, and so forth). (See [23], pp. 349–351.) Shifting of the whole tax or even the bulk of it would tend to create a relative tax advantage for corporate equity investment which could hardly be overlooked by what is sometimes characterized as the "never-ceasing pressure of funds seeking employment" ([19], p. 2).

Burden of Proof on the 100 Per Cent Shifting Thesis

While I would not wish to fall into the trap of Palmstrom logic which Krzyzaniak and Musgrave so appropriately cite (p 46, n. 4), a heavy burden of proof rests upon those who would assert theoretically or ascertain empirically that the whole corporate tax is shifted, let alone more than 100 per cent of the tax, or indeed any fraction of the tax in excess of the differential, as appraised in the collective eye of the capital market. To assert this thesis is tantamount to saying that heavy corporate income taxation itself has made corporate equity investment relatively advantageous. Assume 100 per cent shifting of the corporate tax, as such, at the corporate level so that after-tax rates of return are maintained intact. This would imply not only that dividend distributions were free of any substantive double tax, but also that an opportunity existed for reinvestment of retained earnings essentially without corporate or individual tax burden other than capital gains tax on disposition of appreciated shares. While non-corporate business investment might be considered to be able to withstand the competition of partially "tax-free" corporate investment opportunities by living under the shelter of higher prices and profit margins created by corporate tax shifting, bonds and other debt or contractual forms of investment would be at serious tax disadvantage. As a consequence, interest, rent, etc. would tend to be increased to balance the tax status of corporate equity rewards. Without this equalization, capital would migrate to the corporate equity field away from the "untaxed" uses.

This model of the economy seems implausible. It seems inconsistent with the squeeze on corporate equity returns in general which occurred as the 52 per cent rate became increasingly burdensome after the steam went out of the economy in the late fifties. It suggests that the corporate tax tended to raise interest rates, contrary to the more plausible view that the impact of the tax has been diffused and reflected in lower interest or "capitalization" rates. It may suggest that the real effect of the Krzyzaniak-Musgrave short-term shifting would be a diffused upwards thrust on property incomes unless the economy is considered to be tolerant of substantial investment return differentials for an extended period.[28]

[28] If this upwards thrust on other investment returns also involved general price increases, it would present once again the problem of where the money demand comes from.

Krzyzaniak-Musgrave Findings on the Differential

As we have seen, Krzyzaniak and Musgrave did not flinch at steering a collision course with the differential view of corporate tax incidence any more than with the many other cherished beliefs of neoclassical theory. Their conclusion was that the differential approach did not jibe with the behavior of the economy for two reasons (pp. 57–58):

1) The coefficient for the lagged differential tax variable was insignificant, as was the case for the lagged total corporate tax liability variable.

2) Unlagged, the differential showed a higher degree of shifting (180 per cent) than the whole corporate tax (145 per cent) in the comparable test,[29] but R was lower, error greater, and significance less.

I cannot regard this test of the differential theory as conclusive.

Krzyzaniak and Musgrave treat the differential as a single figure computed as the difference between the combined corporate and individual marginal tax rate on equity income and the individual marginal tax rate on dividends for the average shareholder (Table 3–1, pp. 28–29). Actually, the differential in any year is a whole array of differentials, varying in amount and in algebraic sign, depending on the income bracket of the shareholder. The positive differential may be minimized, or the negative differential maximized, by tailoring the stockholder's holdings to the distribution-retention policy of the corporation. Tax differentials of this type, like the value of the tax exemption reflected in the yield differential on state and local securities, are subject to a process of market evaluation.

Quantitatively, Krzyzaniak and Musgrave measured the nominal differential against the average corporate equity investor as ranging between a negative $\frac{7}{10}$ of 1 percentage point (1947) and a positive 34 per cent (1942) in the years covered

[29] This compares initial period shifting shown in line 11, Table 7–1, pp. 54–55 with that shown in line 1, Table 6–1, pp. 44–45.

by their study. In the late fifties, their differential ran consistently at about 17½ percentage points, or only 8 or 9 percentage points higher than in the late thirties. While the Krzyzaniak-Musgrave method of computing the differential on an average basis seems reasonable, its results over time bear only a general resemblance to those of Holland. Their measure of the differential in 1940 as compared with 1952, for example, seems quite different from that suggested by Holland's figures.[30]

The actual behavior of the differential is of necessity erratic since it varies directly with the corporate tax rate, inversely with the applicable individual tax rate, and generally inversely with the proportion of earnings retained for reinvestment. It is difficult to determine what kind of lagging is appropriate to estimate the effect of the swirling cross-currents of varying burdens and benefits confronting different income-levels investors in any year computed at past, present, and prospective constellations of the pertinent variables. The inclusion of temporary excess profits taxes in the computation of the differential as in the whole Krzyzaniak-Musgrave analysis may have further affected the significance of the lagging procedure.

Difficulty of Econometric Treatment of the Differential

The differential concept of the motivating force behind shifting not only is consistent with marginality and profit maximization, but also helps to explain the impasse reached in empirical studies.

As we have seen, the differential is only a fraction of the corporation income tax: at 17½ percentage points as measured by Krzyzaniak and Musgrave for the average shareholder in the late fifties it was roughly one-third of the prevailing 52 per cent corporate tax rate. If the search for the effects of the full corporate tax has led to conflict and bafflement, it is evident

---

[30] See summary comparison of 1940 and 1952 differentials in (15), p. 63, which indicates a decrease in the differential in 1952 over 1940 at income levels accounting for the bulk of dividends. Krzyzaniak and Musgrave, on the other hand, show almost a tripling of the differential for the average stockholder between these two years.

that it is even more difficult to identify the repercussions of a much smaller tax factor.[31]

It is recognized, of course, that shifting of a differential of, say, 20 per cent under a 52 per cent corporate tax could easily involve blowing up profits at the zero-tax level by some $2\frac{1}{2}$ times that percentage, or by roughly 50 per cent of the original profit level depending on the rate of profits retention,[32] the extent to which higher bracket investors matched their own tax situation by selecting stocks of corporations with high retention ratios, and many other factors. Still, the impact which could be expected is much more likely to be submerged in the complex of economic events than is the gross doubling of earnings rates and profit shares which would reflect full shifting of the corporate tax as such.

Offsets against the Differential

One would not expect a nominal tax differential of 20 per cent to be fully subject to shifting even if the forces making

[31] It may be relevant to note that Krzyzaniak and Musgrave found 180 per cent current-year shifting of the differential as against 123 per cent shifting of the entire tax on the equity base. Cf. lines 1 and 11, Table 7–1, pp. 54–55. These results are numerically inconsistent since 180 per cent of, say, $17\frac{1}{2}$ percentage points is only about half of 123 per cent of 52 percentage points. They imply quite different impacts in pushing up the gross rate of return before tax on equity investment. This underscores the impressionistic nature of the outcome of multiple regressions of this character. I wish to thank Mr. Murray Brown, Office of Business Economics, U.S. Commerce Department, for helpful consultation on this point as well as on the validity of the "economic pressure variable" experiment previously presented in Table 21.

[32] The illustrative figures cited are based on the following simplified analysis. Let us assume a differential against corporate earnings of 20 per cent, resulting from a 50 per cent corporate tax, a 40 per cent individual income tax on dividends, and a distribution ratio of half of corporate earnings after tax. In accordance with the familiar formulation, disregarding capital gains tax complications, the differential $D = r$ plus $R [d(1\text{-}r) - 1]$

where r is the corporate rate,
R the individual rate,
and d the distribution ratio.

Only if corporate earnings of $100 in the absence of tax were blown up by 50 per cent to $150 or $2\frac{1}{2}$ times the 20 per cent differential would the corporate investor be in the same after-tax position as the recipient of $100 of interest. This simplified example assumes that $1 of reinvested earnings are as valuable to the investor as $1 of cash. After a 40 per cent tax, the interest receiver has $60 net income. After a 50 per cent corporate tax on $150, the corporation has $75, of which it retains $37.50 and pays out $37.50 dividends. After a 40 per cent individual tax the stockholder has $22.50 net dividends, which together with his $37.50 retained earnings give him a $60 net increment, equivalent, on the assumptions given, to the net gain to the bondholder.

for shifting were in full operation.[33] The advantages of the corporate form, the advantages of size and market power associated with it, the convenience of corporate equity investment as an inflation hedge, and the promise of relatively trouble free automatic growth, all tend to render corporate equity investment attractive vis à vis debt or non-corporate enterprise and compensate for some tax differential. For the high-income investor, a dollar of retained corporate earnings reinvested in a manner which is at least as satisfactory to the stockholder as any other commitments he could make with the same funds may be worth as much as $10 of taxable interest income. Even if the original corporate earnings are reduced by half through corporate taxation, the corporate equity with complete reinvestment of earnings may be five times as attractive tax-wise as an equivalent dollar investment in taxable bonds. An important and strategic sector of the demand for corporate equities is in the same qualitative position although the multiples expressing this advantage may be lower.

Stockfisch has pointed out that, since property taxes generally impose relatively light obligations on manufacturing assets, property taxes may have an effect opposite to that of the corporate tax on tax differentials and on capital allocation between the corporate and non-corporate sectors.[34]

Denison has also observed that calculations of the Harberger-type differential which do not take the state and local property taxes into account may be misleading. Denison calculated the real property tax, based on 1956–57 assessments, at 22 per cent of income from real property if the rate of return is 6 per cent (or 17 per cent if the return is 8 per cent). Since the property

[33] A part of the nominal differential—apparently some 5 percentage points as measured by Krzyzaniak and Musgrave—antedated 1935, the first year of their coverage, and may have been built into the pre-existing structure of earnings rates. While this is a general observation applicable not only to the status of the pre-1935 tax, the fact that the Krzyzaniak-Musgrave model does not really separate out short-run effects (with the exception of their one differencing experiment) or abstract from the long run (since last year's shifting would presumably carry over to the current year) may account for some of its difficulties in measuring the lagged differential impact.

[34] See J. A. Stockfisch, "The Capitalization, Allocation, and Investment Effects of Asset Taxation," *The Southern Economic Journal*, Vol. XXII, No. 3 (January 1956), pp. 317–329.

tax bears more heavily on real estate and agricultural invest-
ments characterized by the non-corporate form, it may cancel
much of the nominal differential against corporate equities.
(See [6], p. 187.)

A Speculation

While Krzyzaniak and Musgrave found current overshifting
of the differential (without allowance for inflation) they conceded that their 100 per cent shifting measure for the whole
tax after inflation adjustment overstates the degree of shifting
by a substantial margin due to correlation of taxes and expenditures. With allowance for statistical error, partial inefficacy of
the instrumental variable approach, incomplete adjustment for
inflation, and inadequacies of the profit model previously
discussed, I suspect that the remaining modest shifting tendency
disclosed—whether it be regarded as short or long run in
character—could be reconciled with the differential theory.

A DYNAMIC INTERPRETATION

The shifting and incidence of the corporate income tax
cannot be judged in terms of any single indicator or in static
timeless terms. Rather, they must be appraised in relation to
an overall picture and a dynamic course of economic change
which contain the rapid ascent of the profits tax rate.

Most analyses of incidence approach this, however, in the
abstract using essentially static concepts. This is true of empirical investigators, and of times-series and multiple-regression
technicians who, alike, seek a single answer to corporate tax
shifting and incidence regardless of the dynamic course of
events into which corporate tax increases are injected.

Corporate Tax Increases Sustained by Profit Increases

In the absence of a general upwards movement in corporate
earnings due to economic conditions, the application of a substantial increase in the corporation income tax is something of
an abstraction. The large corporate tax increases of the past

30 years have generally been imposed on rising earnings trends for industry. Most of the increases of World War II and the Korean conflict absorbed part but not all of large increases in profits generated by defense spending and inflationary pressures.

Initially designed in part to reach retained corporate earnings as part of a general system of income taxation, the corporate tax entered a new phase after 1936 when coordination of corporate and individual taxes was removed and rates began their upward climb. Capacity to pay was aided first by the recovery from the Great Depression and then by the quickening impulse of defense activities. The differential tax on corporate earnings was kept moderate because of the accompanying increases in the individual tax schedule.

Since the late thirties, the corporate tax has in its various historic phases been sustained by the wartime and postwar boom, which temporarily boosted corporate profits, partly because of the relative shortage of productive facilities and the new prospects of sustained economic growth under the Employment Act of 1946. The real squeeze on profits and the resulting shifting force of increased corporate taxes was felt not when the increases were initially enacted and applied, but as the economy "subsided" and the higher tax gradually bore down upon more normal earning levels. Once having absorbed wartime inflationary margins of profit into regular corporate rates which embodied an element of excess profits taxation, the corporate tax structure by the middle fifties was left holding the tail of a bear which soon turned into straw. Even though the nominal differential against corporate earnings was moderate and the real differential was even less, the total burden on the corporate sector, the heart of the modern industrial economy, was an anachronism.

While the 52 per cent rate was not reduced for more than a decade, recognition was given to its untenability for the long run. To neutralize the impact of the tax on both returns and the rate of investment essential to growth, tax policy depended on a series of features. Depreciation was liberalized in 1954, and in 1962 depreciation guideline lives were shortened and investment credit legislation was enacted pending the major tax reduction legislation of 1964.

Dynamics of Subsidence

Even into the late fifties we witnessed the pre-tax earnings rates of public utilities varying directly with the level of taxation. For manufacturing and corporate industry generally, the problem posed by the historic data is whether the tax has prevented a larger or more rapid decline in profits in recent years than would otherwise have occurred in a lower-tax environment. The dynamics of subsidence in this instance have been complicated by the introduction of incentive features which have had important effects on the true effective rate of tax, after-tax profitability, and cash flow. The full moment of truth needed to test the "resistance level" theory that the corporate economy will pass on taxes which compress returns to the corporation or its investors below certain minimums, has been postponed, let us hope, indefinitely.

"Resistance" versus "Virtual Earnings Increase"
Theories of Shifting

As the above rehearsal of events suggests, there are two distinct theories concerning the clues to the evidence of the shifting of the corporation income tax and its mechanism. One (implicitly embraced by the time-series investigators) is that shifting occurs if the corporate tax invades a basic minimum net return. This concept is akin to Keynes' favorite old saw "John Bull can stand anything but 3 per cent." What happens when economic conditions permit a pre-tax return sufficiently high to exceed the after-tax minimum is less clear, and presumably these interpreters do not assert that shifting necessarily takes place under these conditions. Their relatively simple and straightforward construct does not provide a dynamic moving norm (higher in prosperous periods, lower in less favorable times) against which to gauge actual results. They merely have the historic norms of the twenties or thirties, which can be invoked only when actual results show resistance, or fail to show resistance, to tax compression below that level.

The other more complex behavioral theory is that tax shifting occurs in the form of a virtual increase in pre-tax rates of return at all levels of earnings, that it further inflates already high earnings in boom periods, and that it somehow sustains and boosts abnormally low levels of earnings even in depressed periods. This type of theory, with its overtones of cost-push inflation, underlies the Krzyzaniak-Musgrave approach, which furnishes a dynamic norm against which to appraise earnings results in the light of corporate tax rates in all except the most abnormal circumstances.

CONCLUSION

Krzyzaniak and Musgrave have conducted an important exercise in taking econometric soundings of the short-run correlations between the corporate tax factor and the rate of return on investment. However, what they have captured is a combination of the known collinearity of profitability and profits tax levels in the period of observation (particularly in view of the inclusion of loss companies and excess profits tax in their tax variable) and assumptions of normal profit behavior in their profit equation with which reasonable men and competent experts may disagree. Their model is a highly pragmatic or "econometric" formulation without a strong theoretical rationale. The model represents a special case of one general model of the economy and thus requires a special defense that other experimental equations with equal or greater economic justification would alter or reverse their results has been demonstrated by our economic pressure variable experiment.

After allowance for these factors and for the overstatement of the uptrends in earnings rates due to inflation, there would probably remain only a modest residual reflecting a measure of reserve market power in the manufacturing sector of the economy. The result is not a plausible single answer to the empirical question of corporation tax shifting in the short run. It does not seem to justify a wholesale jettison of the profit-maximizing assumption of neoclassical theory. Neither does it resolve the more basic issue of the impact of the corporate tax on investment and growth in the long run under the conditions we face now and in the future as distinct from the emergency and inflationary periods which accounted for much of their time coverage.

Since so much of the foregoing may seem to have a monotonously critical tone, a final word is in order. Despite its flaws and inconclusiveness, the Krzyzaniak-Musgrave study is an important pioneer effort. It has broken new ground and will certainly provoke new and increasingly fruitful econometric approaches to incidence questions.

Appendix II-A
Richard E. Slitor
Simple Correlation Matrix
All Years 1935–42, 1948–59
(All Manufacturing, Total Capital Base)

Variables	$Y_{g,t}$	L_t	Delta C_{t-1}	V_{t-1}	J_t
L_t	.95				
Delta C_{t-1}	−.01	−.10			
V_{t-1}	−.65	−.64	−.19		
J_t	.18	.33	.38	−.59	
P_t	.93	.95	−.03	−.75	.42

Comment: This matrix shows that the correlation between P_t and $Y_{g,t}$ is almost as great as that between L_t and $Y_{g,t}$. It clearly reflects the high degree of collinearity of P_t and L_t. In an economy characterized by a large number of intercorrelated variables, statistical results are never entirely free of bias due to hidden correlation. However, the omission of such an important variable as the economic pressure variable P_t, collinear with the tax variable L_t on which interest is focused in the Krzyzaniak-Musgrave inquiry, significantly affects the results.

Appendix II-B
Average Contribution of Variables
(Average Value of Variable X Regression Coefficient)

Equation	$Y_{g,t}$ =	Intercept +	Delta C_{t-1} +	V_{t-1} +	J_t +	L_t +	P_t
1.	.1462	.2683	−.0036	−.0868	−.1211	.0895	
2.	.1462	−.3884	−.0032	−.0128	−.1287		.6794
3.	.1462	.0079	−.0037	−.0478	−.1244	.0598	.2544

Note: Owing to rounding, intercept and variables may not add exactly to $Y_{g,t}$.

Key: Equation 1 is standard Model A, total capital base, least squares method (K&M, No. 6, Table 6–1, pp. 44–45), as re-run with rounded data (2, Table 1).
Equation 2 is #1 with P_t substituted for L_t.
Equation 3 is #1 with P_t added to list of independent variables.

Measure of the Individual Importance of
the Independent Variables: Beta Coefficients

Equation	Intercept	Delta C_{t-1}	V_{t-1}	$\mathcal{J}_t$	L_t	P_t
1.	0	.1615	−.2041	−.3091	.9372	
2.	0	.1430	−.0302	−.3283		1.0524
3.	0	.1640	−.1123	−.3173	.6259	.3941

Note: Beta = Regression coefficient times the ratio of the standard deviation of the independent variable to the standard deviation of the dependent variable.

Appendix II-C

1. *Snowballing or Multiple Effect of Tax Shifting.*

Let the multiple effect $M = \dfrac{Y_g}{Y'_{g,t}} = $ ratio of the pretax rate of return after shifting to the rate of return in the absence of tax.

Then $M = \dfrac{1}{1 - Z * S} = $ reciprocal of the complement of the cross-product of the effective rate of tax and the Krzyzaniak-Musgrave shifting measure S (gross formulation).

Derivation:

(1) $\dfrac{Y_{g,t} - Y'_{g,t}}{Z_t * Y_{g,t}} = S$ (by definition)

(2) $Y_{g,t} - Y'_{g t} = Z_t * Y_{g,t} S$

(3) $1 - \dfrac{Y'_{g,t}}{Y_{g,t}} = Z_t * S$

(4) $-\dfrac{Y'_{g,t}}{Y_{g,t}} = Z * S - 1$

(5) $\dfrac{Y'_{g,t}}{Y_{g,t}} = 1 - Z_t * S$

(6) $\dfrac{Y_{g,t}}{Y'_{g,t}} = M = \dfrac{1}{1 - Z_t * S}$

2. *Illustrations of Snowballing Effects of Shifting for Selected Rates of Return with Zero Tax and Estimated Degrees of Shifting*

50 Per Cent Tax Rate

Estimated Degree of Shifting	1	1.25	1.33	1.4	1.5	1.67	2.
Multiple	2	2.67	3.	3.33	4.	6.	inf.

Rates of Return after Shifting

Base of Return with Zero Tax							
5%	10%	13.3 %	15%	16.67%	20%	30%	inf. %
10	20	26.67	30	33.33	40	60	inf.
15	30	40	45	50	60	90	inf.

Appendix II-D

Comparison of Rates of Return on Net Worth in All Industries, Manufacturing, and Public Utilities Excluding Transportation (Before and After Tax 1930–1960)

Corporations

	All Industries		Manufacturing		Utilities	
	Before Tax	After Tax	Before Tax	After Tax	Before Tax	After Tax
1930	1.0%	.5%	2.1%	1.4%	3.0%	2.6%
1931	−2.3	−2.6	−1.7	−2.1	2.3	1.9
1932	−4.2	−4.4	−4.1	−4.3	1.4	1.0
1933	−2.0	−2.3	.5	−*	1.1	0.7
1934	.1	−.4	2.6	1.9	3.1	2.6
1935	1.2	.7	4.8	3.9	3.5	2.9
1936	5.5	4.6	9.6	8.0	5.8	5.1
1937	5.2	4.3	9.0	7.4	7.5	6.5
1938	2.7	2.0	3.9	2.9	5.2	4.5
1939	4.9	4.0	8.4	6.9	6.4	5.5
1940	6.4	4.6	12.0	8.5	7.4	5.7
1941	11.5	6.4	21.5	11.3	8.4	5.5
1942	16.5	7.7	24.8	9.8	8.8	5.2
1943	19.1	8.2	27.3	10.0	9.9	4.9
1944	17.5	7.6	23.5	8.7	9.7	5.1
1945	13.7	6.7	16.0	6.5	9.3	5.0
1946	15.3	9.9	17.3	10.5	9.8	6.6
1947	17.4	11.3	21.7	13.5	8.5	5.7
1948	17.5	11.4	21.5	13.4	8.9	6.0
1949	13.5	8.8	16.0	9.8	9.3	6.0
1950	19.1	11.3	24.4	13.5	11.2	6.7
1951	18.2	9.0	23.7	10.2	12.4	6.4
1952	15.1	7.6	18.6	8.1	12.5	6.2
1953	14.9	7.4	19.6	8.1	12.8	6.3
1954	13.0	7.0	15.4	7.3	12.3	6.0
1955	15.5	8.4	19.9	9.9	13.5	6.6
1956	14.3	7.8	17.7	8.9	12.9	6.3
1957	12.9	6.9	15.5	7.7	12.3	6.0
1958	10.4	5.3	11.9	5.8	12.0	5.8
1959	12.0	6.2	15.4	7.8	13.1	6.4
1960	10.6	5.3	13.1	6.4	12.8	5.9

*Less than .1 percent.

Source: Computed from *Statistics of Income*.

Note: Rates of return represent the net income (less deficit) of the current year as a percentage of net worth from balance sheets as of the end of the same year. This may tend to understate rates of return slightly relative to those computed on an average or mid-year net worth.

Acknowledgment: These and other computations from *Statistics of Income* data were made by Miss Florence M. Roberts, with the helpful advice of Miss Mary Little of the Statistics Division, Internal Revenue Service.

BIBLIOGRAPHY

1. Adelman, M. A. "Reply" and "Rejoinder" (to Arnold Zellner *re* "The Corporate Income Tax in the Long Run: A Comment,") *Journal of Political Economy*, Vol. LXVI, No. 5 (October 1958).
2. Clendenin, John C. "Effect of Corporate Income Taxes on Corporate Earnings," *Taxes*, Vol. XXIV (June 1956).
3. Committee for Economic Development, Research and Policy Committee. "Reducing Tax Rates for Production and Growth," A Statement on National Policy by the Research and Policy Committee, December 1962.
4. *Company Taxation in Western Europe*, 3d rev. ed., Rotterdam: R. Mees and Zoonen, 1962 (published in cooperation with the International Bureau of Fiscal Documentation).
5. Darling, Paul G. "Income Taxation and Dividend Income," *Tax Revision Compendium*, Committee on Ways and Means, U. S. House of Representatives, Vol. 3, Washington: U. S. Government Printing Office, 1959.
6. Denison, Edward F. *The Sources of Economic Growth in the United States and the Alternatives Before Us*, Committee for Economic Development, Supplementary Paper No. 13, January 1962.
7. Eckstein, Otto (with the assistance of Vito Tanzi). Contribution to *The Role of Direct and Indirect Taxes in the Federal Revenue System*, Studies of Government Finance, The Brookings Institution. Princeton: Princeton University Press, 1964.
8. Elwell, Edwin S., and Arthur R. Upgren. "Why the Corporation Income Tax Should be Abolished," Bulletin 15, Series on American Capitalism, Macalester College, St. Paul, 1962.
9. Federal Trade Commission. *Report of the Federal Trade Commission on Rates of Return for Identical Companies in Selected Manufacturing Industries*, 1940, 1947–58. Washington, D. C.
10. Fromm, Gary. "Inventories, Business Cycles and Economic Stabilization," *Inventory Fluctuations and Economic Stabilization*, Part IV, Joint Economic Committee, U. S. Congress. Washington: U. S. Government Printing Office, 1962.
11. Goode, Richard. *The Corporation Income Tax*. New York: John Wiley & Sons, 1951.
12. Hall, Challis A., Jr. "Direct Shifting and the Taxation of Corporate Profits in Manufacturing 1919–1959," Proceedings of the American Economic Associations, 1963.
13. Harberger, Arnold C. "The Corporation Income Tax: An Empirical Appraisal," *Tax Revision Compendium*, Ways and Means Committee, U. S. House of Representatives, Vol. I. Washington: U. S. Government Printing Office, 1959.
14. ———. "The Incidence of the Corporation Income Tax," *Journal of Political Economy*, Vol. LXX, No. 3 (June 1962).

15. Holland, Daniel M. *The Income-Tax Burden on Stockholders*, National Bureau of Economic Research Study. Princeton: Princeton University Press, 1958.
16. Johnston, J. *Econometric Methods.* New York: McGraw-Hill, 1963.
17. Knowles, James W. (with the assistance of Charles B. Warden, Jr.). *The Potential Economic Growth in the United States,* Joint Economic Committee Print, 86th Cong., 2nd Sess., Jan. 30, 1960. Washington: U. S. Government Printing Office, 1960.
18. Krzyzaniak, Marian, and Richard A. Musgrave. *The Shifting of the Corporation Income Tax.* Baltimore: The Johns Hopkins University Press, 1963.
19. Madison Fund, Inc. *Annual Report 1963.*
20. Ratchford, B. U., and R. B. Han. "The Burden of the Corporate Income Tax," *National Tax Journal,* Vol. X, No. 4 (December 1957).
21. Terborgh, George. "Effect of the Corporate Income Tax on Investment," Machinery and Allied Products Institute and Council for Technological Advancement Research Study, 1959.
22. Ture, Norman B. "The Study of Tax Policies for Economic Growth of the National Bureau of Economic Research," *Public Finance,* Vol. XVIII, No. 2, 1963.
23. Slitor, Richard E. "The Enigma of Corporate Tax Incidence," *Public Finance,* Vol. XVIII, Nos. 3–4, 1963.
24. Stockfisch, J. A. "On the Obsolescence of Incidence," *Public Finance,* Vol. XIV, No. 2, 1959.
25. _____. "The Capitalization, Allocation, and Investment Effects of Asset Taxation," *The Southern Economic Journal,* Vol. XII, No. 3 (January 1956).
26. U. S. Treasury Department, Internal Revenue Service. *Statistics of Income.*
27. Walras, Leon. *Elements of Pure Economics,* Edition Definitive (1926) trans. by William Jaffe, American Economic Association and Royal Economic Society, Translation Series. Homewood, Illinois: Richard D. Irwin, Inc., 1954.
28. Weston, J. Fred. "Incidence and Effects of the Corporate Income Tax," *National Tax Journal,* Vol. II, No. 4 (December 1949).
29. Zellner, Arnold. "The Corporate Income Tax in the Long Run: A Comment," *Journal of Political Economy,* Vol. LXVI, No. 5 (October 1958).

In recent years, more and more of those commenting on the corporation income tax have disclaimed knowledge of its incidence. The format of many discussions includes one section based on the assumption that the tax remains on corporations and their shareholders, and another section based on the assumption that the tax is fully passed on, in higher prices, to consumers. This uncertainty has confused both public and legislators and has allowed everyone to choose whatever assumption best fits his own predilections or policy program.

Economists' recent skepticism about the incidence of the corporation income tax reflects a rebellion against previously accepted theories. At the micro level, the assumption that firms attempt to maximize profits has been questioned. At the macro level, there has been increased willingness to accept the hypothesis that any increases in costs or in taxation will provoke a general rise in the price level and that this will be made possible by an accommodating monetary policy.

Supporting the hypothesis of short-run shifting of a tax on net profits requires both the discard of a great part of orthodox price theory and some special assumptions concerning aggre-

* I wish to acknowledge helpful comments and suggestions from John A. Brittain, Edward Denison, Gary Fromm, and Richard E. Slitor. Brittain generously made available his worksheets on corporate profits and related data for manufacturing and collaborated with Slitor and me in formulating and fitting the regression equations described in Appendix III-A.

gate income and monetary policy. This subject, therefore, raises theoretical questions that go far beyond public finance in any narrow sense. Ideally, tax specialists should be able to draw on other theorists for an explanation of both price behavior and the general price level directly applicable to tax incidence. But, in the absence of a consensus on these important matters, anyone who wishes to consider the economic effects of the corporate income tax or other taxes of large yield and broad coverage must try to make his own way through the theoretical difficulties.

The traditional view is that, generally speaking, the corporation income tax cannot be shifted in the short run while the stock of capital remains approximately constant. There has never been any similar consensus about the long run. Whether a tax that is not shifted in the short run will be shifted in the long run depends on the attractiveness of the corporate form and the elasticity of the supply of capital with respect to the rate of return. These are subjects on which opinions differ widely.

Recently Professors Krzyzaniak and Musgrave and Professor Hall have reported two important statistical investigations of corporate tax incidence ([8] and [5]). Unfortunately, these studies do not dispel doubts about the validity of the traditional theory. Whereas Krzyzaniak and Musgrave find the evidence consistent with full or more than full shifting in the short run, Hall finds that, on certain plausible assumptions, the evidence he examines is more compatible with the hypothesis of zero short-run shifting than with that of full shifting.

In this paper, I propose to review some of the general considerations and statistical evidence that seem important in appraising the incidence of the corporation income tax. After a brief examination of the assumptions underlying opposing hypotheses with respect to short-run shifting, I shall comment on the Krzyzaniak-Musgrave study and shall mention other statistical studies of profits. My discussion of long-run incidence draws attention to the conflicting evidence of different statistical indicators and emphasizes the difficulty of separating the possible influence of taxation from that of other factors affecting profits.

SHORT-RUN SHIFTING

Opposing Hypotheses

The traditional conclusion that a tax on net profits does not affect prices in the short run is basically a simple proposition. If firms are maximizing their profits before the tax is imposed, or are attempting to do so, the tax gives them no reason to change their prices. The price and output that will yield maximum profits before the tax is levied will yield maximum profits after the tax is in effect; any increase in prices by a firm operating at its optimum point will reduce profits before taxes and will leave the firm with smaller after-tax profits than it would obtain at the old prices.

Certain qualifications of the no-shifting conclusion have usually been conceded. One is that the imposition of a tax will goad firms into looking more carefully at their opportunities and will cause some of them to make price increases which would have been advantageous in the past but which were overlooked. A closely related reaction is that self-restrained monopolists or oligopolists may find in the tax increase an excuse for exercising their market power. A third qualification arises from the fact that the tax law does not allow a deduction for imputed interest on working capital, a cost of production even in the short run. But these qualifications have usually been regarded as fairly minor exceptions to the broad rule. (For a summary statement and references to the literature, see [8], pp. 1–7, 8.)

The hypothesis that short-run shifting of a profits tax is general, rather than exceptional, may be suggested by a belief that pricing is dominated in the short run by the decisions of restrained oligopolists or by the view that price theory is irrelevant to the understanding of market behavior. A well-supported finding of widespread short-run shifting of the whole corporate tax would constitute a devastating criticism of price theory and would suggest that businessmen were right all along in paying little attention to economists' talk about price determination.

Over the past twenty-five years, a number of surveys of business behavior have cast doubt on the realism of the assumption that firms attempt to maximize profits in the short run by unwavering attention to the equalization of marginal costs and marginal revenue. The alternative patterns of behavior that have been suggested usually take one of two forms. The first is that firms attempt to set prices at a level that will cover their full costs (including overhead costs as well as variable costs) plus a margin for profit. The second, which is only a variation of the first, views the process as one of striving for a target rate of return on invested capital, which would be achieved at a certain normal or standard level of operations. Thus Gordon speaks of "an irresistible tendency to price on the basis of average total cost for some 'normal' level of output," adding that "this is the yardstick, the short-cut, that business men and accountants use, and their aim is more to earn satisfactory profits and play safe than to maximize profits" ([4], p. 275). A study based on extensive interviews with executives of large corporations found the dominant objective to be either the achievement of a target rate of return or the preservation or expansion of a share in a particular market ([6], [10], and [11]). These studies have had the desirable effect of introducing disturbing reports from the world of experience into the tidy system of the theorist. Their findings, nevertheless, have not led to the general discard of the theoretical apparatus founded on the assumption that firms generally try to maximize profits. Partly this reflects scholarly inertia and reluctance to substitute disorderly reality for neat theoretical deductions, but there is also a more creditable basis for the reluctance to accept the survey evidence: businessmen's price decisions may be more influenced by the unseen hand of market forces than they realize. Furthermore, in responding to questions, executives may consciously or unconsciously put a good face on their behavior. An explanation that prices are set so as to recover costs plus a reasonable profit sounds better than a statement that the firm attempts to earn as much profit as it can. Critics have pointed out that rates of return actually earned vary greatly among industries and firms and often differ significantly from the avowed targets ([7] and [13]).

Granted that firms do not always behave in a way that will maximize profits in the short run, it does not follow that the general tendency is to set prices below the level that would yield the greatest profits. Inertia or target-return pricing might equally well result in prices higher than those that would yield maximum profits. Whether departures from short-run profit maximization will tend to be concentrated below or above the maximum will depend on the direction and rate of change of consumption, the degree of utilization of plant and equipment, the behavior of variable costs, the price elasticity of demand, the state of competition, and other considerations.

The hypothesis of full short-run shifting of a tax on net profits goes much farther than the proposition that firms do not continuously maximize profits. It implies that producers always stop short of the price that would yield maximum profits. If prices are already above the point at which profits would be maximized, a further increase intended to recoup the corporate tax will be unsuccessful and indeed will depress profits. Even if full-cost pricing on the basis of a fixed target rate of return were the general practice, it would not assure successful short-run shifting of the corporation income tax.

An increase in a tax on net profits, it should be emphasized, differs sharply from increases in wage rates or raw-material prices. The latter raise marginal variable costs and, according to partial-equilibrium theory, are likely to bring about higher prices in either a competitive or oligopolistic industry. The recognition of this fact underlies the opinion that inflation may result from a cost push. Doubts about the importance of cost-push inflation relate to the implied assumptions regarding aggregate demand and monetary conditions. The hypothesis of full short-run shifting of the corporate tax requires conditions at the macro level similar to those necessary to allow cost-push inflation, plus the special assumption that producers generally possess a high degree of unused market power.

Krzyzaniak and Musgrave's Econometric Analysis

Having examined certain broad indicators of the possible degree of shifting of the corporation income tax and finding them unsatisfactory because they do not permit an allowance for the influence of nontax factors, Krzyzaniak and Musgrave (hereinafter abbreviated K & M) resort to an econometric analysis designed to isolate the tax influence. Their technique is to attempt to explain short-run changes in the before-tax rate of return on capital in manufacturing corporations by an econometric model that includes the corporate tax as an independent variable.[1]

K & M deserve much credit for their ingenuity and persistence in carrying through a study which encountered formidable difficulties with respect to concepts, statistical methods, and data. Especially valuable are the authors' efforts to define precisely what is meant by different degrees of shifting, a question which has received little attention in the past, and to test for degree of shifting.

K & M's standard model includes, in addition to the corporate tax, three other variables that are supposed to account for changes in the rate of return on invested capital of manufacturing corporations: (1) the change in the ratio of consumption expenditures to gross national product (GNP); (2) the ratio of inventory to sales for all manufacturing establishments; and (3) the ratio of accruals of all federal, state, and local taxes other than the corporate income tax (minus government transfer payments) to GNP. The first two of these three variables are lagged one year. The corporate tax is usually

[1] The K-M study is not confined to a period in which the capital stock remains approximately fixed, the traditional short run, and in fact covers, with an interruption, a span of twenty-five years. It is, nevertheless, a study of short-run shifting in two senses: (1) the shifting mechanism visualized by the authors does not depend on changes in the capital stock; and (2) their standard econometric model includes as the tax variable only the current-year tax without explicit allowance for prior-year taxes. (See [8], pp. 29–30. Further page references to this publication are noted in parentheses in the text where the source is clear from the context.)

represented by the effective rates of federal corporate income and excess profits tax for all manufacturing corporations, but the statutory rates of income and excess profits taxes are also used to some extent.

K & M find that the corporate tax was more than 100 per cent shifted in the years 1935–42, 1948–59. The results for their so-called "standard model" indicate that the degree of shifting was 134 per cent, and many of their other results are close to this figure (p. 45).

Now, the startling findings are entitled to no more credence than the model that is intended to explain profit behavior. K & M remind critics that there is "no a priori insight which tells us . . . that such a result *must* be wrong" because it conflicts with certain long-accepted theoretical propositions (p. 46). I agree. But their quotation of a telling satiric verse on this point, "Weil, so schliesst er messerscharf, Nicht sein *kann*, was nicht sein *darf*," prompts me to paraphrase a wise maxim of David Hume: No evidence is sufficient to establish an implausible result unless the unreliability of the evidence would be more remarkable than the result which it endeavors to establish.[2]

Frankly, I would find a judgment that the K-M model or data are inadequate less remarkable than the conclusion which they purport to establish.

In my opinion, the best way to evaluate these findings is, not to look at the statistical measures of correlation and errors of estimate, but to consider their economic implications. I believe that econometricians will agree that choices among statistical explanations of economic behavior must be made on the basis of economic theory, independent knowledge, and common sense—not merely by formal statistical tests. I propose to consider the K-M model from several points of view: its implications concerning aggregate consumer demand and monetary conditions, the variables included in the model or

[2] What Hume said was: "No Testimony is sufficient to establish a Miracle, unless the Testimony be of such a Kind, that its Falshood [sic] would be more miraculous, than the Fact, which it endeavours to establish . . . " (David Hume, *An Enquiry Concerning Human Understanding and Other Essays*, ed. Ernest C. Mossner [New York: Washington Square Press, 1963], p. 114).

excluded from it, the plausibility of estimates of rates of return derived from the K-M model and from modified versions of it or alternative models, the degree of tax shifting indicated by the K-M model, and by a comparison of rates of return which does not attempt to hold constant nontax factors. I shall then call attention to other econometric studies of profits and, finally, mention several technical questions relating to the statistical data used by K & M.

Aggregate Demand and Monetary Conditions K & M believe that the corporate tax does not depress the total capital stock (p. 64). Since capital coefficients presumably are not affected, it seems to follow that real output is also unaffected. Aggregate money expenditures must rise if the tax is to be shifted through higher prices. The ratio of consumption expenditures to disposable income of consumers apparently will have to rise, despite a decrease in the real value of cash balances and other fixed claims. The monetary authorities are assumed to allow any expansion which may be needed to support higher prices.

All this seems to imply that—within the broad range of conditions covered by the K-M study—there were virtually no market nor monetary limitations on the extent to which firms could raise prices. They could have obtained huge increases in profits, in the absence of any change in taxes, if they had acted in informal concert. Nor do K & M suggest that, if corporate tax rates had been raised more or had been increased more quickly, shifting would have been less complete. Prices of manufactured goods appear to rotate on an axis that has no visible connection with a solid base.

Variables Among the independent variables selected by K & M to explain corporate profits, the ratio of inventory to sales has some appeal, but, on economic grounds, the one-year lag is curious. The relevance of the change in the ratio of consumption to GNP $\left(\Delta \left[\dfrac{C}{GNP} \right] \right)$ escapes me. A rise in this ratio, for example, might be due to causes as diverse as a reduction in private investment or a cut in personal taxes. The ratio of

the change in consumption to GNP $\left(\dfrac{\Delta C}{GNP}\right)$ might be regarded
as a measure of the accelerator. For this purpose, however, a
more general measure of activity—say the rate of change in
GNP or in private consumption plus investment—or a specific
measure of the change in manufacturing production would seem
preferable. Also obscure is the reason why the average effective
rate of all taxes other than the federal corporation income tax—
measured by the ratio of tax accruals to GNP—should affect
profits. Should the sign of the coefficient for this variable be
expected to be positive or negative? A positive sign might be
rationalized on the grounds that rising tax ratios have accompanied increases of government expenditures, which are expansionary even when financed by taxation. A negative sign might
be taken as an indication that, given the level of government
expenditures, a tax increase is deflationary. K & M find the
sign to be negative but do not explain why this should be true.

Variables omitted from K & M's standard model which might
be expected to help account for profits of manufacturing corporations include measures of pressure on total economic
resources, the rate of utilization of manufacturing capacity,
the rate of change in manufacturing production or sales, the
level and rate of change of government expenditures, and the
relation between prices and labor costs as determined by productivity and wage rates. A more elaborate listing would
include still other items some of which are mentioned in the
section on long-run shifting which follows.

K & M did experiment with a variable representing the ratio
of federal government expenditures to GNP; however this
variable received a negative coefficient, which is hard to explain.
When it was dropped from the standard model, there was a
gain in reliability in the other statistical coefficients.

K & M nevertheless agree that an increase in government
expenditures probably is favorable to profits and concede that
they have not been able to separate the effect of corporate
taxation from that of government expenditures because cor-

porate tax rates and the ratio of government expenditures to GNP are correlated.[3] They state that the rise in the before-tax rate of return on capital "reflects tax shifting in the sense of administered price adjustments, as well as responses to changes in government expenditures" (p. 47). This is a highly important point, especially since the rise in government expenditures after the mid-1930's was intimately associated with the growth of money income and real output which was conducive to better profits. K & M, to be sure, argue that the statistical results "suggest" that the tax factor is "much stronger" than the government-expenditures ratio as an influence on profits. However, I am most reluctant to rest such a judgment on the statistical evidence presented by the authors.

Plausibility of Estimates of Rate of Return Perhaps the simplest way of posing the issues with respect to the adequacy of the K-M estimates of the degree of short-run shifting of the corporation income tax is to look at estimates of the before-tax rate of return on capital of manufacturing corporations made on the basis of the K-M model but assuming different tax rates, appraising these estimates in the light of what we know, or think we know, about the economy. Several such estimates for 1936–39 and 1955–57 are brought together in Table 26.

Lines 1 and 2 of Table 26 show the average actual rate of return on total capital in corporate manufacturing and the estimates produced by application of one of the versions of the K-M Model A. The version chosen is the one which K & M call the "naive least squares" approach (line 5 of their Table 6–1, pp. 44–45). This particular version is used because it does not require resort to the complex instrumental-variable technique. Although K & M consider the "naive least squares" technique less satisfactory than the instrumental-variable technique, the measure of shifting and the coefficient of multiple correlation are not very different from those obtained by their preferred technique. It will be seen that the K-M estimates are close indeed to the actual rates of return obtained in 1936–39 and 1955–57.

---

[3] See the simple correlation matrix, [8], p. 46.

Table 26

Before-Tax Rate of Return on Total Capital of Manufacturing
Corporations: Actual and Alternative Statistical Estimates, 1936–39
and 1955–57[a]

(*In Per Cent*)

Description	1936–39	1955–57
1. Actual	7.46	16.15
Estimated by K-M Equation [b]		
2. With Actual Tax Rates	7.55	16.33
3. With Constant 1936–39 Tax Rates	7.55	7.21
4. With Constant 1955–57 Tax Rates	16.66	16.33
Estimated by K-M Equation Modified by:		
5. Substitution of "Pressure" Variable for Tax Variable [c]	8.40	16.15
6. Substitution of Capacity-Utilization Variable for Tax Variable [d]	7.60	17.26
7. Estimated Solely from "Pressure" Variable [e]	7.86	17.04
8. Estimated Solely from Capacity-Utilization Variable [f]	7.24	18.14

[a] Arithmetic means of annual percentages. Data on rates of return and tax rates are from [8], p. 74. The before-tax rate of return is the sum of profits and interest paid as a percentage of equity + debt at the beginning of the year; the tax-rate variable is computed with respect to invested capital (K & M's *L*). For additional details, see Appendix III-A.

[b] Standard model, "naive least squares" technique; equation 1.1 given in Appendix III-A.

[c] Equation 2, Appendix III-A.

[d] Equation 3, Appendix III-A.

[e] Equation 4, Appendix III-A.

[f] Equation 5, Appendix III-A.

Lines 3 and 4 of Table 26 were derived by substituting in the K-M equation two sets of constant tax rates to replace the actual tax rates which were in effect each year. Line 3 shows the before-tax rate of return estimated from the K-M equation on the assumption that corporate income tax rates were constant at the 1936–39 level, whereas line 4 shows estimates based on the assumption that corporate tax rates were constant at the 1955–57 level. These estimates imply that, except for the difference in corporate tax rates, the before-tax rate of return would have been approximately the same in 1936–39 and in 1955–57. With the lower 1936–39 tax rates, the estimated rate of return in 1955–57 would have been less than half the actual rate; with the higher 1955–57 tax rates, the estimated rate of return in 1936–39 would have been more than double the actual rate. These estimates allow for the influence of the other independent variables which K & M include in their model explaining corporate profits. They are based on the assumption that only corporate tax rates are held constant while the other relevant variables follow their actual historical course.

I consider the estimates shown in lines 3 and 4 of Table 26 implausible. Is it likely that, except for differences in corporate tax rates, profits would have been substantially the same in 1936–39 and in 1955–57, considering the differences between the two periods with respect to unemployment rates, the apparent intensity of use of plant and equipment, price developments, and other factors which are widely regarded as influential in determining profits? Notice that, since K & M argue that short-run shifting occurs without affecting the capital stock, their model implies that the absolute amounts of profits would differ as much as the rates of return under alternative assumptions.

Lines 5 and 6 of Table 26 show estimates made on the basis of the K-M model and data but with alternative variables substituted for the tax variable. Three of the four estimates are farther from the actual figures than the estimates produced by the K-M model (line 2), but the difference in the size of the error is not striking. The alternative variables that are substituted for the tax variable in lines 5 and 6 are intended to provide rough measures of the pressure on total resources and of the rate of capacity utilization in manufacturing. The "pressure" variable which is substituted in line 5 is a general measure of the rate of utilization of resources based on Knowles's estimate of the ratio of actual GNP to "potential" GNP. The capacity-utilization variable that is substituted in line 6 represents the ratio of actual current manufacturing production to a high-level growth trend. (The substitute variables are described in Appendix III–A and are shown in Appendix Table A–1.)

The increase in rate of return between 1936–39 and 1955–57 shown in lines 5 and 6 of Table 26 seems to me to correspond better with the pattern that might have been expected to obtain with constant corporate income tax rates—and with all other relevant variables unaffected by the constancy of corporate tax rates—than does the stability shown in lines 3 and 4. After all, 1955–57 was a more prosperous period than 1936–39.

Lines 7 and 8 of Table 26 show that fairly good estimates of the rate of return on corporate capital in manufacturing can be made solely on the basis of the two variables which were substituted for the tax variable in lines 5 and 6. The estimates produced in this way again seem reasonably consistent with what one would expect to find about the behavior of profits in the light of general knowledge of economic conditions in 1936–39 and 1955–57. (I do not intend to imply that the simple equations underlying lines 7 and 8 offer adequate structural estimates of profits, only that they call attention to the importance of capacity utilization as a factor accounting for profits.)

Estimates of Shifting A further test is provided by comparing the degree of shifting of the corporate tax that is indicated simply by the changes in rate of return and tax rates between 1936–39 and 1955–57, without allowance for other factors, with the estimates of shifting derived from K & M's preferred model. For manufacturing, the percentages of shifting estimated by the crude method and the econometric model are as follows:[4] The remarkable correspondence between the estimates derived by the two methods leaves me more worried than reassured. The model suggests, not merely that the corporate tax influenced rates of return, but that nothing else did, on balance, between 1936–39 and 1955–57.

Measure	Crude Method	Econometric Model
All manufacturing corporations		
Equity capital base	136	123
Total capital base	134	134
Equity capital, with correction		
for inflation	99	101
Manufacturing corporations with assets		
Above $50 million (equity base)	121	121
Below $50 million (equity base)	129	129

[4] The crude method is a comparison of before-tax rates of return in 1936–39 with those in 1955–57; the econometric model is Model A, 1935–42, 1948–59 ([8], p. 64).

The fact is, of course, that measured rates of return on corporate capital tended to rise after the mid-1930's simultaneously with the increase in production, the reduction in idle capacity, the growth of government expenditures, and general inflationary pressures. Corporate tax rates also rose during World War II, were cut after the war, were increased during the Korean War, and then were cut again but not to the 1936–39 level. Except in the years immediately after World War II, the movement of tax rates was roughly coincident with that of forces that would have tended to raise or depress profits in the absence of short-run shifting. The forces that raised profits after 1939 also pushed up wage rates. Perhaps an ingenious person, following the lead of K & M, could construct a model that would indicate that the increase in individual income taxes payable by wage earners was fully shifted.

Other Models

Other econometric studies have developed statistical explanations of corporate profits on the basis of models quite different from that of K & M and, in some cases, have obtained reasonably satisfactory results. Without undertaking a broad survey, I shall refer to five general models and to two studies directed specifically toward the question of corporate tax incidence. The general models are intended to explain the amount of corporate profits before tax or the share of profits in income rather than the rate of return on invested capital. In the short run, there is no great difference between the approaches, but for the long run they differ.

Duesenberry, Eckstein, and Fromm, in a paper published in 1960, explained the change in corporate profits, before tax and before depreciation allowances but after inventory valuation adjustment (IVA), by changes in final sales and in inventory investment, all changes being measured from the previous peak (2). They fitted their equation to pooled quarterly data for the recessions of 1949 and 1954. They justified their use of profits before depreciation on the grounds that depreciation allowances are "no more than an accounting convention," and their use of final sales rather than GNP because profits are earned on sales not on production.

Kuh explained quarter-to-quarter variations in before-tax corporate profits during the postwar period (1947–59–II) by fluctuations in the net markup, which he found to be related to variations in the level of output (9).

Schultze explained the share of gross profits (corporate profits before taxes plus IVA plus depreciation) by two elements: (1) a secular or trend component and (2) a cyclical component represented by deviations of corporate product from its full capacity "norm." Schultze's statistical estimates were impressive for the period of 1922–41 but less satisfactory for the period 1949–59 (15). It is possible that changes in the corporate tax rate may be obscured in Schultze's trend component.

Fromm, in a 1962 study, explained postwar profits before taxes as a function of sales, inventory change, and the gap between actual and potential or normal output (3). He viewed the sales term as a representation of "the normal share of profits in GNP," the inventory term as an indication of "the tendency for the commodity output share to vary inversely with cyclical swings in output," and the gap between potential and actual GNP as a representation of "the cyclical variation in the corporate share of total national product." Fromm also gave his equation a microeconomic interpretation, suggesting that "the coefficient of the sales term is the normal profit margin, the inventory term is an adjustment for the differential effect of selling goods out of stock, and the gap term is an indicator of the pressure on unit costs and prices as capacity utilization declines."

Liu, in a recent quarterly model of the postwar economy, treated corporate profits before taxes (+IVA) as a function of GNP, the ratio of money wage rates to prices, and profits of the two preceding quarters (12). His equation was fitted to observations for the 50 quarters 1947–III to 1959–IV.

Though none of these econometric models was developed in a way which permits one to test the influence of changes in the corporate tax rate, it is interesting that the independent variables

selected by the separate authors differ from those employed by
K & M and that none of the other scholars called on corporate
tax rates to help explain corporate profits.[5]

Brannon, in an unpublished paper presented at a meeting of
the Econometric Society in December 1960, addressed himself
directly to the issue of tax shifting. He explained corporate
profits, before taxes and before depreciation allowances, over
the period 1923–41, 1946–59 as a function of GNP originating
in the corporate sector, capital stock valued at current prices,
the year-to-year change in GNP originating in the corporate
sector, and effective corporate tax rates. He found the coefficient for the tax variable to be a small negative figure which
was statistically insignificant and concluded that this was strong
evidence of the absence of shifting.[6] Brannon attributed the
high rate of gross return on corporate capital in the postwar
period to a capital shortage rather than high corporate tax rates.

Hall studied the question of short-run shifting of corporate
profits taxes in manufacturing, 1919–59, by fitting a production
function of the Cobb-Douglas type to data on output, capital
employed, and labor input. He found that, if technological
progress was neutral (that is, if it increased the productive
contributions of capital and labor in the same proportions), the
statistical results were more consistent with the hypothesis of
zero short-run shifting than with that of full shifting [5].

Questions Relating to Statistical Data Employed by K & M

While I do not propose to undertake a thorough examination
of the statistical data underlying the K-M study, I do wish to
make a few remarks about certain key variables and to comment
on a problem of comparability of data drawn from the Treasury
Department publication, *Statistics of Income.*

Tax Rates For most of their regressions, K & M use effective

[5] An estimate of after-tax magnitudes is an equation developed by the staff of the
Joint Economic Committee, which explains corporate cash flow (profits after tax plus
capital consumption allowances) as a function of potential GNP, the difference between
actual and potential GNP, and the change in GNP over that of the previous year. (See
[16], p. 687.)

[6] Gerard M. Brannon, "Some Investigations of the Incidence of the Corporate
Income Tax." Public utilities were excluded to the extent feasible.

corporate tax rates as an instrumental variable or independent variable. For industry groups or subgroups, effective tax rates are the ratio of (1) federal corporate income, excess profits, declared-value excess profits, and undistributed profits tax liabilities of all firms to (2) combined net income of all firms. Effective tax rates so measured change from year to year for any of three reasons: (a) changes in statutory rates, (b) changes in the rates paid by profit-making firms because marginal rates exceed average rates owing to graduation of statutory rates and the existence of the excess profits tax in some years, and (c) changes in the ratio of deficits of firms with no net income to the positive profits of profit-making firms. The first kind of change must receive attention in a study of short-run shifting, but the significance of changes due to the other two factors is not so clear. It is hard to see how firms in setting current-year prices could take account of their current excess profits tax liabilities since the computation of excess profits tax requires precise knowledge of the final operating results of the year. When the excess profits tax was in existence, moreover, renegotiation of government contracts also prevailed. Whether profits were subject to excess profits tax or were taken by renegotiation was to a considerable extent an accidental or arbitrary matter.[7] There is a real question whether the excess profits tax can properly be brought into a behavioral model such as that employed in the K-M study.

Also questionable is the significance of changes in effective tax rates due solely to the change in the size of deficits realized by firms that made no profit. Surely the deficit firms do not shift a tax which they do not pay; they are not even able to pass on all of their ordinary costs. To illustrate the point, sup-

[7] For the years in which renegotiation was in effect, the amounts of profits and tax liabilities reported in *Statistics of Income* reflect renegotiation completed prior to the filing of the tax return but not renegotiation completed later. For 1942, renegotiation procedures completed after the filing of tax returns reduced the profits of manufacturing corporations reported in *Statistics of Income* by at least $1,675 million, or 12 per cent, and reported tax liability of these corporations by at least $1,237 million, or 15 per cent. These figures reflect renegotiation settlements tabulated by the Bureau of Internal Revenue up to December 31, 1945; there may also have been later settlements. (See U. S. Treasury Department, Bureau of Internal Revenue, *Statistics of Income for 1942*, Part 2, pp. 24–25, 93.)

pose that in year 1 firm with net income realize profits of 100 while deficit firms suffer losses of 10, making combined net income 90. If the corporate tax rate is 50 per cent on the firms with net profits, the effective rate as K & M compute it will be 50/90 or 55.6 per cent. Now if in year 2 the firms with net income again realize profits of 100, but those with no net income suffer losses of 25, combined net income will fall to 75, tax liability will remain unchanged, and the effective rate of tax will rise to 66.7 per cent. Can this be expected to lead to price increases that will "shift" the increase in the effective tax rate?

Effective tax rates, of course, are somewhat higher for all corporations than for net-income corporations only. In general, the series move together, but there are divergencies, particularly in recession years. The biggest differences are in 1937–38, when the effective rate for all manufacturing corporations rose 5.8 percentage points while that for net-income corporations declined 0.2 percentage points, and in 1938–39, when the changes for these two groups were −5.6 percentage points and +0.5 percentage points, respectively.[8]

Statutory rates seem more directly related to the behavior that is alleged to bring about short-run shifting than are effective rates. Over the years 1935–42, 1948–59, there were twenty different effective rates, compared with eleven different statutory rates if the excess profits tax and income tax are both included, ten if only income tax changes are taken into account. K & M made one set of estimates for their preferred model using the statutory marginal rates rather than the effective rates. There is no statistically significant difference between the coefficients of the independent variables, the measure of shifting, or the percentage of variance in the rate of return explained; indeed all these measures are virtually identical (pp. 44–45). For the whole period, therefore, it appears that the effective and statutory rates, as measured by K & M, are equally satisfactory instrumental variables in the K-M preferred model. This suggests that my worries on this score are ground-

[8] Computed from *Statistics of Income*, and [8], p. 74.

less. Nevertheless, I would feel more reassured if there had been more experimentation with the use of statutory rates, for sub-periods and industry groups, and with different treatment of changes in the statutory rates of excess profits tax.[9]

Invested Capital A second problem of statistical data relates to the measurement of invested capital. While there are serious questions about the reliability and comparability of statistics of book value of invested capital extending over a long period of years, and questions about the relative suitability of net worth and the total of net worth plus debt, these questions are less important for a short-run analysis. I am not able to judge whether the difficulties are serious for the K-M model, but I am disturbed by the possibility that true relations will be obscured by inaccuracies in the measurement of capital. Further comments on these issues appear in the discussion of long-range shifting.

Leaving aside the more fundamental issues, the K-M statistics are subject to criticism because invested capital at the beginning of the year serves as the base for measuring the rate of return. It seems fairly clear that the behaviorally relevant capital base is the average for the year. Nevertheless, K & M's procedure would be acceptable if invested capital were growing at a steady pace over the period examined because in that case their computations would be an accurate index of changes in rates of return if not of the actual level of return. But invested capital in fact grew at different rates—slowly in the 1930's and rapidly in the 1940's and 1950's. If K & M had computed their rates of return on the basis of the average invested capital during the year (approximated by the mean of the figures for the beginning and end of year), the indicated rates in the 1930's would have been little affected, but the rates in the postwar period would have been somewhat lower. To illustrate, the return on equity capital, as K & M compute it, was 9.61 per cent in 1936 and 21.64 per cent in 1955 (p. 74); computed on average capital, these figures are 9.49 per cent and 20.62

[9] K & M use statutory marginal rates in their Model B, which yields higher degrees of shifting than their preferred Model A. Statutory marginal rates are the maximum combined rates of income and excess profits taxes.

per cent, respectively. The rise in the rate of return from 1936 to 1955 is one-twelfth greater according to the K-M computation than it is according to the other computation.

Profits   K & M's profits figures represent net income of all manufacturing corporations (the combined total for those with net income and those with deficits) as reported in *Statistics of Income*. A preferable figure would be compiled net profits, which includes nontaxable profits that are omitted from net income. The difference between the two figures is small in the years covered by K & M's regression equations but was greater in certain earlier years, when intercorporate dividends and substantial amounts of interest on government securities were not included in net income. In comparisons extending back to the 1920's, use of net income gives a downward bias to the rate of return for the earlier years.[10]

Inflation also distorts reported profits. K & M attempt to correct corporate net income and equity capital for inflation. With this correction, they find that their preferred model still yields statistically significant results and that the degree of shifting is reduced to approximately 100 per cent (compared with 123 per cent in an otherwise comparable regression that does not allow for inflation [pp. 54–55]). Another approach to the problem of correcting for inflation is described below.

Further comments on alternative measures of profits and rates of return appear in the section on long-run shifting.

Consolidated Returns   The data drawn from *Statistics of Income* are subject to noncomparability due to changes in the extent to which consolidated returns were filed by affiliated corporations. Consolidated returns by manufacturing corporations were not allowed in the years 1935–41 but were permitted again in 1942 and in subsequent years covered by the K & M estimates of the coefficients for their model. In the years 1935–41, balance sheets and income statements included items previously

[10] The effect of correcting for both the difference between average and beginning-of-year capital and the difference between compiled net profit and net income can be seen by comparing my figures for 1927–29 (Table 27) with K & M's pp. 17–18. The two corrections were partly offsetting. For 1936 and later years, the difference between compiled net profit and net income is small, and I have used K & M's figures for net income. The difference between my averages for 1936–39 and 1955–57 and theirs presumably is due to my use of the average capital base rather than the beginning-of-year capital.

and subsequently consolidated out by "intercompany elimina-
tions." The industrial classification of many corporations was
also affected. The quantitative importance of the resulting
noncomparability of data for 1935–41 with those for 1942 and
1948–59 cannot be exactly gauged. However, some information
is available with respect to 1934, which was the first year in
which consolidated returns were not permitted. Although this
information does not show the full effect of the change in basis
of reporting, it makes clear that the change was important in
1934. For manufacturing, the rate of return on equity capital
in 1934 is 4.14 per cent with consolidation and 3.64 per cent
without consolidation; the effective tax rate is 14.75 per cent
with consolidation and 18.96 per cent without consolidation.[11]
This element of noncomparability casts doubt on the usefulness
of the statistics for 1935–41. These statistics play an important
part in the K-M hypothesis because they relate to years in
which tax rates and investment returns were much lower than
in the later years during which consolidated returns were permitted. Generally, the K-M regression coefficients for their
preferred model indicate less shifting in the postwar years than
in the whole period studied (pp. 54–55).

Conclusions with Respect to Short Run

My conclusion is that the case for short-run shifting of a
large fraction of the corporation income tax remains unproved.
My own inclination is to continue to employ the working
hypothesis that little short-run shifting occurs and that, with
a given capital stock, changes in the corporate tax rate affect
mainly profits. In brief, I have not been persuaded that short-
run shifting occurs on a large scale by the survey evidence
regarding business pricing behavior or the K-M statistical
analysis. While my position would be bolstered if I could present a full econometric analysis of profit behavior, I have neither
the inclination nor the resources to attempt that.

It may be helpful if, in concluding this section, I try to state

[11] The rate of return is compiled net profit as a percentage of end-of-year net worth;
the effective tax rate is total tax as a percentage of compiled net profit. (For discussions
of the consolidated-returns problem, see *Statistics of Income, 1934*, Part 2, pp. 19–29;
[18], p. 576.)

somewhat more exactly how I account for the K-M findings. Briefly, my position is that K & M have not succeeded in isolating the tax variable from the other, and in my judgment more important, factors that determine corporate profits. This I attribute to shortcomings of their model and data and to inherent difficulties due to intercorrelation of relevant variables.

My hypothesis is that short-run changes in corporate profits reflect mainly changes in the economic environment, particularly the rate of capacity utilization and the degree of inflationary pressures. The level and rate of change of government expenditures contribute importantly to capacity utilization and inflationary or deflationary pressures and are also associated with statutory and effective corporate tax rates. A large fraction of the variance of before-tax corporate profits can be explained merely by reference to the rate of capacity utilization. The addition of certain nontax variables increases the fraction of variance explained to a high figure. While the inclusion of corporate tax rates, in models similar to those developed by K & M, reduces the unexplained variance still further, I do not concede that the regression coefficient for the tax variable provides an acceptable measure of the separate influence of corporate tax rates. That coefficient, in my opinion, measures whatever influence corporate tax rates may have plus part of the influence of other variables with which tax rates are associated.

LONG-RUN SHIFTING

The absence of short-run shifting of the corporate tax would not mean that long-range shifting could not occur. Indeed, the traditional view is that long-run shifting may occur because short-run shifting does not. In the absence of short-run shifting, the tax will reduce rates of return on corporate equity and will cause capital to be diverted into corporate debt and to the noncorporate sector. In time, the appropriate yield differentials will be re-established by some increase in before-tax yields on corporate equity and some reduction in other yields. If investment is elastic with respect to the rate of return, the capital stock will tend to fall, and this will restore part of the decline in yields. If investment as a whole is not elastic with respect to the rate of return, capitalists throughout the economy will have to bear the whole corporate tax. The extent to which the tax will affect returns on capital other than corporate equity depends on the importance attached to the corporate form and economic and institutional limits to debt financing by corporations. Reallocations of capital between the corporate and noncorporate sectors—and perhaps also between debt and equity within the corporate sector—will affect relative commodity prices. Any retardation of total capital formation which may occur will tend, in the long run, to affect output and shares of the productive factors in national income.

While it may take many years for long-run shifting to work itself out completely, the forces that affect the capital stock will begin to operate immediately by influencing current investment or disinvestment in fixed capital and working capital.

A quick look at the statistics reveals no trend away from the corporate form of business after two decades of comparatively high corporate tax rates. Concentrating on manufacturing, in order to minimize complications due to changes in the industrial composition of output, we find that the share of corporations in value added by all establishments rose from 91.5 per cent in 1929 to 94.7 per cent in 1958.[12] The ratio of debt to the book value of debt and equity combined changed little between the late 1920's and 1950 but increased over the next few years from about 15 percent to about 20 percent. (*Statistics of Income*, annual volumes.) Without an analysis of other factors we cannot say what if any influence the corporate tax had on the debt-equity ratio or the role of corporations in manufacturing.

The available statistics show that the before-tax rate of return on corporate capital was considerably higher in prosperous years after World War II than in the 1920's. The profit margin on sales was also higher after World War II, but the difference was less marked. On the other hand, profits in relation to national income originating in corporations were little,

[12] Census data reported in *Historical Statistics*, p. 413; and U. S. Bureau of the Census, *Census of Manufactures*, 1958, Vol. 1, p. 3–2.

if any, greater than in the 1920's. Inasmuch as corporate tax rates have been much higher since World War II than they were during the 1920's, the rate-of-return statistics—and, to a lesser degree, the sales-margin figures—seem to be consistent with a large amount of shifting of the tax, whereas the income-share statistics seem to be inconsistent with shifting.

Selected statistics for manufacturing corporations are brought together in Tables 27, 28, and 29. Manufacturing is a particularly interesting case for study since corporations have been dominant in this sector for a long time and the industry is more homogeneous than the whole corporate universe. The K-M study also concentrates on manufacturing.

Table 27

Rate of Return on Book Value of Invested Capital of Manufacturing Corporations: *Statistics of Income* Basis, Selected Years, 1927–60 [a]
(In Per Cent)

Measure	1927–29	1936–39	1955–57	1958–60
Return on Equity				
Before Tax	8.8	7.8	18.2	13.8
After Tax	7.8	6.4	9.1	6.8
Return on Total Capital [b]				
Before Tax	8.7	7.3	15.5	11.9
After Tax	7.8	6.2	8.2	6.4
Memo: Statutory Corporation				
Income Tax Rate [c]	12.2	17.0	52.0	52.0

[a] Arithmetic means of annual percentages. Calculations based on *Statistics of Income* and data from [8], p. 73. (For details, see Appendix III-B.)

[b] Profits + interest paid as percentage of equity + debt capital.

[c] Statutory rate of federal corporation income tax applicable to large firms (arithmetic mean of annual figures).

Table 27, based on *Statistics of Income*, shows rates of return computed from profits reported for tax purposes and the book value of invested capital. It will be seen that the before-tax return on equity capital was more than twice as high in 1955–57 as in 1927–29, while the after-tax return was about one-sixth higher in 1955–57. Computed on total capital, the rise in the rate of return was smaller.

Table 28

Profits Share of Income Originating in Manufacturing Corporations,
with Alternative Profit Concepts, Selected Years, 1927–60 [a]
(In Per Cent)

Profits Concept	1927–29	1936–39	1955–57	1958–60
1. Profits before Tax	22.4	19.4	24.5	20.4
2. Line 1 + Depreciation Charges	28.9	26.0	30.1	27.0
3. Line 2 + Inventory Valuation Adjustment (IVA)	29.7	25.6	28.9	26.8
4. Profits before Tax, with Current Cost Depreciation Allowances, + IVA	23.8	18.2	23.9	20.9
5. Memo: Effective Rate of Federal, State, and Local Corporate Profits Taxes	14.0	22.6	49.0	49.3

[a] Arithmetic means of annual percentages. Calculations are based primarily on estimates of Office of Business Economics, U. S. Department of Commerce. National income originating is adjusted to correspond to the profits concept in lines 2, 3, and 4. (For sources and details, see Appendix III-B.)

Table 29

Profit Margin on Sales of Manufacturing Corporations,
Selected Years, 1927–60 [a]
(In Per Cent of Sales)

Profits Concept	1927–29	1936–39	1955–57	1958–60
Profits before Tax	6.7	5.8	8.6	6.7
Profits before Tax + Depreciation Charges	9.7	8.6	11.7	10.1

[a] Arithmetic means of annual percentages. Profit margin is computed as percentage of profit to corporate sales minus profit. Calculations are based primarily on estimates of Office of Business Economics, U. S. Department of Commerce. (For sources and details, see Appendix III-B.)

The before-tax profits share of national income produced by manufacturing corporations was roughly the same in 1927–29 and 1955–57 on four bases of calculation (Table 28). The after-tax share, not shown in the table, was of course substantially smaller in 1955–57.[13]

[13] Interest paid might appropriately have been added to profits, but, according to the national income and product accounts, net interest originating in manufacturing is a small item in most years (average, $45 million in 1955–57). This is because interest originating is calculated net of monetary and imputed interest received. (See [19], Table VI-12.)

The before-tax margin of profit on sales of manufacturing corporations rose between 1927–29 and 1955–57 but much less than the rate of return on capital (Table 29). The difference between the behavior of the sales-margin and income-share figures is due mainly to changes in the amounts of purchased materials from other industries and changes in excises and sales taxes.

No conclusions can be drawn without considering the possible influence of nontax factors, but, before doing that, some attention should be given to the suitability of the three different indicators of possible shifting.

If the statistics on the rate of return on invested capital, income shares, and profit margins on sales were equally reliable, much could be said for preferring the rate-of-return measure. The great advantage of this approach would be its relation to incentives for new investment. The income-share measure, nevertheless, would have considerable interest because it is directly relevant to the estimation of production functions and because it is connected with the size distribution of income and other questions of social policy. The sales margin would be the least interesting of the three figures because it is influenced by changes in the relation between sales and value added which may have no clear significance for tax shifting or public policy.

The difficulty of accurately measuring invested capital, however, is so great that in my view the usefulness of rate-of-return data is questionable. The book value of capital at any moment of time is an aggregation of figures developed by diverse accounting methods and reflecting the original cost of items acquired at widely different price levels. Balance sheet items are influenced by past and expected future profitability. The degree of consolidation of balance sheets and income statements, as noted above, can have an important effect on aggregates.

Though the measurement of profits, income shares, and sales margins is subject to some of the same limitations as the rate-of-return statistics, the difficulties of obtaining reliable estimates of flows are far less serious than those associated with the data on the value of invested capital.

An attempted correction for some of the shortcomings of the usual rate-of-return statistics is reported in Table 30. In the

Table 30

Rate of Return on Reproducible Tangible Capital of Manufacturing Corporations: OBE Basis, with Capital and Profits in 1954 Dollars, Selected Years, 1929–60 [a]
(In Per Cent)

Measure	1929	1936–39	1955–57	1958–60
Before Tax				
Profits	15.2	10.3	18.3	13.6
Profits + Depreciation				
Charges	20.8	14.8	24.2	19.6
After Tax				
Profits	13.3	8.1	9.3	6.9
Profits + Depreciation				
Charges	18.8	12.6	15.2	12.9

[a] Arithmetic means of annual percentages. Reproducible tangible capital consists of structures, equipment, and inventory. Calculations are based on estimates of Office of Business Economics, U. S. Department of Commerce. (For sources and details, see Appendix III-B.)

statistics underlying this table, capital is restricted to structures, equipment, and inventory, omitting land and all intangibles. In arriving at the estimates of net capital stocks, the Office of Business Economics of the Department of Commerce employed consistent depreciation methods and evaluated stocks in constant prices. I have converted estimated profits and gross cash flow (profits before tax plus depreciation charges) to constant prices by deflating by an implicit price index for private purchases of plant and equipment in manufacturing. This approach is different from other adjustments for inflation in that it simply takes profits or cash flows as reported and deflates them without any attempt to make detailed adjustments for distortions due to inflation. The procedure is intended to state profits or cash flow and the rate of return in terms of purchasing power over new plant and equipment. The use of the particular price deflator which I have chosen is debatable; if the implicit price deflator for the consumption component of GNP or for GNP as a whole had been used, the rate of return obtained for 1955–57 would have been higher relative to 1929 than that shown in Table 30.

Estimates such as those given in Table 30 are subject to wide margins of error. Nevertheless, I consider them more reliable than unadjusted statistics on the rate of return such as those shown in Table 27. The adjusted figures in Table 30 show a much smaller rise in the before-tax rate of return between 1929 and 1955–57 than is indicated by the unadjusted figures and a decline in the after-tax rate of return. The adjusted figures, therefore, suggest less shifting of the additional corporate profits tax.[14]

The difference between the behavior of the rate of return, as reported in Table 30, and the profits share shown in Table 28 is far less striking than the difference between the course of the rate of return on book value of invested capital (Table 27) and the profits share. Nevertheless, there is enough difference between the movements of the corrected rate-of-return estimates and the profits share to call for explanation. Aside from differences in corporate tax rates, how could the two indicators of profitability be expected to behave in the years under consideration?

Economic Conditions in the 1920's and after World War II

The rate of capacity utilization in the economy as a whole seems to have been at roughly comparable high levels in 1927–29 and 1955–57 and at appreciably lower levels in 1958–60 and 1936–39. This is indicated by unemployment rates and the relation between GNP and estimated potential GNP (Table 31). In manufacturing, pressure on capacity may have been greater in 1955–57 than in the late 1920's, as is suggested by the ratio of current production to its high-level growth trend (Table 31). Inasmuch as the degree of utilization of resources is an important influence on profitability, the periods 1927–29 and 1955–57 may reasonably be compared. An increase in profitability between 1936–39 and 1955–57 and a decrease in

[14] In Table 30, as in Table 28, interest paid is omitted from the return to capital because, according to the national income and product accounts, net interest originating in manufacturing is a small item.

Table 31

Indexes of Resource Utilization, Selected Years, 1927–60 [a]
(In Per Cent)

Item	1927–29	1936–39	1955–57	1958–60
Unemployment Rate	3.9	16.8	4.3	6.0
Ratio of Actual GNP to Potential GNP	100	85	99	93
Ratio of Actual Manufacturing Production to Its High-Level Trend	97	69	103	94

[a] Arithmetic means of annual percentages. (For sources, see Appendix III-B.)

1958–60 could be expected, regardless of corporate tax rates. In addition to cyclical changes in capacity utilization, there are several other factors that may affect profitability.

The figures on rate of return on capital in corporate manufacturing and the profit share in this industry imply that, at comparable stages of the business cycle, the capital-output ratio has recently been lower than in the 1920's. This is amply supported by independent evidence. The capital-output ratio in manufacturing rose from 1880 to 1919, but sometime between 1919 and 1929 it began to decline. It fell from 1.02 in 1919 to 0.88 in 1929 and to 0.59 in 1953.[15] A decline in the capital-output ratio tends to be favorable to profits.

A secular decline in the capital-output ratio could be due to a capital shortage, which would tend to push up profit rates. If associated with high corporate tax rates, these conditions might be taken as evidence of tax shifting. It is significant, however, that the decline in the capital-output ratio began in a period of low taxes.

A secular decline in the capital-output ratio need not imply a greater scarcity of capital. Kuznets points out that it "may be easily ascribed to the pressure for reducing costs and maximizing profits," and he adds that "since profits are, at least in part, a function of sales volume, a lower capital-output ratio would mean a higher rate of profit for total capital—and an even higher rate on the equity share of it" ([1], p. xxxv).

Another reason for expecting a decline in the capital-output

[15] Measured in constant 1929 prices. (See [1], p. 40.)

ratio to be favorable to profits is that high ratios often reflect excess capacity built up in a period of rapid growth of an industry because of indivisibilities and the long average life of plant and equipment (see [1], p. xxxvii). Cyclical increases in the rate of capacity utilization are known to be very favorable to rising profits.

A development which may have contributed to a rise in the rate of return realized on capital is the change in the composition of physical capital. The proportion of reproducible tangible capital in manufacturing represented by structures has declined greatly, and the proportions accounted for by equipment and inventories have risen. According to estimates of the Office of Business Economics of the Department of Commerce, structures represented 49 per cent of the total (structures, equipment, and inventories) in 1928–29 and only 31.5 per cent at the end of 1957 (values in constant 1954 prices) ([19]).

If the typical or required rate of return is different for structures from that for equipment and inventories, the change in capital mix could have a considerable influence on the over-all rate of return. It seems plausible to suppose that the rate of return on equipment and inventories should be expected to be higher than that on buildings because buildings usually have more alternative uses than equipment and can be more easily and cheaply financed by mortgage credit. Suppose, for example, that the required rate of return on structures is only half that on equipment and inventories. Then the required or normal rate of return for the 1957 mix would be 11 per cent higher than that for the 1928–29 mix. Leaving aside inventories, and looking only at the change in the relation between structures and equipment, it appears that the change in the mix between 1928–29 and 1957, on the foregoing assumption, would raise the required or normal over-all rate of return by 15 per cent.

Direct evidence is not available on the differential, if any, between normal or required rates of return on structures, equipment, and inventories. An investigation of this point might be a worthwhile subject of research. It is interesting to notice, nevertheless, that the earnings-price ratio of industrial common stock in 1957 was 1.9 times the market yield of industrial bonds.[16] May not this relationship give some indication of the appropriate differential between the yields on structures and those on equipment and inventories? (I am not suggesting that the bond yield and the earning-price ratio indicate the required levels but only the differential.)

Price behavior was also more favorable to profits in the years after World War II than in the 1920's. Wholesale prices fell by 8 per cent from 1926 to 1929, whereas from 1954 to 1957 they rose 10 per cent. More important, the wholesale price index in 1929 was 29 per cent lower than it had been ten years earlier; in 1957, it was 32 per cent higher than in 1947.[17] These price movements were attributable to broad developments with respect to liquidity, aggregate income, and productive capacity. Rising prices lift profit rates on the book value of invested capital. To a lesser extent, the return is increased when measured from capital values and profits stated in dollars of the same purchasing power. This is true because certain contractual costs lag, because debtors make real gains, and because buoyant demand is associated with inflation.

The effects of price changes were not offset by wage changes, since the movement of labor costs per unit of output in manufacturing was broadly parallel to that of wholesale prices both in the 1920's and after World War II. In the period 1919–29, labor costs declined, as productivity increased faster than wages, and prices fell by about the same percentage as unit labor costs. In 1948–57, labor costs rose, as wages increased faster than productivity, and prices rose almost as much as unit labor costs.[18] When prices of finished goods and labor costs per unit of output fall or rise in exactly equal proportions, the relative

[16] Yield of industrial corporate bonds in 1957, 4.12 per cent ([14], p. 351); earnings-price ratio of common stocks, 7.8 per cent (Standard and Poor's, from [20], p. 288).

[17] BLS index of wholesale prices of all commodities other than farm products and foods ([18], p. 117).

[18] From 1919 to 1929, labor costs per unit of output in manufacturing declined 31 per cent, while wholesale prices of all commodities other than farm products and foods declined 29 per cent. From 1948 to 1957, labor costs per unit of output rose 22 per cent, while wholesale prices of manufactures rose 19 per cent. (For sources, see Appendix III-B.)

share of capital and other factors in the value of output remains unchanged; the absolute size of the nonlabor share increases in proportion to the growth of output and the rate of return on invested capital increases.

While I cannot pretend that these unsystematic remarks offer a satisfactory explanation of profit behavior, I believe that they suggest reasons for expecting higher rates of return on capital in prosperous years of the 1950's than in the 1920's, regardless of the corporate tax rate. Further study of factors bearing on rates of return and profit shares would be an important subject of research which would go far beyond the question of tax incidence but which might shed more light on that question.

Conclusions with Respect to Long Run Shifting

I am left uncertain about the degree of long-run shifting of the corporation income tax. On deductive grounds, I believe that the tax causes some reallocation of capital, which tends to cushion its impact on the return on corporate equity while depressing rates of return elsewhere. This is a kind of long-run shifting, but it does not necessarily indicate that capitalists as a group succeed in throwing off the tax. That is a more doubtful proposition. I do not think that either deductive considerations or the available statistics suggest anything close to full shifting in the latter sense. However, so many influences are at work that extreme caution in drawing conclusions is wise.

Perhaps the narrow question of shifting is unanswerable because we cannot conceptually or statistically hold constant all the relevant variables except corporate tax rates. Powerful political forces are at work to raise profits tax rates at the same time that economic conditions are conducive to rising profits. Would anyone contend that corporate tax rates would have risen so sharply in the 1940's except for the war and accompanying conditions which were very favorable to profits? And going a step farther, is it likely that corporate tax rates would have remained at their recent high levels so long if the postwar economic environment had offered no better profit opportunities than those of the late 1930's? At the same time, high tax rates may contribute to conditions which make for high profits because of long-run shifting or because the revenue yield relaxes political restraints on government spending.

Appendix III-A
Richard Goode
*The Krzyzaniak-Musgrave Profits Equation and Alternative Equations**

The following symbols are employed:

Y_g Before-tax rate of return on total capital (equity + debt), manufacturing corporations.

ΔC Increase in the ratio of consumption expenditures to GNP over the ratio for the previous year.

V Ratio of inventory to sales in manufacturing.

$\mathcal{J}$ Ratio of (1) federal, state, and local government receipts (national income and product account basis), *minus* federal corporate profits tax accruals, *minus* government transfer payments to persons, to (2) GNP.

L Ratio of federal corporation income, excess profits tax, declared-value excess profits tax, and undistributed profits tax liabilities to total capital, manufacturing corporations.

P Ratio of actual GNP to potential GNP.

$\mathcal{Q}$ Ratio of actual manufacturing production to its high-level trend.

$\bar{R}^2$ Coefficient of multiple correlation, squared, and adjusted for degrees of freedom.

$\bar{r}^2$ Coefficient of simple correlation, squared, and adjusted for degrees of freedom.

$\overline{S.E.}$ Standard error of estimate, adjusted for degrees of freedom.

$D–W$ Durbin-Watson statistic.

The subscripts t and t–1 refer to values of the current year and the preceding year, respectively.

Y_g, ΔC, V, $\mathcal{J}$, and L are from Krzyzaniak and Musgrave, *Shifting of the Corporation Income Tax*, pp. 74–75. The figures for V, which differ from published statistics, are an index of some kind.

P is the ratio of actual GNP in 1954 dollars to potential GNP in 1954 dollars, as estimated by James W. Knowles ("The Potential Economic Growth

* The estimates reported in this appendix were made in collaboration with Richard E. Slitor and John A. Brittain. Interpretations, however, are my own.

in the United States," Joint Economic Committee, *Study of Employment, Growth, and Price Levels* [86 Cong. 2 sess., 1960], Study Paper 20, p. 37). Knowles's estimates of potential output are based on a production function statistically derived from data for the period 1909–58. Values for P appear in Table A–1.

$\mathcal{Q}$ is the ratio of actual manufacturing production to its estimated "high-level trend." Actual production for the period up to 1948 is measured by an index with the base 1929 = 100 (John W. Kendrick, *Productivity Trends in the United States* [Princeton, N.J.: Princeton University Press for National Bureau of Economic Research], pp. 465–66). For 1948 and later years, actual manufacturing production is measured by the index of the Board of Governors of the Federal Reserve System, with the base 1957–59 = 100 (*Economic Report of the President, January 1964*, p. 247). The high-level trend of output is estimated by connecting actual production indexes for 1919 and 1929, 1929 and 1941, and 1948 and 1957 by exponential growth curves. The estimates are based on the assumption that the economy was operating at substantially full normal capacity in 1919, 1929, 1941, 1948, and 1957. For 1958–59, the high-level growth trend is estimated by extrapolating the curve connecting 1948 and 1957. Values for $\mathcal{Q}$ appear in Table A–1.

Table A–2 gives the coefficients of simple correlation between P and $\mathcal{Q}$ and the other variables. Other relationships between variables are shown in the simple correlation matrix appearing on p. 46 of K & M.

The equations shown below provide alternative estimates of Y_g. Equation 1 is the K-M Model A for all years, "naive least squares" technique (Table 6–1, line 6, pp. 44–45). Equation 1.1 is a recomputation of equation 1 with the values for the K-M variables rounded. Equations 2 and 3 show the effect of substituting P and $\mathcal{Q}$ respectively, for the K-M tax variable (L). Equations 4 and 5 employ P and $\mathcal{Q}$ as the only independent variables. All equations were fitted to annual data 1935–42, 1948–59. The figures in square brackets below the coefficients are the ratios of the coefficients to their standard errors.

(1) $\quad Y_{g,t} = \quad n.c. + \quad 0.4966 \Delta C_{t-1} - \quad 0.4681 V_{t-1} - \quad 0.8967 \mathcal{I}_t + \quad 1.4199 L_t$
$\qquad\qquad\qquad\qquad [3.5440] \qquad\quad [-3.0253] \qquad\quad [-5.4347] \qquad [15.3468]$
$\quad \overline{R}{}^2 = \quad 0.9614 \qquad\qquad S.E. = \qquad \ldots \qquad\qquad\qquad D\text{-}W = \quad 2.6526$

(1.1) $\quad Y_{g,t} = \quad 0.2683 + \quad 0.4338 \Delta C_{t-1} - \quad 0.4556 V_{t-1} - \quad 0.8355 \mathcal{I}_t + \quad 1.410 L_t$
$\qquad\qquad\qquad\qquad [2.9333] \qquad\quad [2.7140] \qquad\quad [4.8100] \qquad [14.1051]$
$\quad \overline{R}{}^2 = \quad 0.955 \qquad\qquad\quad S.E. = \quad 0.0126 \qquad\qquad\quad D\text{-}W = \quad 2.660$

(2) $\quad Y_{g,t} = -0.3884 + \quad 0.3841 \Delta C_{t-1} - \quad 0.0673 V_{t-1} - \quad 0.8875 \mathcal{I}_t + \quad 0.7131 P_t$
$\qquad\qquad\qquad\qquad [1.9993] \qquad\quad [0.2744] \qquad\quad [3.9116] \qquad [10.5175]$
$\quad \overline{R}{}^2 = \quad 0.923 \qquad\qquad\quad S.E. = \quad 0.0164 \qquad\qquad\quad D\text{-}W = \quad 1.380$

(3) $\quad Y_{g,t} = \quad 0.0749 + \quad 0.3407 \Delta C_{t-1} - \quad 0.4103 V_{t-1} - \quad 1.178 \mathcal{I}_t + \quad 0.3507 \mathcal{Q}_t$
$\qquad\qquad\qquad\qquad [1.5331] \qquad\quad [1.5632] \qquad\quad [4.4081] \qquad [8.8381]$
$\quad \overline{R}{}^2 = \quad 0.897 \qquad\qquad\quad S.E. = \quad 0.0191 \qquad\qquad\quad D\text{-}W = \quad 1.342$

(4) $Y_{g,t} = -0.4561 + 0.6322 P_t$
            [11.0089]

$\overline{r^2}$ = 0.864 $\overline{S.E.}$ = 0.0220 $D\text{-}W$ = 1.140

(5) $Y_{g,t} = -0.1521 + 0.3238 \mathcal{Q}_t$
            [8.8350]

$\overline{r^2}$ = 0.802 $\overline{S.E.}$ = 0.0264 $D\text{-}W$ = 0.795

Table A-1.

Ratio of Actual GNP to Potential GNP in 1954 Dollars (P) and
Ratio of Actual Manufacturing Production to Its High-Level Trend
($\mathcal{Q}$), 1927–29, 1935–42, 1948–60[a]

Year	P	$\mathcal{Q}$
1927	1.012	0.959
28	.981	.944
29	1.018	1.000
1935	.766	.658
36	.849	.741
37	.875	.761
38	.809	.573
39	.850	.699
40	.899	.779
41	1.008	1.000
42	1.085	1.200
1948	1.008	1.000
49	.966	.905
50	1.013	1.011
51	1.047	1.047
52	1.039	1.045
53	1.041	1.091
54	.983	.973
55	1.017	1.052
56	.991	1.039
57	.965	1.000
58	.912[b]	.888
59	.931[b]	.968
60	.931[b]	.954

a For sources, see text.

b The figures for 1958–59 are preliminary estimates used in fitting equations 2 and 4. Revised estimates are 0.917 for 1958 and 0.939 for 1959; these revisions and the estimate for 1960 were supplied by Knowles.

Table A-2.

Simple Correlation Between P and $\mathcal{Q}$ and Between P and $\mathcal{Q}$ and
Other Variables, 1935–42, 1948–59

Variable	$\mathcal{Q}_t$	L_t	ΔC_{t-1}	V_{t-1}	J_t	$Y_{g,t}$
P_t	0.96	0.95	−0.03	−0.75	0.42	0.93
$\mathcal{Q}_t$		0.94	−0.01	−0.72	0.47	0.90

Appendix III-B

Statistical Sources

Table 27

Equity capital and interest-bearing debt are taken as the arithmetic means of the values for the end of the current year and the end of the preceding year. For the years 1927–29, the return on equity capital is represented by compiled net profits; for other years, by net income. The difference between compiled net profits and net income of manufacturing corporations is small for 1936 and later years. Interest-bearing debt includes bonded debt, mortgages, and notes payable but excludes accounts payable. Amounts of notes payable at the end of the years 1928 and 1929 were estimated on the assumption that notes payable constituted the same fraction of notes and accounts payable as at the end of 1927. Data for 1927–29 and 1960 are from U. S. Treasury Department, Bureau of Internal Revenue, *Statistics of Income*, annual volumes; for other years, from Krzyzaniak and Musgrave, *Shifting of the Corporation Income Tax*, p. 73.

Table 28

For 1929 and later years, the underlying statistics on corporate profits in manufacturing; inventory valuation adjustment; and federal, state, and local corporate profits tax liabilities are estimates of the Office of Business Economics, U. S. Department of Commerce (OBE), published in *U. S. Income and Output* (1958) and *Survey of Current Business*, July 1962 and July 1963. Statistics on depreciation charges, 1946–60, are OBE estimates from the same sources. For 1927–28, profits are estimates by John A. Brittain. For 1927–45, depreciation charges are estimates by Brittain, based on Raymond W. Goldsmith, *Study of Saving in the United States* (Princeton, N. J.: Princeton University Press, 1955), vol. I, and *Statistics of Income*.

Estimates of current-cost depreciation allowances for all years are also by Brittain and are based on the OBE estimates for manufacturing establishments.

Estimates of national income originating in manufacturing corporations were derived from estimates of national income originating in manufacturing establishments. The latter series for the period 1929–60 was obtained from OBE estimates (*National Income* [1954], *U. S. Income and Output*, and *Survey of Current Business*, July 1962 and July 1963). For 1927–28, the estimates are by Challis A. Hall, Jr. I estimated the corporate component of the total on the basis of Census data on the fraction of value added in manufacturing establishments which was produced by corporations. The Census statistics are available for 1919, 1929, 1939, 1947, 1954, and 1958 (U. S. Bureau of the Census, *Historical Statistics of the United States, Colonial Times to 1957*, p. 413, and *Census of Manufactures, 1958*, vol. 1, p. 3–2). For intervening years, I obtained the corporate fraction by interpolation; for 1959–60, the corporate fraction was assumed to be the same as in 1958.

In the ratios of profits plus depreciation charges to income originating (lines 2 and 3), the denominator is national income originating plus depreciation charges. In the ratios in which profits are measured on the basis of current-cost depreciation allowances (line 4), national income originating is adjusted by substituting the current-cost depreciation allowances for reported depreciation charges.

The effective rate of corporate profits tax is the percentage ratio of federal, state, and local corporate tax liabilities to profits before taxes.

Table 29

Corporate profits in manufacturing are measured by the same statistics as in Table 28. Corporate sales, 1929–60, are OBE estimates, from *National Income, U. S. Income and Output*, and *Survey of Current Business*, July 1962 and July 1963. For 1927–28, the estimates are by John A. Brittain.

Table 30

The statistics underlying text Table 30 are given in Table B–1. The estimates of the value of structures, equipment, and inventory of manufacturing corporations, in 1954 dollars, are based on OBE estimates of the value of privately owned structures, equipment, and inventory in manufacturing establishments. The corporate total was derived from the establishment total by multiplying by the estimated fraction of national income originating in manufacturing which was produced by corporations (see notes on Table 28). Since corporate manufacturing is likely more capital intensive than noncorporate, my method may somewhat understate the corporate component of reproducible tangible capital; however, the error cannot be large, inasmuch as the bulk of the total is attributed to corporations in each year (91.5 per cent in 1929 and 94.7 per cent in 1958–60).

The underlying statistics on profits and depreciation charges of manufacturing corporations, in current prices, are from the following sources: profits before taxes and profits after taxes, OBE estimates (*National Income, U. S. Income and Output*, and *Survey of Current Business*, July 1962 and July 1963); depreciation charges, 1946–60, *ibid.*; depreciation charges, 1929–45, estimates by John A. Brittain (see notes to Table 28). Current-price amounts were converted to amounts in 1954 dollars by deflating by the OBE implicit price index for private purchases of structures and equipment in manufacturing, 1954 = 100 (*U. S. Income and Output*, Table V–12, and *Survey of Current Business*, July 1962 and July 1963).

Table B-1

Value of Structures, Equipment, and Inventory; Profits; and Profits Plus Depreciation Charges: Manufacturing Corporations, Selected Years, 1928–60 [a]

(Money Amounts in Billions of 1954 Dollars)

Year	S. E. I. End of Year	Aver-age [b]	Implicit Price Deflator	Profits and Depreciation Charges in 1954 Dollars			
				π	$\pi + D$	$\pi - T$	$\pi + D - T$
1928	70.1	.....	...	....	....	....	......
1929	74.2	72.2	44	11.0	15.0	9.6	13.6
1935	64.5	.....	...	....	....	....	....
1936	66.2	65.4	42	8.4	11.5	6.7	9.8
1937	70.2	68.2	45	8.1	11.2	6.4	9.5
1938	68.2	69.2	46	3.4	6.4	2.4	5.4
1939	68.5	68.4	46	7.9	11.0	6.3	9.4
1954	118.2	.....	100	....	....	....	....
1955	121.9	120.0	102	25.8	33.1	12.9	20.3
1956	128.9	125.4	111	22.7	30.0	11.7	19.0
1957	132.2	130.0	119	20.0	27.5	10.3	17.7
1958	131.4	131.8	121	15.3	23.1	7.7	15.5
1959	135.0	133.2	123	20.9	28.9	10.7	18.7
1960	136.8	135.9	124	18.3	26.6	9.2	17.5

[a] For derivation, see text. Symbols: *S. E. I.*, value of privately owned structures, equipment, and inventory of manufacturing corporations; π, corporate profits before taxes; D, corporate depreciation charges; T, federal, state, and local corporate profits tax liabilities.

[b] Arithmetic mean of values for end of current year and end of preceding year.

Table 31

The unemployment rate is expressed as a percentage of the civilian labor force. Definitions for 1955–60 differ from those for the earlier years. The source for 1927–29 is *Historical Statistics*, p. 73; for later years, *Economic Report of the President, January 1964*, p. 230.

The ratio of actual GNP to potential GNP, both expressed in 1954 dollars, is *P* from Table A-1. In Table 31, the revised estimates for 1958 and 1959, shown in a footnote to Table A-1, are used.

The ratio of actual manufacturing production to its high-level trend is *2* from Table A-1.

Labor Costs and Prices

In manufacturing, the change in labor costs per unit of output and in wholesale prices from 1919 to 1929 and from 1948 to 1957 can be compared on the basis of the following ratios of indexes for the terminal years to those for the initial years of the two periods:

	1919–29	1948–57
1. Output per manhour	1.724	1.267
2. Average hourly earnings	1.187	1.541
3. Labor costs per unit (line 2 ÷ line 1)	0.689	1.216
4. Wholesale prices	0.711	1.187

The estimates of output per manhour in manufacturing for 1919 and 1929 are an index (1929 = 100) from John W. Kendrick, *Productivity Trends in the United States* (Princeton, N. J.: Princeton University Press for National Bureau of Economic Research, 1961), p. 465. For 1948 and 1957, the estimates are an index of the Bureau of Labor Statistics (BLS), 1957–59 = 100 (*Economic Report of the President, January 1964*, p. 245).

Average hourly earnings of production workers in manufacturing are represented by a BLS series. For 1919 and 1929, it is from *Historical Statistics*, p. 92; for 1948 and 1957, from *Economic Report, 1964*, p. 240.

Wholesale prices in 1919 and 1929 are measured by the BLS index for all commodities other than farm products and foods (*Historical Statistics*, p. 116) and in 1948 and 1957 by the BLS index for manufactured goods (U.S. Department of Labor, Bureau of Labor Statistics, *Wholesale Prices and Price Indexes, January 1962*, p. 32).

BIBLIOGRAPHY

1. Creamer, Daniel B., Sergei P. Dobrovolsky, and Israel Borenstein, introduction Simon Kuznets. *Capital in Manufacturing and Mining.* Princeton: Princeton University Press for National Bureau of Economic Research, 1960.

2. Duesenberry, James S., Otto Eckstein, and Gary Fromm. "A Simulation of the United States Economy in Recession," *Econometrica*, XXVIII (October 1960), 749–809.

3. Fromm, Gary. "Inventories, Business Cycles, and Economic Stabilization," in Joint Economic Committee, *Inventory Fluctuations and Economic Stabilization* (87 Cong. 2 sess., 1962), Part IV, pp. 50–133.

4. Gordon, R. A. "Short-Period Price Determination in Theory and Practice," *AER*, XXXVIII (June 1948), 265–288.

5. Hall, Challis A., Jr. "Direct Shifting of the Corporation Income Tax in Manufacturing," *AER*, LIV, Papers and Proceedings (May 1964), 258–271.

6. Kaplan, A. D. H., Joel B. Dirlam, and Robert F. Lanzillotti. *Pricing in Big Business: A Case Approach.* Washington: Brookings, 1959.

7. Kahn, Alfred E. "Pricing Objectives in Large Companies: Comment," *AER*, IL (September 1959), 670–678.

8. Krzyzaniak, Marian, and Richard A. Musgrave. *The Shifting of the Corporation Income Tax.* Baltimore: Johns Hopkins University Press, 1963.

9. Kuh, Edwin. "Profits, Profit Markups, and Productivity: An Examination of Corporate Behavior since 1947," in Joint Economic Committee, *Study of Employment, Growth, and Price Levels*, Study Paper 15 (86 Cong. 1 sess., 1960).

10. Lanzillotti, Robert F. "Pricing Objectives in Large Companies," *AER*, XLVIII (December 1958), 921–940.

11. ____. "Reply," *AER*, IL (September 1959), 679–687.

12. Liu, Ta-Chung. "An Exploratory Quarterly Econometric Model of Effective Demand in the Postwar U. S. Economy," *Econometrica*, XXXI (July 1963), 301–348.

13. Markham, Jesse W. Review of [6], *AER*, IL (June 1959), 473–475.

14. National Industrial Conference Board. *Economic Almanac, 1962.*

15. Schultze, Charles L. "Short-Run Movement of Income Shares," in *Behavior of Income Shares*, Studies in Income and Wealth, XXVII. Princeton: Princeton University Press for National Bureau of Economic Research, 1964.

16. U. S. Congress. Joint Economic Committee. *State of the Economy and Policies for Full Employment.* (Hearings, 87 Cong. 2 sess., 1962.)

17. U. S. Department of Commerce. Bureau of the Census. *Census of Manufactures,* 1958.

18. ____. *Historical Statistics of the United States, Colonial Times to 1957.*

19. ____. Office of Business Economics, *U. S. Income and Output* (1958), and *Survey of Current Business* (July 1962).

20. U. S. President. *Economic Report of the President, January 1964.*

21. U. S. Treasury Department. Internal Revenue Service. *Statistics of Income,* annual volumes.

DISCUSSION

Marian Krzyzaniak and Richard Musgrave

The papers by R. Goode and R. Slitor have raised many interesting points, including some which we accept and others which we do not find compelling. In order to keep this response within brief limits, we shall comment on the most important items only; and where both critics take similar views, we shall treat their comments jointly.

1. These critics argue that our results would be of little value if substitution or addition of other variables in our estimating equation gave equally good results in predicting the rate of return, while yielding a substantially reduced tax rate coefficient. We agree, and indeed were quite aware of this problem. Going further, they attempt to demonstrate that the tax rate coefficient is in fact highly sensitive to the specifications of the model. We do not believe that their evidence makes the point.

Goode and Slitor both argue that the rate of return in any one year may be expected to depend on the "pressure" under which the economy operates, i.e., on the general state of business conditions. They take this degree of pressure to be measured by the GNP gap. Adding an unlagged gap variable P to the system, or substituting it for some other variables, they find that estimated shifting is reduced. For the standard case the coefficient drops from 134 to below 100 per cent. They conclude that this demonstrates the fickleness of our tax rate coefficient.

We agree, of course, that the rate of return in any one year will depend on the prevailing "pressure," and that a very high correlation between the pressure index and the rate of return is to be expected. But we object to the technique used to estimate the rate of return with "pressure" as an explanatory variable. The pressure variable stands for economic conditions of the period for which the rate of return is observed, conditions which in turn depend on many other variables including the corporate income tax. The result is an equation containing two dependent variables in which case least squares technique is liable to yield biased and inconsistent estimates.

Moreover, we think it inappropriate to use the pressure variable in a model designed to measure the tax effect upon the rate of return. The pressure variable is itself a function of the corporate income tax. Hence, if the pressure variable is included, the coefficient of the tax variable does not represent the isolated tax effect upon the rate of return, part of this effect being hidden in the coefficient of the pressure variable.

Measurement of a tax effect upon the rate of return is a prediction of the businessman's behavior. To permit such prediction, the rate of return function should be in reduced form. In a truly reduced form, these conditions should be met: (1) the equation should contain only one dependent variable; (2) the function should be linear and in explicit form, i.e., the coefficient of the dependent variable in the equation should be a constant, namely equal one; and the equation should (3) account for all the relevant variables in the system.

Our model B meets condition 1 since all predetermined variables are lagged. It also meets condition 2. Condition 3 is not met as well as one might wish. The model is not as comprehensive as we would like it to be, but the number of available observations is limited and the use of independent variables had to be economized.

Our model A does not fare quite as well. Condition 1 is still satisfied. Although the L_t variable is dependent, no new dependent variable is introduced because $L_t = Z_t^* Y_{g,t}$. Introduction of L_t in place of Z_t^*, however, renders the predicting equation non-linear, leaving condition 2 unmet. In fact, our model A equation may be also written as:

$$Y_{g,t} = a_0 \frac{1}{1 - a_4 Z_t^*} + a_1 \frac{\Delta C_{t-1}}{1 - a_4 Z_t^*} + a_2 \frac{V_{t-1}}{1 - a_4 Z_t^*} + a_3 \frac{L_t}{1 - a_4 Z_t^*} + \frac{U_t}{1 - a_4 Z_t^*}.$$

Despite the non-linearity of this equation there is no reason to doubt its predictive power. Condition 1, which still holds, is the more important for prediction purposes. The tax variable coefficient isolates the whole tax effect and is still suitable for prediction. However, the non-linearity of the reduced form does pose a computational problem, and this was resolved by the use of the instrumental variable technique. A check by using other techniques, like Klein's approximation, yielded coefficients that were close.

Both models were included in our study since both reflect reasonable hypotheses regarding the businessman's reaction to the tax. Model B implies that he endeavors to recover a fraction of the negative rate of return which is imposed by the tax. Model A tests the more likely hypothesis that he tries to recover a certain fraction of his tax liability. As pointed out in our study, the latter hypothesis yields the better results.

The critics' model fails to meet either conditions 1 or 2. Inclusion of the P_t variable, defined as the unlagged value of the GNP gap, is not permissible in a prediction model. The coefficient of the gap variable already contains a tax effect, hence the tax variable coefficient does not measure and isolate the whole tax effect on the rate of return.[1] Estimation by the least squares technique renders coefficients biased and inconsistent as well.

What then is the proper way of allowing for the pressure variable? Let us assume for a moment that our estimating

[1] At an earlier stage in our project, sales and quantity variables (unlagged) were used. Inclusion of the sales variable showed lower shifting for the first period, and yielded a hard-to-explain result of negative shifting for the second period. The error involved in the inclusion of the endogenous quantity or sales variable was pointed out to us by Professor Carl Christ at a Brookings Conference held to discuss a preliminary version of our study, and the model was then revised accordingly.

equation already satisfies conditions 1 and 3, and possibly 2. Due to satisfaction of condition 3, all relevant predetermined variables are already included. In such a case, the current state of "pressure" is a function of these predetermined variables and is already reflected in them. No separate "pressure" variable would have to be added.

While no claim of completeness is made for our model, inclusion of predetermined variables which determine the current level of expenditures (such as ΔC_{t-1}, V_{t-1} and G_t) as well as allowance for the capital stock in the denominator of the dependent variable should go pretty far to account for the current state of pressure. This is the case especially if "pressure" is defined more appropriately as the degree of capacity use of capital rather than the GNP gap. Moreover, it may be noted that our V_{t-1} and G_t variables show a fairly high correlation with the gap type of pressure variable used by our critics.[2]

Nevertheless, we made some further attempts to see whether the tax coefficients would change substantially in response to alternative selections of predetermined variables. The results are shown in Table 32. Line 1 repeats our standard case. (See [2], Table 7–1, l. 2.) In line 2 the critics' gap variable P, now lagged one period, is substituted for the V_{t-1} variable. Contrary to their result for the unlagged P, the degree of shifting remains practically unchanged. Used in lagged form, the P variable is acceptable as predetermined, but it merely substitutes for other forces already reflected in the system.

In lines 5 and 6 an alternative measure of pressure or P_c is used. Defined now as Professor Klein's percentage utilization of capacity (see 4 and 1), this measure is available for the postwar period only and must thus be compared with our standard model for that period, as shown in line 4. To permit comparison with the critics' result, the P_c variable is used unlagged in line 5. The degree of shifting is lower, although less dramatically so, than in their version. If P_c is used in lagged form, as it again should be, the P_c variable becomes insignificant and the fit is reduced. A perhaps more helpful way of looking at the capacity

[2] See Appendix Table A-2 to the Goode paper in this volume.

Table 32

Alternative Estimates of Rate of Return Equation for All Manufacturing

No.	Description	Years	No. of Observations	Intercept a_0	Regression Coefficients, [ ] as Fractions of Standard Error — Variables								R Adjusted	Shifting Measure, ( ) Its Standard Error
					ΔC_{t-1}	C_{t-1}	V_{t-1}	$\mathcal{J}_t$	P_{t-1}[1]	$P_{o,t}$[2]	$P_{o,t-1}$	L_t		
1.[3]	All manufacturing, total capital, all years	1935–42 1948–59	20	.2859	.4038 [2.6690]		−.5272 [−3.0043]	−.8333 [−4.7168]				1.3394 [12.2165]	.9765	1.3394 (.1096)
2.	No. 1	1935–42 1948–59	20	.0607	.4750 [2.7104]			.9232 [−3.5564]	.1507 [1.7918]			1.2949 [7.6451]	.9675	1.2949 (.1694)
3.[4]	No. 1	1936–42 1949–59	18	.0031		.5009 [1.8538]	−.4024 [−1.2641]	−.4978 [−1.0589]				1.2486 [5.4969]	.8903	1.2486 (.2271)
4.[5]	All manufacturing, total capital, postwar	1948–59	12	.2698	.1593 [.5962]		−.1044 [−2.5218]	−1.1223 [−3.1541]				1.2050 [4.3398]	.9191	1.2050 (.2777)
5.	No. 4	1948–59	12	.0305	−.1185 [−.8463]		−.0113 [−.0614]	−1.6748 [−8.3920]		.3563 [4.5883]		1.0558 [7.2947]	.9843	1.0558 (.1447)
6.	No. 4	1948–59	12	.3308				−1.1775 [−3.6647]			−.0686 [−.5706]	1.1046 [3.7130]	.9150	1.1046 (.2975)

[1] P_t Pressure variable as given by Goode's Table A-1, Appendix to this volume.

[2] $P_{o,t}$ Averaged for the annual capacity variable as given in "Statement of Lawrence R. Klein," *Measures of Productive Capacity*, Hearings before the Subcommittee on Economic Statistics of the Joint Economic Committee (May 14, 22, 23, 24, 1962), p. 9, reprinted in American Economic Association, *Papers and Proceedings*, May 1963, p. 283.

[3] For this estimate see (2), Table 7-1, 1. 1, p. 54.

[4] The whole model was differenced.

[5] For this estimate see (2), Table 7-1, 1. 2, p. 54.

problem is to change the consumption variable from ΔC_{-1} to C_{-1}. The result, using differenced values throughout and applied to the entire period, is shown in line 3. Shifting is slightly lower, but the general picture is unchanged.

In all, we grant that the value of our results would be greatly reduced if the tax coefficient were shown to be quite sensitive to admissible changes in specification of the estimating equation. We do not deny the possibility that a more ambitious model, applied to a larger number of observations, may in time yield different results. This, after all, is a very difficult problem to tackle by quantitative techniques. We do not think, however, that the critics have shown the model to be unreliable nor is this suggested by the further experimentation which we have undertaken.

2. We now turn to the general plausibility test, contained in Table 26 of Goode's paper. Let us reproduce lines 1, 3, and 8 of his table, comparing the 36–39 and 55–57 periods; and for lines 1 and 8 let us add the 27–29 period.

Table 33

Gross Rates of Return (total capital) in Manufacturing

	27–29	36–39	55–57
1. Actual	8.1%	7.5%	16.1%
2. Our estimate with tax rates constant at 36–39 level	n.a.	7.6	7.2
3. Goode estimate solely from capacity utilization variable	17.5	7.2	18.1

Goode notes that, according to our model, rates of return (line 2) would have been unchanged from 36–39 to 55–57 had tax rates remained at 36–39 levels. This he finds highly implausible, as conditions were more prosperous in the second period. Proceeding on the hypothesis that gross rates of return do not respond to changes in tax rates but are a function of "pressure" as measured by the unlagged gap P_t variable, he estimates the rate of return for 55–57 at 18.1%. As shown in Table 33, this is fairly close to the observed rate. If Goode's hypothesis is correct, so that a conclusion of no-shifting may be drawn from this evidence, it should also hold for other periods. Let us extend his estimate back to the 27–29 period. Proceeding as Goode does, we estimate the rate of return for 27–29 at 17.5%, which differs greatly from the observed value of 8.1. If the pressure variable fails so grossly in explaining the rate of return over this period, why should it be the correct predictor for the later period? Evidently, changes in the rate of return cannot be predicted in this simple fashion.

Putting it differently, Goode's hypothesis renders it rather difficult to explain both the 27–29 to 36–39 and the 36–39 to 55–57 sequences. Such an explanation follows more readily from the hypothesis that non-tax factors were near to neutral on balance, while the tax was shifted. With the tax rate rising but slightly from 27–29 to 36–39, the modest decrease in the observed rate of return reflects the worsening of business conditions. With the tax rate rising sharply from 36–39 to 55–57, the gross rate of return responded accordingly. The implication of our model (i.e., the unchanged rate of return in absence of tax change) may be surprising on intuitive grounds, but we do not find it as incredible as Goode suggests. The periods of 36–39 and 55–57 may have differed less in terms of capacity use of capital than the sharp difference in unemployment rates suggests; [3] and many factors other than "pressure" variables may have affected the rate of return.

Turning to a somewhat related point, we are puzzled by the critics' suggestion that our analysis merely recaptures the results of earlier authors who observed that the gross rate of return doubled over the decades of rate increase, while the net rate showed little change (see [3]). These authors interpreted this to indicate shifting by *assuming* that non-tax influences upon the gross rate of return were neutral on balance. Our analysis makes no such assumption but applies econometric methods to *measure* the *ceteris paribus* effect of tax change. While the model shows that non-tax effects did wash out. This conclusion follows from, rather than provides, the basis for

[3] Unfortunately, no comparable indices of capacity use in all manufacturing are available for the 1930's and 1950's. The only available index, i.e., The American Iron and Steel Institute's index of steel production as a per cent of capacity, averages at 63.5 for the 36–39 period as against 89.1% for the 55–57 period. This compares with a differential in umemployment rates of 16.9 and 4.2 per cent, respectively.

Table 34

Additional Estimates of Rate of Return Equation

No.	Description	Years	No. of Observations	Regression Coefficients, [ ] as Fractions of Standard Error					R Adjusted	Instrument or Technique	d Statistics	Shifting Measures, ( ) its Standard Error
				Intercept	C_{t-1}	V_{t-1}	$\mathcal{J}_t$	L_t				
1[1]	All manufacturing, equity capital (with and without profits)	1935–42 1948–59	20	.4234	.3431 [1.8180]	−.9429 [−4.2971]	−1.1778 [−5.3266]	1.2331 [10.4348]	.9745	Z^*_t	2.4285	1.2331 (.1182)
2	All manufacturing, equity capital (with profits only)	1935–42 1948–53	20	.3434	.5556 [3.0954]	−.4547 [−2.2093]	−1.0984 [−5.1662]	1.2128 [11.3377]	.9594	Z^*_t	2.5498	1.2128 (.1070)
3	Utilities, equity capital (with and without profits)	1935–42 1948–59	20	.1425	−.0992 [−.8701]	−.2213 [−1.4003]	−.5681 [−2.2768]	1.8290 [5.2029]	.9603	Z^*_t	n.c.	1.8290 (.3515)
4	No. 3	1935–42 1948–59	20	.1383	.0436 [n.c.]	−.3122 [n.c.]	−.3612 [n.c.]	1.9044 [n.c.]	.9683	Klein's approx.	n.c.	1.9044 (n.c.)

[1] For this estimate see (2), Table 7-1., l. 3, pp. 54–55.

The remaining estimates were made by students in an Econometrics Seminar at Wayne State University.

our analysis. Moreover, our model differs in that only the short-run tax effect is considered, whereas the earlier discussion included longer-run effects as well.

3. Among the many suggestions made by the critics two were followed up by additional computations. The hypothesis that including loss firms caused us to overstate shifting was tested by computing the model for profit firms only. Line 1 of Table 34 repeats our standard case which includes all firms, and line 2 shows the corresponding result for profit firms only. The degree of shifting is barely reduced. Another suggestion was that utilities should show a higher degree of shifting than other industries. As shown in lines 3 and 4 the estimated degree of shifting is indeed substantially higher than for the total group.[4]

4. The critics believe that acceptance of our results required the most drastic reorientation not only of tax policy but of economic theory, and that it seriously implicates the efficiency of our economic system. We agree that the place of the corporation tax in the tax structure depends quite fundamentally on whether or not it is taken to be shifted in the short-run sense. But beyond this, we feel that the critics' alarm rather overstates the significance of our results.

Empirical evidence of market behavior which does not quite follow traditional profit-maximizing lines, may impair the predictive usefulness of traditional price theory, but it does not affect its normative (efficiency criteria) function. Moreover, price theorists have become increasingly aware that entrepreneurial behavior does not follow a simple profit-maximizing pattern of the perfect competition-monopoly variety. Complex oligopoly reactions, sales maximization, maintenance of market shares, long- as distinct from short-run objectives, political or social restraints regarding the exploitation of potential monopoly profits, profitability as a factor in wage bargaining, are but some of the complications which need to be accounted for, and which may explain short-run shifting. Slitor's helpful concept of over-

---

[4] The extremely high degree of shifting is in line with the hypothesis that utility regulations do little to restrain profitability. See for instance George J. Stigler and Claire Friedland, "Regulation: The New Laissez-Faire —?" unpublished mineographed paper offered in June 1963 at the "Economics of Regulated Public Utilities," a program supported by the Bell Telephone Companies and the University of Chicago.

shifting via "umbrella effects" further illustrates this pattern and may well explain how high degrees of shifting (or even over-shifting) can come about.

In view of all this, we do not find it so difficult to conceive that firm behavior does, in fact, lead to shifting. Nor do we feel that such shifting would require so drastic an adjustment in the macro-magnitude of the system as has been suggested. Suppose that the entire tax of 50% (effective rate) was imposed in one year, say 1957. Assuming the entire shifting to be into higher prices, this would add a tax liability of $21 billion to a gross national product of $443 billion. Thus, the increase in total payments would have been about 5 per cent, an order of magnitude well within the range of minor annual cyclical changes. Moreover, the increase in tax rates did not occur at once but over a considerable number of years. Even the 40–41 increase in effective rate (by 18 points) and the 45–46 decrease (by 21 points) involved payment changes of hardly more than 2 per cent; and apart from these two changes, the annual fluctuations during our period were over a rather narrow range, requiring changes in total "payments" of well below 1 per cent. Given these orders of magnitude and allowing for the responsiveness of the monetary system to changes in the demand for transaction funds, we do not believe that "macro-restraints" can do much to Hume-anize Mr. Goode's case.

Finally, it does not seem to us that even the existence of full shifting of the corporation tax would be grounds for revolutionizing one's views regarding the efficiency of the pricing system. Even though resource allocation in line with purely competitive pricing does not always secure efficient resource use, let it be accepted as a pretty good bench mark for this purpose. Now there are many respects in which actual allocation differs from this bench mark: many sorts of imperfections exist in both product and factor markets, and would so exist even in the absence of a corporation tax. The existence of these imperfections does not mean that the market mechanism results in wholly inefficient allocation. It only means that efficiency is already impaired to some degree. As we see it, this picture is not changed greatly if short-run shifting of the corporation tax is allowed for.

BIBLIOGRAPHY

1. Eckstein, Otto, and Vito Tanzi. "Comparison of European and United States Tax Structures and Growth Implications," *The Role of Direct and Indirect Taxes in the Federal Revenue System*. Princeton: Princeton University Press, 1964. (A Conference Report of the National Bureau of Economic Research and the Brookings Institution.)
2. Hall, Challis A., Jr. "Direct Shifting of the Corporation Income Tax in Manufacturing," *AER*, LIV, Papers and Proceedings (May 1964), 258–272.
3. Krzyzaniak, Marian, and Richard A. Musgrave. *The Shifting of the Corporation Income Tax*. Baltimore: The Johns Hopkins University Press, 1963.
4. Musgrave, Richard A., and Peggy Brewer Richman. "Allocation Aspects, Domestic and International," *The Role of Direct and Indirect Taxes in the Federal Revenue System*. Princeton: Princeton University Press, 1964. (A Conference Report of the National Bureau of Economic Research and the Brookings Institution.)
5. Neumark Committee. *Report of the Fiscal and Financial Committee of the EEC on Tax Harmonization, 1962*. English edition: Commerce Clearing House.

The response by Professors Krzyzaniak and Musgrave clarifies the issues and makes further valuable contributions to the econometric analysis. Our rejoinder is limited to four subjects: (1) the admissibility of an unlagged pressure variable; (2) the independence of the tax rate variable; (3) the comparative shifting experience of utilities and manufacturing; and (4) the plausibility of the findings. The discussion of points 1 and 3 is mainly by Slitor and of points 2 and 4 mainly by Goode.

ADMISSIBILITY OF UNLAGGED
PRESSURE VARIABLE

The contention by Professors Krzyzaniak and Musgrave that our experimentation with a pressure variable in the profit-estimating equation is impermissible because it fails to meet the reduced-form requirement merits special comment. This involves such related matters as the comprehensiveness of the Krzyzaniak-Musgrave model, the predetermined or exogenous character of the independent variables, the influence of other variables on the pressure variable, and the issue of "causation" in the model.

The justification for our experimentation was in fact the serious question raised as to whether the Krzyzaniak-Musgrave Model A adequately specified the corporate rate of return. In their original study an exercise was conducted to show that the

Model A equation is a reduced form derived from a macro model based on a series of structural relationships reflected in consistent estimating equations. However, this demonstration is not persuasive.[1] In theory, procedures to avoid problems of simultaneity by progressing from a comprehensive general model through consistent structural equations to the desired reduced-form relationship would rule out the introduction of a fifth wheel in the profit-estimating equation. In reality, the formulation of the regression equation almost necessarily involves a process of semi-arbitrary selection and modification of variables. This problem, frequently encountered in econometric analysis, leads, as we believe it has done in the Krzyzaniak-Musgrave model, to a semi-structural relationship which cannot realistically be regarded as a sacrosanct reduced form.

Krzyzaniak and Musgrave concede that their estimating equation is less than comprehensive. They offer little or nothing in the way of economic rationale for their selection of variables. As to the question whether the pressure variable is itself dependent on other elements in the equation, it seems evident to us that, whatever inevitable intercorrelation there may exist between this and the other variables, it is subordinate to the substantial contribution which the pressure variable makes to the explanation of corporate earnings rates. If one is to take a purist view of this matter, it should be observed that the $\mathcal{J}_t$ variable actually employed by Krzyzaniak and Musgrave (the ratio of general tax receipts, adjusted, to the GNP for the current year), as distinct from the $\mathcal{J}_t$ variable (personal tax rate) appearing in the macro-model sketch, is equally open to the charge that it is not independent or predetermined. Both the numerator and the denominator of this variable are interdependent with each other and with other factors in the equation. If the pressure variable brings some impurity into the estimating operation, it may not have added more than was already present in the environment.

In short, we feel that it is only realistic to recognize that the Krzyzaniak-Musgrave model is in reality not a rigorously

[1] See their presentation under the heading "Note on General Model" in *The Shifting of the Corporation Income Tax*, pp. 35–36.

developed, reduced form equation, but a semi-structural, behavioral relationship. It inadequately explains corporate earnings rates, thrusting undue explanatory weight on the corporate tax variable L_t (correlated as it is with the dependent variable via government expenditures). The result is an overestimate of shifting. Under these circumstances, the experimentation we have made with a pressure variable is justified and revealing. Lagging of the pressure variable as suggested and tentatively tested by Krzyzaniak and Musgrave is inappropriate since it is inconsistent with the functional relationship which exists. Earnings rates depend primarily on this year's capacity utilization, not last year's.

INDEPENDENCE OF THE TAX RATE VARIABLE

We seriously doubt that the influence of corporate tax rates can be properly measured by the coefficient of L_t, Z^*, or Z in the Krzyzaniak-Musgrave equations. As they note, L_t is not an independent variable since it includes as one of its components the dependent variable $Y_{g,t}$. The naive least-squares regressions including L_t, therefore, involve the regression of $Y_{g,t}$ on itself. We are not sure that this difficulty is obviated by the instrumental variable technique.

The instrument for L_t is Z^*, the effective corporate tax rate computed as the ratio of corporate tax liabilities to gross profits. While Z^* does not directly involve $Y_{g,t}$, it responds to changes in Y_g through associated changes in the ratio of taxable net income to gross profits and because of the existence of the excess profits tax in several of the years under study. Z^*, in our opinion, cannot be considered a fully independent variable.

Even the statutory tax rate Z depends on the trend of profit rates and on the forces accounting for the general level of activity. Over the period studied by Krzyzaniak and Musgrave, both Z and Y_g increased sharply in response to war and inflationary pressures and later declined somewhat as the pressure on resources subsided.

COMPARATIVE EXPERIENCE OF UTILITIES

The new regressions, developed by Krzyzaniak and Musgrave

for the utility group, tend, as we interpret them, to confirm the suspicion that their model over-estimates shifting. The tax-return time series seem to show approximately 100 per cent shifting for the individually regulated utilities. The 183 to 190 per cent measures shown in Items 3 and 4 of the new Table 34 suggest an explosively large increase in after-tax profitability, in the short run at least, attendant upon corporate income taxation. Unless this result is to be interpreted merely as applying to relatively small year-to-year differences and is to be very short-lived, we feel that it implies more over-reaction than can be attributed to inertia or lack of effective restraint in utility regulation.

PLAUSIBILITY OF FINDINGS

As Krzyzaniak and Musgrave show, the simple relation between capacity utilization and the profit rate that existed in 1935–42, 1948–59 does not satisfactorily account for differences between profit rates in 1927–29, 1936–39, and 1955–57. While Goode's plausibility test would be stronger if the same relation held for the earlier period, we do not believe that its failure to hold does much to buttress the Krzyzaniak and Musgrave findings. Owing to lack of data, their equations cannot be tested to see how well they would explain profit rates in the twenties. Certain alternative measures indicate a smaller rise in profit rates from 1927–29 to 1955–57 than do the statistics used by Krzyzaniak and Musgrave, and there are several factors other than tax rates which may help account for the rise in profit rates that did occur.

We still consider it remarkable and disturbing that the Krzyzaniak and Musgrave findings with respect to shifting correspond so closely with those obtainable without any allowance for non-tax factors. They imply a closer resemblance between other relevant economic conditions in the 1930's and 1950's than we consider plausible. We doubt that Krzyzaniak and Musgrave have indeed succeeded in allowing for the non-tax factors and thus measuring the *ceteris paribus* effect of tax changes.

Dr. Marian Krzyzaniak, Associate Professor of Economics, Rice University. Born February 4, 1911; received M. Economics and Political Science from the University of Poznan in 1932; M.A. from the University of Alberta in 1954; and Ph.D. from Massachusetts Institute of Technology in 1959. Held positions of research associate with the University of Michigan in 1958–59, and with Johns Hopkins University in 1960–61. Taught at Montana State University in 1959–60, at Johns Hopkins University in 1960–61, and at Wayne State University in 1961–64. Prior to teaching, held business and civil service positions in Poland, England, and Canada. Co-author with Professor Richard A. Musgrave, *The Shifting of the Corporation Income Tax: An Empirical Study of Its Short-Run Effect upon the Rate of Return* (1963).

Dr. Arnold C. Harberger, Professor of Economics, University of Chicago. Born July 27, 1924; received M.A. in 1947; Ph.D. in 1950 from the University of Chicago. Taught at Johns Hopkins University from 1949 to 1953, then at the University of Chicago. Received Guggenheim and other fellowships, was consultant to International Monetary Fund, U.S. Government agencies, World Bank, and Pan American Union. Has published numerous articles on corporation income taxes and other topics.

Dr. Richard A. Musgrave, Professor of Economics, Harvard University. Born December 12, 1910; received A.M. from Harvard in 1936; Ph.D. from Harvard in 1937. Was resident economist with Federal Reserve Board from 1940 to 1948; taught at the University of Michigan from 1948 to 1958, at Johns Hopkins University from 1958 to 1962, at Princeton University from 1962 to 1965, and since then at Harvard University. Was consultant to private and government agencies. Published numerous articles and a public finance text for graduate studies: *The Theory of Public Finance*. Co-author with Professor Marian Krzyzaniak, *The Shifting of the Corporation Income Tax: An Empirical Study of Its Short Run Effect upon the Rate of Return* (1963).

Dr. Richard E. Slitor, Assistant Director, Office of Tax Analysis, U. S. Treasury. Born July 1, 1911; received S.B. from Harvard in 1932; M.A. from Colgate

262

in 1934; and Ph.D. from Harvard in 1940. Taught at Colgate from 1932 to 1934; taught and tutored at Harvard from 1934 to 1941; taught at Mount Union College from 1941 to 1942. Held various positions as staff economist, U. S. Treasury from 1942 to the present. Is currently Assistant Director, Office of Tax Analysis, U. S. Treasury. In 1963–64 when his contribution to this volume was written was on leave to hold appointment as Federal Executive Fellow, The Brookings Institution. Has published several leading articles covering topics related to problems of corporate income taxation.

Dr. Richard Goode, Director of the Fiscal Affairs Department, International Monetary Fund. Born July 31, 1916; received B.A. from Baylor, 1937; A.M. from Kentucky, 1939; and Ph.D. from Wisconsin, 1947. Was economist at U. S. Bureau of the Budget and Treasury Department from 1941 to 1947. Taught at the University of Chicago from 1947 to 1951. Held positions with International Monetary Fund as assistant chief, finance division, from 1951 to 1954; chief from 1954 to 1958; assistant director, Asian department, from 1958 to 1959. From 1959 to 1965, member, senior staff, The Brookings Institution. Was also associate editor of *National Tax Journal*, 1948–50, and editor, 1950–51. Published several journal articles on the corporation income tax and a book entitled *The Corporation Income Tax* (1951).

The manuscript was edited by Mary Garner. The book is designed by Peter Nothstein. The text type face is Caslon Old Style based on a type originally designed by William Caslon in the Eighteenth Century. The display face is Venus Bold Extended designed by Bauer Type Foundry, 1907–13.

This book is printed on Glatfelter RR Antique paper and bound in Columbia Mills' Atlantic Vellum. Manufactured in the United States of America.